WILL

WILL

A Portrait of
William Douglas Home

David Fraser

ANDRE DEUTSCH

First published in 1995 by
André Deutsch Limited
106 Great Russell Street
London WC1B 3LJ

CIP data for this title is available
from the British Library

ISBN 0 233 98915 3

Printed in Great Britain by
St Edmundsbury Press, Bury St Edmunds, Suffolk

CONTENTS

FOREWORD
WITH ACKNOWLEDGEMENTS

I knew the subject of this portrait for over fifty years and I am very aware that long acquaintance and great affection can distort perspective. Cromwell may have urged the artist to paint him 'warts and all' but it is not certain how fond of Cromwell the artist was, nor – if he was – how smoothly or accurately he managed the warts. I have done my best to depict the shortcomings and describe the failures as well as recount the triumphs and celebrate the virtues of a complex man, but partiality has no doubt sometimes won the day; not least because every fancied defect or contradiction seemed, both in life and in retrospect, only to make him more interesting – and, often, more endearing.

There is no shortage of primary sources. William Douglas Home – 'Will' to many, 'Willie' to some, 'Wills' or 'Wilks' to his father – lives in the memory and perceptions of a great legion of friends. He had the gift of making anyone he was with feel important and unique and when two or more of his intimates met it was likely that an account of the latest encounter with him soon bubbled to the top of the conversation. Yet at the superficial level, or with those he did not know well, his exchanges with people – light, amused, deprecatory – left them often with sensations of some perplexity. They had been amused but were uncertain why. He had been elusive – his talk abrupt, allusive, timed. He had given the impression of a performer, but a performer who was also directing a cast into which his companions for the moment had somewhat bemusedly strayed. He never used endearments – something of a family characteristic. For conversation, in the sense of serious, sustained exchanges of ideas, he seemed to have little taste and he appeared never to stick to any subject for long. Conversation indeed – social intercourse – needed to shade into banter or to become dialogue of the kind he wrote: to become an exchange of something like wit rather than an exchange of something like ideas. He appreciated ideas, but he had to mature them inside himself, quietly. Then they had a chance of emerging as plots, lines.

For most things, whether he was conscious of it or not, were adapted by him to the forms of drama. The process could be rapid – he never appeared to lack spontaneity. But he was always observing, listening, weaving within his mind the text and texture of a theatrical event. He was always – unknown by others, often no doubt unknown by himself – setting scenes, evoking responses, prompting lines from friends, instantly trying them on other friends (sometimes disconcertingly; he reported talk, if it intrigued him, without scruple), moving from one person or group to another, often with a memorable curtain line: all done with a half-suppressed chuckle, a whimsical, half-distorted smile. From all this come a mass of affectionate, laughter-filled, sometimes half-puzzled recollections. One definition of eternity, he thought and wrote, is to be remembered with devotion. This may make a huge concept too subject to the vagaries and limited span of human memory, but it was the way he reconciled his philosophic doubts with his 'almost instinct' that, as Philip Larkin wrote, 'what will survive of us is love'.

But William was above all a writer; and the key to a writer's character and opinions must lie in his principal writings. More even than in his remembered personal effect on others he is to be found in his work.

There is a huge amount of it. He was an exceptionally prolific author and his plays have been translated into many languages and performed on stages the world over. He produced over forty stage plays. He wrote for television and radio. He published three volumes of autobiography, was tireless in turning out articles, contributions to periodicals, light verse. He brought laughter – not only laughter but laughter primarily and irresistibly – to theatregoers in many countries for an extraordinarily long time. And into a large number of his plays (for his plays are the memorable core of his work) he put, either explicitly or by inference, a great deal of himself. In his autobiographical books he disclosed a certain amount, and told plenty of personal anecdotes (some reproduced here), often more than once and differently as to detail, for he had a fine disregard for consistency in such matters. But to find the man it is to the plays that one must go.

And there is a difficulty. He was generally reckoned a superb 'actors' author'. He had trained for the stage, he understood and was fascinated by stagecraft and direction, he wrote with well-spoken lines ringing in his head, and as he wrote he could see a scene and an actor or actress's interpretation of it with absolute clarity. But because he wrote so much to the players' own skills his work does not always read particularly effectively – except to a fellow professional of comparable intuition. He did not often write instantly quotable lines. He seldom made his characters 'speak prose'. They talked, wittily, convincingly: they did not recite. His silences were eloquent; so were gestures, expressions. Unlike Shaw, for instance, he did not produce 'literary' plays stuffed with ideas, aphorisms, complexity, para-dox. His technique was light, easy, conversational. He gave his actors scope to develop. His unwritten – unspoken – touches were often as theatrically compulsive as his words since he could envisage with such clarity and imagination. Thus the written text of his plays, while conveying much of the man, provides the beginning rather than the end of self-disclosure. His father once, apologetically, told him that he found plays, including Shakes-peare's, impossible to read. To detect and exemplify William's particular quality, whether of character or talent, from the written versions of his dramatic work is always hard. He needed voices. The cast are missing. Much, however, is still on the page for the eye and the mind to discern.

William's family and friends, therefore, together with his own output and the public record – both amiable and hostile – of his activities and work, have been the chief sources of information and inspiration for this book. First and foremost I owe a great debt to his widow Rachel, Lady Dacre, who has honoured me with her confidence in what must surely be the most difficult of all transactions. William's children have been equally helpful and trusting. I am indebted to the great army of his relatives, friends and professional associates (few of whom did not also become counted as his treasured friends) who have been gen-erous with their time, encouragement and hospitality. I should especially mention the Hon. Sir John Astor, Mr David Barton, Lord Bruntisfield, Mme Helene Catsiapis, Mr Ray Cooney, Mr Allan Davis, Mr Michael Denison and Mrs Michael Denison (Dulcie Gray), the Hon. David Douglas-Home and the Hon. Mrs David Douglas-Home, the Hon. Edward Douglas-Home, Mr Lawrence Evans, Sir Edward Ford, Mr John Gale, Mrs Janet

Glass, Lord Glendevon, Mr Otto Herschan, Lord Home of the Hirsel, the Marquess of Lansdowne, Colonel Michael Lyle, Mr Kenneth Macksey, Lady William Montagu-Douglas-Scott, Mr Ian Mullins, Mrs Sue Mumford Smith, Mrs Charles Pretzlik, Mr Anthony Roye, Mr John Rubinstein, Colonel Nigel Ryle, Sir Peter Saunders.

The staff of the National Library of Scotland, where the extensive collection of William Douglas Home papers is held, have been most helpful and I am grateful. I am also grateful to the staff of the Public Record Office, Kew, for prompt response to my requests, particularly for War Diaries in connection with the battles at Le Havre in September 1944. To the staff of the London Library, as usual, and to the staff of the British Library (Newspaper Library, Colindale), whose speed and efficiency were admirable, I owe my thanks.

I have quoted frequently from the text of the Douglas Home plays, both performed and unperformed. Will wrote – or scribbled – in (mostly large) notebooks, and his scripts were then somehow turned into excellent typescripts by other skilled and devoted hands. I am grateful to Lady Dacre and the Estate of the late William Douglas Home for the use of all this material and for leave to quote from these and other writings. In two cases – *The Reluctant Debutante* and *The Bad Soldier Smith* – I have also quoted from the Production Note (by Jack Minster) and the Author's Note (W. DH), using the published edition and acting edition, and I am additionally grateful to the publishers (Samuel French) and to the previous Douglas Home agents, Curtis Brown, for permission to quote from the former and the latter respectively. For leave to quote an extended extract from *Half-Term Report* I thank Messrs Longman, and for permission to use an extract from *Ego 9*, James Agate's works, I owe thanks to Messrs George Harrop. The bronze sculptured head of Will shown on the jacket of this book is by Rosie Sturgis, to whom I owe gratitude not only for permission to show it here, but for executing it to widespread acclaim.

Finally, as ever, the work could not have been done without the skilful perseverance of my wife at the word-processor, and her perceptive advice, at every stage, on this attempt to portray a man we both loved.

Isington
1995   David Fraser

PART I
1912–1944

DOUGLAS and HOME

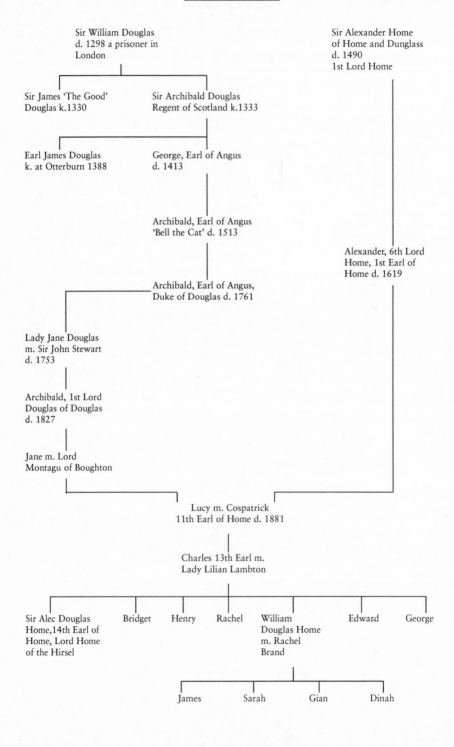

Sir William Douglas
d. 1298 a prisoner in
London

Sir Alexander Home
of Home and Dunglass
d. 1490
1st Lord Home

Sir James 'The Good'
Douglas k.1330

Sir Archibald Douglas
Regent of Scotland k.1333

Earl James Douglas
k. at Otterburn 1388

George, Earl of Angus
d. 1413

Archibald, Earl of Angus
'Bell the Cat' d. 1513

Alexander, 6th Lord
Home, 1st Earl of
Home d. 1619

Archibald, Earl of Angus,
Duke of Douglas d. 1761

Lady Jane Douglas
m. Sir John Stewart
d. 1753

Archibald, 1st Lord
Douglas of Douglas
d. 1827

Jane m. Lord
Montagu of Boughton

Lucy m. Cospatrick
11th Earl of Home d. 1881

Charles 13th Earl m.
Lady Lilian Lambton

Sir Alec Douglas
Home,14th Earl of
Home, Lord Home
of the Hirsel

Bridget

Henry

Rachel

William
Douglas Home
m. Rachel
Brand

Edward

George

James

Sarah

Gian

Dinah

CHAPTER I

Sight and Sound of Tweed

William Douglas-Home generally dispensed with the hyphen in 'Douglas-Home', but the hyphen – of respectable age as hyphens go – marked an historic and profitable connection. Alexander Home, fifteenth Lord and tenth Earl of Home, was born in 1769[1] and his eldest son, Cospatrick Home – born in 1799 – married Lucy, the eldest daughter and co-heiress of Lord Montagu of Boughton. Lucy's mother, Lady Montagu, had been born Jane Douglas. This Jane, Cospatrick's mother-in-law, was the eldest daughter (and ultimate co-heiress) of Archibald, first Lord Douglas of Douglas. Henceforth Douglas-Home it was formally to be.

The Douglas connection brought to the Homes not only a hyphen but the lands of Douglas in Lanarkshire. It also brought the residue of a notorious dispute. The first Duke of Douglas, who died without children in 1761, was succeeded in those of his many honours which did not become extinct by his distant cousin, the Duke of Hamilton. Douglas, however, had had a sister, Lady Jane Douglas, who had married a Highland soldier, Sir John Stewart of Grandtully; and this lady, at the age of fifty, had given birth (or claimed to have given birth) in Paris to twin sons in the summer of 1748. She had died in 1753, but on her brother, the Duke's, death the elder twin, Archibald – aged thirteen – claimed the Douglas lands of his uncle.[2] The Duke of Hamilton

1. A vintage year, which also saw the births of the first Duke of Wellington and the first Emperor Napoleon.
2. The younger twin died in infancy. William Douglas Home's play *The Douglas Cause* (1971) – splendidly featuring Andrew Cruickshank – gave a robust and almost impartial account of the whole extraordinary business. Sir Bernard Burke, in *Vicissitudes of Families* (Longman, Green, 1893) observed that the case produced 'feuds among the gentry and rioting among the people'. He added, temperately, that 'when the question is considered after the lapse of a century . . . it seems impossible to reconcile the contradictory assertions connected with the strange story of Mr Douglas's birth, or to resist the strong appearance of imposture.'

counter-claimed, alleging that the twins were no Douglasses, no
Stewarts, but had been bought or stolen by Stewart and Lady
Jane in France. The case was heard in the Court of Sessions in
Edinburgh in 1767 and decided in the Hamilton favour by the
casting vote of the President, after the judges divided seven–seven;
but two years later the Edinburgh judgement was reversed by the
House of Lords and Archibald Stewart came into his Douglas
inheritance. He was, in 1790, created Lord Douglas of Douglas,
and since his own sons died without children his lands passed to
the descendants of his daughter, Jane: Douglas-Homes.

The lands of Douglas, at issue in *The Douglas Cause* and cradle
of the enormous Douglas tribe, lay astride the Douglas Water,
itself a tributary of the Upper Clyde, separated by the watershed
of the Tinto Hills from the headwaters of the east-running Tweed.
Archibald Douglas, when he claimed his inheritance, claimed
a name and a descent as bold, as chivalrous but often as blood-
stained as any in Scottish history. It was a descent from Archibald
Douglas, Regent of Scotland in 1333, whose brother, 'Good Sir
James Douglas', had been killed in Spain, escorting the heart of
King Robert Bruce to the Holy Land; and whose grandson, Earl
James Douglas, had reached as far as York on a raid into England,
had taken Harry Hotspur prisoner and had fallen at the battle in
the moonlight at Otterburn in 1388 – thanking God that, like his
forebears, Douglas was dying not abed but by the enemy's sword.
The Douglas lords were, as often as not, Wardens of the Marches,
responsible for order in the wild country between Scotland and
England; while as often themselves raiding deep into England.

Earl James had a bastard brother, George Douglas, created Earl
of Angus in 1389: forebear of that so-called 'Great Earl of Angus'
who earned the name 'Bell-the-Cat' for brutally confronting and
destroying King James III's favourite, Cochrane, while the other
nobles hesitated[3] – tearing the King's present, a jewelled collar,
from Cochrane's neck and hanging him from the bridge at Lauder.
From the line of Angus came (according to the House of Lords'
judgement) Cospatrick Home's wife and descendants; and, in particular, Cospatrick's grandson, Charles Douglas-Home, thirteenth

---

3. W.DH's play *The Thistle and the Rose* (1949) dealt with the incident, as well
as with Angus's disapproval of James IV giving battle to the English at Flodden, a
battle wherein his two sons – as well as the king, and a large part of the nobility
of Scotland – were killed.

Earl of Home. The latter had two daughters and five sons. Of these the third, born on June 1912, was christened William.

The Home lands lay on the north bank of the Tweed, in Berwickshire for the most part; and the Homes, like the Douglasses, were often Wardens of the Marches or East Marches. Like the Douglasses, too, the Homes often died in battle – or on the scaffold for some alleged act of treason, as did the third Lord Home, executed (his brother dying by the axe the following day) in October 1516. Created Earls of Home by James VI in 1604, immediately after he ascended the English throne as James I, the Homes thereafter played a full part in the affairs not only of Scotland but of the whole realm. In the troubled seventeenth century the third Earl signed the Solemn League and Covenant in 1638, but, like others, became disenchanted with the way the Covenanting party was going and with the influence of Argyll. He joined Montrose, and from 1640 supported the King. Deprived of his lands after Cromwell's victories, he recovered them at the Restoration.

Thereafter the Home of the day opposed the Williamite succession of 1688; opposed the Union with England in 1707; was arrested, suspected of Jacobitism, in 1715, but, as with many other families, was reconciled to the Government after the failure of the Rising in that year. The eighth Earl of Home, indeed, fought with the Government troops at Prestonpans in the Rising of 1745, when Sir John Cope was routed by the Highlanders marching with Prince Charlie; and later became a Lieutenant-General. His great-nephew and ultimate successor sired Cospatrick, grandfather of Charles, thirteenth Earl: great-grandfather of William.

In William's generation the eldest of the Douglas-Home family, Alec, was styled Lord Dunglass after his father's succession to the Earldom. Next came Bridget, and next Henry, a brilliant ornithologist. Rachel was William's nearest in age and was followed by William, Edward and George – a span of nineteen years, with George born ten years after William, in 1922.

Playwright, rebel, aspiring politician, William Douglas Home – 'Will' henceforth – was often described with varying (and frequently hostile) nuances as coming from a background of privilege. The word is imprecise. If simply indicating a long-recorded lineage, of names distinguished in his country's history and possessing wide lands, the description is factual and fair. Will was, however, not one of those numerous Scots who take a particular relish in genealogy; if he spoke of family history at all he would generally do so with deprecatory mockery.

Nevertheless it meant a good deal to him to belong to one of Scotland's great families; and, like most Scots, he could not resist the magic of an occasional roll-call from a brightly coloured past. Here is his forebear, the Douglas Earl of Angus, telling James IV's widowed young queen of the tragedy of Scotland's defeat at Flodden, the loss of her king, the slaughter of her nobility in *The Thistle and the Rose*: 'The Lord Archbishop of St Andrews died'; and Will gave Angus a concluding speech, a sounding list of the great names of Scottish chivalry who had fallen on that day – Lennox, Crawford, Montrose, Errol, Argyll and many more – while 'The Flowers of the Forest' sounded off-stage. He enjoyed the music of it and – deprecatory or not – found his blood stirred by the tragedy Flodden represented.

Few playwrights are at their most successful with historical themes. The Scottish vernacular, too, needs convincing handling. Will's friend Jakie Astor, who had made a modest investment in the production of *The Thistle and the Rose*, telephoned after the first night, as Will ruefully recounted: 'When that boy came on shouting "Mither, Mither", and Mither dropped a bucket of water which splashed over me, and a lot of men in armour rushed on stage in total darkness, I knew we'd had it!' They had. But there was poetry in *The Thistle and the Rose*, which was written with a near versical rhythm as well as great feeling, and it came from one, seldom paraded, part of Will's heart. He was privileged to possess it.

'Privilege' also, and very importantly, meant that he grew up in beautiful surroundings, with sporting and social pleasures taken for granted, without pressures of poverty or insecurity in childhood and youth. The love of beauty as well as the confidence which early memories transmitted remained always with him. Often shy of attempting a lyrical note in his writings, he touched it here and there. John Brown, in *The Queen's Highland Servant* (1968), knows himself dying and recalls the sights and smells of Scotland – although his own Highlands rather than Will's beloved Borders.

> I dinna want them burying me here,
> Remember that – I'm wanting up to Deeside,
> wi' the curlews calling and the plover tumbling where
> I was born and reared. Remember that.

The Hirsel, the Homes' principal home on the Tweed, by Coldstream, was a large house, run on traditional lines of punctuality and decorum, but with routine always tempered by liveliness and laughter; and it was the same at the other family home at Douglas, where they went, throughout Will's youth, for summers – for the grouse shooting, the snipe, the roe deer. Will was always devoted to waiting for a chance of a rifle shot at a roe deer, a solitary pursuit requiring knowledge and patience as well as marksmanship. The grace and shyness of these beautiful creatures intrigued him – all sportsmen understand that there is no natural discord between admiring and killing, a discord only imaginable by those unfamiliar with the countryside. Will shot his first roe in 1924 at the age of twelve and in 1929 bagged and mounted the best roebuck head yet got in Scotland. Throughout life he was an excellent pigeon shot, again enjoying the waiting and the solitude. Throughout life, too, Will had an artistic as well as a naturalist's sense of countryside, and a knowledge of beasts and birds which, although he did not match his brother Henry's ornithological expertise, made him a particularly enchanting companion when there were rivers to inspect, animals to observe, birds to listen to or watch.

He had, of course, learned much from Henry, who achieved a great reputation as 'The Birdman', particularly on radio; and whose story may or may not have been apocryphal about one especially penetrating evening birdcall which he had evoked in a wood for a radio programme, in company with Will. Will, a little bored with waiting, had gone off for a while. Henry, long afterwards, recalled: 'That was a good one, that evening! It impressed the BBC people no end.'

'Good,' said Will, 'it was me!'

Hirsel, Douglas, grouse, snipe, roe deer, waiting for pigeon; gamebook record meticulously kept; salmon, trout, beauty of the cloud-shadowed hills: all this, as well as history, poetry and the call of the blood meant much to Will. Like John Buchan[4] he could surely have said, 'If Paradise be a renewal of what was happy and innocent in our earthly days, mine will be some golden afternoon within sight and sound of Tweed.'

That all this was privilege Will never attempted to deny. It created background. Foreground, however, involves, for an

---

4. *Memory Hold the Door*, Hodder & Stoughton, 1941.

adult, the dramas, triumphs and trials of adult life – fortune and failure; and if the word 'privilege' is used to imply dependence on family and connections, on inherited circumstances rather than personal effort for advancement, then in Will's case the word is inappropriate. Primogeniture – the concentration of family wealth in the hands of an elder son and heir – is a system with much to commend it, and nowhere has it been more stringently applied than in Scotland and by Scottish families. Estates sometimes produced (and sometimes did not) substantial revenues, but they bore heavy expenses as well as the upkeep, as often as not, of some great house. Subdivided they could not last. The Scottish tradition was for younger sons to be given an education and a childhood home, and, if family affections were strong (as they certainly were in the case of the Homes), a base and a sort of general headquarters for descendants of the tribe; but as adults they were expected to make their own way, perhaps to a greater extent than in England. A younger son might be given an allowance from estate income but it would certainly not enable him even to exist without personal endeavour. Will received £250 a year from the strict legal administrators of the Home fortunes. The sum remained unchanged until a moment came in the 1940s when he opened a lawyers' letter. This explained that they were very aware how time, taxation and the depredations of inflation were placing every budget under difficulties. 'Thank God,' said Will. 'They've at last realised the sort of problems I've got.'

He read on. The Home estates were suffering from this universal budgetary problem. His allowance was to be cut by £50.

Such it was to be a younger son, and such it was for Will. But the system had benefits beyond the preservation of inheritances, and, knowing or not, he gained from them. Younger sons of distinguished houses in Scotland made their own way because they had to. In so doing they often enriched both themselves and the nation's life. There was, for instance, little of the aversion from 'trade' which is said to have confined the younger sons of comparable English families to the Law, the Church, the Army, the Navy. On the contrary, Scottish sprigs of the nobility[5] often became merchants, manufacturers, bankers, entrepreneurs. The concept of 'gentlemen's professions' in the snobbish and exclusive sense barely existed in Scotland, although in no country was

5.'Nobility' has, anyway, a different historic significance in Scotland, having nothing to do with title, everything to do with blood.

there more pride in birth as opposed to money, or more profound respect for learning. But Will's 'privilege' – and it was real – was certainly not financial. Throughout life, what he spent he earned.

Privilege, however, Will certainly possessed in one sense, and that the most important of all. He was a member of an exceptionally close-knit and internally loyal family, a family, furthermore, as tolerant as it was affectionate. Charles, Earl of Home, was a man greatly beloved throughout Scotland, not only in his own Border lands. Small of stature – he was known locally as 'the wee Lordie' – he was, like his children, a countryman through and through. He was gentle-tempered, generous, genial and upright, with an excellent memory for people (the most endearing of qualities) and a complete lack of self-importance or pomposity. The most kindly of men, he was eccentric in the way that men and women often appear eccentric if they are totally without self-consciousness. He generally moved about humming or singing some little song. When inclined (frequently) to prayer, he prayed aloud and very audibly. He lived according to simple and, it was generally and understandably reckoned, saintly principles. A favourite work of his was Jerome K. Jerome's *Passing of the Third Floor Back*, the moving, mystical account of an unknown stranger's visit to a London boarding house, a visit during which he transforms the life of every occupant by confidently showing he sees the best in each, and sees it as the true reality. That was Lord Home – seeing and expecting only the best and, far more often than with most men, getting it. 'Read this?' he'd say to one of the family. 'Only take you ten minutes!' Will loved him deeply. He devoted his life to the stewardship of his considerable properties in Lanarkshire, Roxburghshire and Berwickshire; and to public and charitable service in Scotland. He served in the Army in the Middle East in the First World War. To his family he showed the same affectionate but principled 'persona' that he did to the world in general. A Communist Member of Parliament noticed him once, late in life, and nudged a fellow member of the Party:

'Who's yon?'

'If there were more people like yon there'd be less people like us,' was the reply.

He married Will's mother, Lady Lilian Lambton, in 1902. The Lambtons of Lambton were great landowners in Durham from time almost immemorial. Will claimed for that side of his parentage a strong element of rebellion, of refusal to conform.

He drew for fact, as far as he could, on 'Radical Jack' Lambton, first Earl of Durham, Governor-General of Canada in 1838, a member of the government of Earl Grey (whose daughter he married as his second wife), described as 'the most Radical of the aristocratic members of that [Whig] Party'[6] – which was not, perhaps, saying very much. The Lambtons, like the Homes, also numbered in the family a considerable count of generals, admirals and fighting men, including a cavalry commander who died for King Charles at Marston Moor.

Will enjoyed the character and reputation of 'Radical Jack'. He may have been ignorant (or properly contemptuous) of the *Times*' assessment of Durham's character. That paper obituarised him, amid some diluted praise, as 'a flashy politician, ambitious and without ballast', and as one whose autocracy (in Canada) was 'vainglorious, perverse and reckless of national consequence – beginning in buoyant self-conceit and ending in feeble-minded petulance and mortification'. Whether these disobliging references (1841) from the great 'Jupiter' had any justice in them or not, Will savoured the notorious eccentricity and wilfulness of this great-great-grandfather and the Lambton blood, just as he admired the high principle and independence of mind of his own mother. And Will's mother to some extent counter-balanced his father in the strictness with which she regulated her family's consciences. She was a frequent critic of Will's plays later in life – 'Why must you be so vulgar, William?' – and would reprimand him vigorously with a 'William, you were born a gentleman: try to remain one!'

Will relished his mother's asperity and nonconformity. He chuckled at the way his father was convinced that her health would suffer unless she went to bed sharp at ten o'clock – 'Come on, Lil, time for bed!' He enjoyed describing her typical response to a newspaper enquiry as to how she felt on learning that her eldest son had become Prime Minister in 1963. 'I thought it should have been Mr Butler!'

Will's family, therefore – parents and the four brothers and two sisters he loved – represented for him not only a dependable background of loyalty, rooted in unsentimental mutual regard and tolerance, but a rich seam of comedy from which to tap anecdote and drama. His parents provided him with the Earl and Countess of Lister in *The Chiltern Hundreds* (1947) and its sequel

6. Vicary Gibbs, *The Complete Peerage*, Vol. VI. Earl Grey's administration was in office when the Reform Bill of 1832 was enacted.

The Manor of Northstead (1954). Both were admirably cast, A. E. Matthews giving London a memorable Lord Lister; while the magnificent and long-serving butler at The Hirsel, Collingwood, was given a stage personality, 'Beecham', first by Michael Shepley and then by Charles Heslop. In *The Manor of Northstead*, the Listers are staying in a remote Hebridean fishing lodge during a General Election, and about to undergo a visit from Lord Lister's sister, married (in the dénouement of *The Chiltern Hundreds*) to the Labour peer, Lord Cleghorn.

LADY LISTER (to Beecham):
And the same applies to Lord and Lady Cleghorn in a different way. Since he was made a Labour peer my sister-in-law tells me that Lord Cleghorn gets extremely restless in Elections. He was all right when he was Lord Privy Seal, of course, but now that he's lost that she says he's like a war horse in the stable snorting when he hears the trumpet call.

LORD LISTER: Well, why the devil should he come and snort up here? Besides we haven't got a stable.

BEECHAM: I scarcely think he will, my Lord. I feel that Lady Caroline assumes, quite rightly, that the tumult and the shouting of a General Election bypasses this little island. Thus one hopes Lord Cleghorn will survive the period without a single whinny, so to speak.

LORD LISTER: What happens if he fishes, Beecham? Every time another fellow catches one it means that I catch less.

BEECHAM: Few members of the Labour Party fish for salmon, anyway with rod and line, my Lord. They seem to lack the enterprise required for private rod-fishing, while favouring the more cooperative method of approach inherent in the casting of the midnight net.

As a child Will was particularly shy, nervous and often tearful. But no boy of Will's generation and background could escape one traditional penance: boarding school.

The penance was initially harder the more loved and loving the home. Ludgrove, the preparatory school where Will went when nine years old, was not disagreeable as such institutions went, and Will recalled it in later years with tolerance, even a certain amused affection; but he hated leaving home. He wrote afterwards that he never made a friend during his years there. This was probably untrue, but he had a black temper if provoked and he was not difficult to provoke. At yells of 'Codfish', his nickname, he could react violently and bring the mob against him. Young boys easily compose gangs; find cruelty natural; and mob an isolated victim. Will, throughout life, never joined a gang or in the mobbing of a victim. School was not a naturally agreeable environment for him.

Furthermore he was not particularly good at games, although very adequate at his books, ultimately taking 'Upper Fourth' (at that time the second out of five possible ratings) in the Common Entrance examination to Eton. His reports were good, especially in Classics and 'Repetition' – learning by heart; and he was generally commended for industry, although towards the end of his time observed as 'a little too independent'. And he was shy – another point of vulnerability in communal life – and easy to embarrass. On Sundays when singing the 'Te Deum' (English version, Book of Common Prayer) Will always blushed so furiously and suffered such agonies at the verse 'Thou didst not abhor the Virgin's womb' that the Ludgrove authorities arranged (with uncommon forbearance) that he be escorted from church by a master until the service entered calmer waters. 'He used to sit on a tombstone and smoke a pipe,' Will would recount, with his usual inscrutable smile.

Nevertheless Will was so naturally lovable – and so naturally funny – that despite the temper, the shyness and the lack of athletic skill it is doubtful whether he was ever such a misfit as he later pretended. When he went to Eton in 1925 he wrote of a friend, Penrose Tennyson, that 'he was the first person who had ever really liked me for myself'.[7] This may be doubted. There was, in adulthood anyway, something so instantly endearing, entertaining and sympathetic about Will that it is hard to believe some slender indicators of the man were wholly absent in boyhood. Perhaps he felt himself disliked in those early days but the perception cannot have lasted long. At Eton he was soon popular. He was popular because he was irresistibly good company and at home, at Hirsel or Douglas, he always managed to make the family chuckle, although his father probably found him more entertaining than did his mother.

Will's Eton career was, in fact, successful, in schoolboy terms – Captain of his house; a member of 'Pop', the Eton society elected by the members themselves; a boy surrounded by friends, shyness greatly diminished, confidence enhanced. And at Eton he

7. *Half-Term Report*, Longman, 1954.

started to write. He wrote two articles for the *Chronicle*, the Eton periodical edited by boys, and first felt the warm thrill of seeing his words in print. And at least some schoolmasters enjoyed his economy with words, a facet which lay at the root of some of his future success. Asked to write an essay on 'The future of coal' when studying political and economic subjects, Will submitted a one-word answer: 'Smoke.' He was given seven marks out of ten for accuracy and brevity. He tried his hand at humour, writing a romance between (it was ultimately disclosed) two fountain pens. He found that with his pen as well as his tongue he could make people laugh.

He found a facility for versifying which he always retained. After the annual Harrow Match at Lords (Will was about eighteen), he wrote:

> Though we sit tired out by the hours of play
> When the shadows of evening fall
> We have watched through the dancing heat of the day
> The struggle 'twixt bat and ball;
> For we love the changes and chances of cricket
> Though the bat succeeds or fails,
> Though the ball is striking the fatal wicket
> Or the white pavilion rails;
> For cricket's a glorious game, say we,
> And cricket will never cease to be.
>
> Yes, cricket will live till the trumpet trumps
> From the wide pavilioned sky,
> And time, the umpire, lays low the stumps
> As his scythe goes sweeping by –
> Till the mighty seed of humanity fails
> At the light of another birth,
> And God stoops down to remove the bails
> From the dark deserted earth;
>
> Yes, cricket's a glorious game, say we,
> And cricket will live in eternity.

And he wrote a one-act play (about a murder at Eton) which was put on at the school. He was, furthermore, a good chess player, a finalist in the school competition. The skill may have been indicative – chess involves the ability to envisage a board and what it will look like under varying cases several moves ahead. Will could always envisage – scenes as well as chessboards.

This play, however, was not Will's only dramatic effort at

13

Eton. He wrote another, *Child's Mistake*, in which most of the cast ended dead, with the family nanny opening the window (it was raining) with the curtain line: 'I think God must be crying!'

Will took this round to a friend, Charlie Hopetoun, to read. Hopetoun, who shared a room with his twin, John Hope, finally roared with a mixture of exasperation and mockery, opened the window and threw the play into the shrubbery of his house-master's garden. 'I think God must be crying!'

But a little later into the Hope brothers' room strode a famous Eton master, by name Headlam, housemaster of another house. Headlam had formed a high opinion of Will's potential and he told the offenders that they were in the wrong – one day Will would do great things with his pen! Nevertheless, in later life some of Will's older friends, when he had a disappointment in the theatre, would occasionally murmur to him, 'I think God must be crying!'[8]

From Eton, in 1931, Will went up to Oxford. To New College.

New College had the reputation of a serious and learned institution, much frequented by Wykehamists.[9] Will's two elder brothers, Alec Dunglass[10] and Henry Douglas-Home, had been at Christ Church where they had been respectively distinguished for cricket and horsemanship. Will sensed that his father imagined New College, with its scholastic reputation, might evoke some academic ambitions, more appropriate for one who would undoubtedly need to make his own way in the world.

In this Lord Home was to be disappointed. Will devoted minimum time to learning. He claimed that he found New College austere and uncongenial, and that both its architecture and its atmosphere depressed him.

Depression did not last. He came to appreciate Oxford hugely, although more so when he lived out of college in lodgings for his last year. He particularly cherished Eton friends, friends of longer standing rather than those new-found (although there were plenty of the latter): and this was something of a constant in Will. He was affable and charming with anybody – or almost anybody –

---

8. Will, in his first volume of autobiography, placed this incident at Oxford, but it almost certainly happened at Eton.
9. New College, like Winchester, was founded by William of Wykeham.
10. Later 14th Earl of Home, then Prime Minister as Sir Alec Douglas-Home, having disclaimed his peerage; ultimately Lord Home of the Hirsel, as a Life Peer.

who swam into his life, but he generally preferred the familiar, and the longer the familiarity the better. But Will loved Oxford. His Oxford acquaintance was wide and took him to its heart. He was something of a jester – a witty, argumentative jester – and so he remained, on the surface.

Will tried most things Oxford could provide. He joined the Union, although not at that time involving himself in Oxford politics. He broke the rules, climbed into college, overstayed leaves, was sent down. He lost his driving licence and thereafter went round Oxford, including to lectures, in a phaeton with hired horse, persuading Brian Johnston, a lifelong friend, to act as groom – holding up the traffic intolerably but attracting affection (particularly for the horse) as well as laughter. He even rode in a point-to-point. Since he couldn't ride, and simply took the minimum of lessons to reach the saddle, from which he departed abruptly soon after the start, this involved considerable courage.

Conventionally, Will was idle. He did only as much work as he needed to get by (he read History); and he did it without much difficulty, for he had a good brain, an excellent memory, read and absorbed quickly, and always found in history much of interest. He also, of course, discovered in tutors and mentors a good deal of unintentional entertainment. But he claimed that he felt, at Oxford, an immature ignoramus – undereducated, unsophisticated, ignorant of art, society and the ways of the world; only at ease in the open spaces of the Scottish Border, with rod and gun. He claimed that at Oxford he had few opinions and fewer ambitions beyond the hope of a job and a salary one day, sufficient to enable him to live and to keep up friendships with (in many cases) men whose wealth and prospects were certainly greater than his.

The self-portrait[11] is of a somewhat lazy, certainly impoverished, and essentially unmotivated young man, without intellectual convictions or direction; a gauche and uncertain adolescent, privileged in one sense but immature and ill-equipped for life; a youth pitchforked into an often gilded world without the resources to make much of it. The self-portrait contains a good deal of travesty. Will experienced uncertainties common to most people of his age who are not grossly insensitive, and since he had both imagination and a sense of drama, he dramatised them.

11. *Half-Term Report.*

He was romantic, he built walls round his emotions and inner feelings, he had in many ways a skin too few.

In reality, however, he was popular, a central figure in a lively and loving circle of friends. He gained in sophistication as he gained in confidence, realising that socially he was successful. He might have arrived with few formed opinions, but he made up for it rapidly. And although he may have supposed he lacked the sort of ambition or life-plan some of his friends were evolving, he in fact had purposes of his own which were already taking shape in his mind. Indeed, probably more than any of his contemporaries, he started on a road from Oxford which he would follow until the end. He wrote a play.

Great Possessions (1937), Will's first play to reach a stage (apart from his *Eton Murder*, produced at school), was written during his last year at Oxford. The earlier efforts, even *Child's Mistake*, had helped prepare him for this. He now knew that he wanted to write plays. He knew that he wanted to learn about the art of writing plays. And he soon knew that he wanted this more than anything else in life.

Will – oddly, perhaps – had taken no part in Oxford's dramatic undertakings. He had never joined the Dramatic Society, the OUDS. He had not until now felt particularly drawn to the theatre. Now he felt that the theatre must be his destiny, if humanly possible. Furthermore he now felt that it *was* possible, because he found within himself the power to use words to effect. He found that his ear was sharp. His imagination had always been lively, although he created more from observation of others than from any design evolved from within. The rest he would learn.

Great Possessions is a play on the theme of a rich young man who, like Nicodemus, wanted salvation and worried that his wealth was an impediment. It was not only Will's first presented play, it was the first of many in which both his wit and his conscience found expression. And there were, perhaps, three particular dictates of that conscience which repeatedly surfaced in his writing; which, indeed, provided much of the motive power for much of the writing. These three dictates – in so far as they can be distinguished and defined – often fused, so that a play reflected two or all three of them; sometimes in the lines given to the same character.

The first of these was simple – indeed, they were all simple. It was Will's sense of fairness. He was never conventionally egalitarian in a political sense, and would one day be pilloried by those who were. Nevertheless he had a vivid understanding that life is a great deal harder on some than on others, and it hurt him. He wanted a fair deal for all and a world which would be arranged to promote it. He was naturally very aware that he personally was fortunate – as would incessantly be said later, 'privileged' – albeit without wealth. It never made him feel exactly guilty. That would have been difficult and, in his view, inappropriate since so much of what he was privileged to possess was both intangible and intrinsically good – the love of family, the conventions of an affectionate home, the experience of nature. But he realised that for many people there is not only a complete absence of such blessings, but poverty and want as well. He disliked this elementary fact of life, and he disliked very heartily those who, in his own perception, were indifferent to inequality, were complacent about their own good luck, were insensitive and smug. These he could pursue in the way he came to know best – with humour and irony.

The second dictate of conscience often, but not always, coincided with the first. Will hated double standards. His inherent sense of justice led him always to try to see a problem, a struggle, an argument from an opposing point of view. Where most of his contemporaries – or family – might condemn a particular cause or viewpoint or person, Will would instinctively ask them to consider how they might feel or act or react if their own circumstances were nearer the one condemned. Too often, he believed, men and nations apply to their opponents or rivals very different – and generally more exacting – principles than those they apply to themselves. Will detested this, and in his writing he could, again, give vent to his detestation with wit and mockery. He abominated self-righteousness and self-deceiving humbug.

The third imperative Will's conscience gave him was also simple. But while the first two led to comments on the behaviour and attitudes of individuals as well as nations, the third was wholly political and lay in the public domain. It was an instinctive loathing of war. Some of what he later wrote about this derived from more mature reflection, but there is no reason to doubt his sense of incongruity as a child in 1916 when told that his father was away at the war, killing Germans. Why, Will wondered, should such a kindly man want to do that? And this ingenuousness, this instinctive revulsion from the extremes of violence which war represents, persisted. Even in the small transactions of life Will intensely disliked confrontation.

Questions of peace and war, of course, were political and international questions, and Will – an historian, after all – naturally realised that they were and are complicated. Nevertheless, 'Look at the whole matter from the other's viewpoint,' he would think and say and write. And, 'Is there really no solution except to *kill*?' Sometimes – for Will was generally honest with himself – he admitted there might not be. But his instincts, which in this area often coincided with his detestation of double standards, were fundamentally pacific. They derived from conscience, and from a nature to which hatred itself was alien. They derived from the same principle which guided his father, to look for and presume the best in others rather than the worst. At Eton he had, after a while, found it disagreeable to continue belonging to the Officers' Training Corps, the OTC, and had been allowed to leave it. He had, he wrote, stumbled on the obvious truth that the training was necessarily based on a readiness to kill. Will may not have wholly condemned this, but he found it unpalatable.

This antipathy to the idea of war – its brutality, its destructiveness, the suffering it creates – may be thought exaggerated, even peculiar, in one whose antecedents often served as conventionally patriotic warriors as well as citizens; and in one for whose more remote antecedents warfare was a way of life. Will's antipathy, however, was rooted less in doctrinaire pacifism – which he always disclaimed, albeit with sympathy – than in his hatred of hatred itself, his instinctive need to find some point of empathy with others, however apparently hostile. Love was strong in him and always would be, however reserved his expression of it.

Great Possessions, however, was inspired by his sense of fairness. The young lead part, Jerry, is the younger son of a sporting and landowning peer and is at Oxford when the play begins. He has come under the influence of a devoutly sincere, and lower middle-class, convert to the Oxford Group, the Buchmanite movement enjoying a certain vogue at the time although a little disguised in the play. Jerry is in process of turning his back on the atmosphere of his family's home, his sporting interests, above all his wealth – he has, although a younger son, inherited from a grandparent great possessions.

Jerry castigates his elder brother, Charles – one of Will's many creations of an insensitive, boorish and ill-tempered upper-class young man – for his lack of sympathy, his arrogance, his ill-mannered snobbery. He rounds on his parents – Lord and Lady

Stormont, affectionately portrayed despite their conventionality and lack of understanding – for their easy acceptance of inequality and the misfortunes of others. He rejects expensive twenty-first birthday presents – he doesn't need such extravagance. He is a prig, but a sincere prig.

LORD STORMONT: Damn it, it's my own money!
JERRY: In that case you oughtn't to have it.

And after Oxford, Jerry (whose elder, the insufferable Charles, has left him as Lord Stormont's heir by getting killed in the hunting field, untypically of Will, an infrequent butcher of his characters!) gives up his inherited way of life and works in a dockland settlement. There he is, we learn, prodigal in helping others, many of them undeserving and unscrupulous exploiters of his wealth and naivety.

Jerry rejects urgings to return to his family – and to the false social values he associates with them. They visit him, pleading, and are met with: 'Misery and poverty and hopelessness are more than words down here. They're characters that aren't very nice to have to meet.'

Great Possessions was written sixty years ago. The idiom naturally reflects the times – the dialogue, although already fluent and easy, shows a certain contrived frivolity which dates it – and the attitudes it pillories (or exalts, or ultimately excuses) are to some extent caricatured. Nevertheless it still conveys sincerity and is often moving. It sprang from conscience. It showed Will's impatience with the complacency of the materially fortunate. It also showed his aversion from doctrinaire condemnation. Lord Stormont has more than a touch of Lord Lister, yet to come, and of Will's father, for that matter; he is kindly, good-mannered and tolerant to Jerry's religious-fanatic friend although finding him unsympathetic and distrusting his influence.

The exchanges between father and son show an unchanging characteristic of Will's thinking and writing – the wish to give each side of an argument a fair run. Will didn't always succeed in this but he always tried. And it is Fred, the Oxford Group 'mentor' of Jerry, who, while explicitly retaining his own integrity, is clear-headed in seeing that Jerry is being taken in too often, is mistaking easy generosity and naive kindness for a true conviction of the heart. 'I don't idealise the poor simply because they're poor.' There is a strong dénouement.

In the Caledonian Hotel in Edinburgh, shortly after coming

down from Oxford, Will saw across the lounge the unmistakable profile of John Gielgud, whom he greatly admired but had never met. He approached the already distinguished actor, introduced himself, said that he had written a play, and asked – shy but presumptuous – whether Gielgud would read it. Will saw the look of panic in Gielgud's eye. 'Send it to me!'

There was, Will explained afterwards, no safe exit from the room. He was blocking it. 'I've got it here,' Will said, and pressed a copy of *Great Possessions* into the Gielgud hand.

CHAPTER II

Greasepaint and Shadow

The encounter with Gielgud bore fruit. The great man – he had achieved an enormous success as the tragic young King Richard II in *Richard of Bordeaux* – read Will's play and was encouraging. John Gielgud was as generous as he was brilliant. He wrote to Will about *Great Possessions* in critical but constructive terms. He took trouble. He sent it to another actor who did the same. Ultimately it reached a theatrical manager, Anthony Ellis, who undertook production.

This took time. Will, meanwhile, had come down from Oxford with a Fourth Class degree in history and was living in London. He had never aimed at academic distinction, he had learned something about life and a little about himself, and he had made up his mind about where his future must lie. Sensibly, he decided that if he wanted to make a living from writing plays he must learn more about the stage and what it means to perform on it. He applied for and achieved a place at the Royal Academy of Dramatic Art, beginning in the summer of 1935 at fees of sixteen guineas a term.

Will spent two years at RADA and always recognised the debt he owed it. He gained his diploma. He learned something of stage craft and stage management. He overcame – or began to overcome – his innate nervousness about appearing before an audience, his haunting shyness, his conviction that he could too easily appear absurd. His confidence as a performer grew. Sometimes it grew too fast and was sharply corrected. The Academy were performing Shaw's *Candida* and Will had successfully laid claim to the good part of Marchbanks. After a little the instructress called him over. 'Mr Douglas Home, I am going to take away the part of Marchbanks and give you the part of Lexy, the curate.'

She explained, very kindly, to a crestfallen Will that it was unfair to ask him to try to play Marchbanks. Marchbanks was the son of a peer – the sons of peers were eccentric people, the kind of people 'we middle-class people' don't quite understand. Will took his relegation with good grace – 'So much for type-casting,' he said afterwards. Will wrote another play, *Marry Bachelor*, which was produced (by Will) at RADA, with the author/producer taking the leading part – a novelty at the Academy, perhaps never repeated.

After RADA, Will got a job playing in a repertory company in Brighton for £3 a week – a new play each week. He next got a part in Dodie Smith's *Bonnet over the Windmill* at £8 a week, opening at Leeds and then moving to the New Theatre in London for what turned out to be only a three-month run. He then joined the cast of Thomas Browne's *Plan for a Hostess* which ran for six months at the St Martin's Theatre in London and for a further six months on tour; Will played with Ronald Squire, his daughter Jacqueline Squire and Yvonne Arnaud. He became briefly engaged to Jacqueline Squire during the tour – a matter of some embarrassment when it ended, since they were playing an engaged couple on stage. The episode naturally caused some pain.

In later life Will occasionally stepped into a breach and took a part for a brief spell in one of his own plays. He had few illusions about his acting skill – he had early realised that he could never vary or disguise his distinctive tones, so that a part had to fit, to some extent, his own voice and his own person-ality. This still admitted of a certain limited range, because it was a charming voice with undertones of suppressed laughter[1] and it was an immediately entertaining personality, but he was not designed by God to be a great or versatile actor. He may have been too modest about his ability to play a part, to induce that 'suspension of disbelief' which acting requires. He was a good mimic. When his brother Alec became engaged to Elizabeth Alington, Will presented himself to an aunt, his father's sister, as the fiancée – pretending to have been asked to precede Alec to tea as the latter 'had been delayed at the House of Commons' – and got away with the impersonation for a satisfactory amount of time.

His experience at RADA, however, and on stage was invalu-able. Thereafter, in writing scenes he knew what he was doing. He learned, from practice of the actor's craft as well as from

---

1. Will said that he knew he had a voice like a constipated bishop. He was unfair to himself as well as to the Episcopacy.

his own naturally good ear, the importance of rhythm and it can be seen and heard in most of his plays. In his writing he took increasing care with the juxtaposition of sounds when one actor's or actress's voice is succeeded by another, what he called the 'beat' of the dialogue. He developed an expert understanding of how to avoid what he termed 'air pauses' – the way a word at the start of a line can break the rhythm of an exchange and, for a split second, lose an audience.

Later in life he gave examples. In one of their exchanges, described by a critic as like watching an elegant and apparently effortless rally at Wimbledon, Wilfrid Hyde White and Celia Johnson glance at the morning papers over breakfast.[2]

> 'Hullo, the Duke of Positano's dead.'
> 'Who cares?'
> 'The Duchess, probably. Oh no, she's dead as well.'

Will pointed out that 'Probably the Duchess', instead of the way he wrote it, would have damaged rhythm, created a tiny break in the flow, lost smoothness and attention. 'Obviously!' one may rejoin, but such things are seldom obvious until analysed. Sometimes the point is identical with skill in versifying – and Will wrote verses with impudent (and occasionally moving) felicity. Sometimes it is simply a question of theatrical flow, of giving to an actor the best possible chance.

The technique became second nature. There was inborn aptitude but technique always needs development and practice; Will's development derived greatly from his apprenticeship at RADA and on stage. It gave him insights he never lost. He was, throughout life, an 'actor's playwright'. He could see and hear a scene on a stage even as his pen moved across paper. He could imagine, before any director started on one of his plays, how a gifted actor or actress could get maximum effect from a few apparently inconsequential or insubstantial lines of dialogue – and from the silences between them. Actors and actresses of great distinction wanted to perform in Will's plays, and most were or became devoted friends because he loved and admired the men and women of the theatre. But he was the indispensable source of their success when it came, the third party, the invisible agent of the laughter Hyde White and Johnson and many others so happily evoked. He needed them as his instruments, and they

2. *The Reluctant Debutante*, 1955.

needed his way with words. Stars of the theatre recognised his quality when they read his plays. They read lines they wanted to speak.

While he was still at RADA, Will's *Great Possessions* was produced in London. *Great Possessions* demonstrated another and sometimes unsuspected characteristic of Will. Because he generally displayed a very sweet temper, anxious to oblige a friend, slow to oppose, and because his antipathy to war and war-like attitudes often led him to make virtually common cause with pacifism, he was sometimes imagined to be easy-going about things which mattered to him. Nothing could be less true. He was extremely combative, never failing to take up a challenge, never leaving a contentious point unanswered. He never ran away from a fight and he seldom gave one up before a knockout, but a fight had to be over what he regarded as fundamentals. And one fundamental – in this, his first play – was what he conceived to be his professional integrity.

He was twenty-four. He had no track record of playwriting. He was learning, but only learning, how to act. He knew nothing of the theatre. Nevertheless when Anthony Ellis, the producer, told Will that *Great Possessions* needed a completely different ending he at first dug in his toes. He refused. Ellis wanted not only a different ending but a new character – a girl whom Jerry, the starry-eyed young idealist with great possessions, has met in Dockland and with whom (he believes) he has fathered a child. Jerry, wretched and ashamed, intends to marry her. This, of course, greatly altered the thrust of the final part of the play – indeed, arguably, of the whole play. It still led to a strong dénouement (the girl and her husband, posing as brother and sister, are confidence tricksters and blackmailers). Will, per-suaded by the superior experience of producer and director, wrote a revised last act on these lines. He attended rehearsals.

Will then found himself appalled. His play, his child, had been deformed. He indulged in an indiscretion which he soon found (he was learning all the time) was near unforgivable in the theatre – he started talking to members of the cast about how differently he had envisaged the last act and how much he still preferred his first thoughts. The immediate result was that Anthony Ellis, discovering that Will was not far from instigating mutiny, made the author sign a letter promising not to talk to the cast except with the producer present. Furthermore the letter

– signed in January 1937 – also contained an undertaking never to attend rehearsals unless invited. Will, still unrepentant on the substance of the quarrel although chastened about his tactics in pursuing it, tried to enlist the sympathy of the theatre manager, Jack de Leon. Without success.

Now Will's combativeness and obstinacy emerged. He took the line that he had opposed revision of the last act, had rewritten it under protest, and that the revised version, in his opinion, didn't work. He argued that, as author, he had a right to insist on reversion to the original. Anthony Ellis said that the author had no such right. He, Ellis, was the producer of the play, Will had agreed (admittedly with reluctance) to revise it and the revised version worked well. Since no agreement between them was possible Will decided that he would publicise the quarrel. He told a newspaper reporter, and just before the First Night the papers carried a headline, 'Author disowns last act of Play!' Coming events were casting shadows before!

Anthony Ellis, an old hand, simply went ahead with the play. Jack de Leon, another old hand, assessing accurately that news of a row would be more likely to fill than empty a theatre, was unmoved. Will's démarche had done a lot for the play's publicity, and a fashionable audience thick – as ever – with Will's friends and relations attended the First Night. On stage at the final curtain, together with Ellis, Will made a few remarks about how inferior the play was to what the audience might have seen, and shook the Ellis hand. The play was quite well received, reviewers using such expressions as 'remarkably moving', 'sincere', 'clever'. *Great Possessions* then moved to the Duke of York's Theatre in St Martin's Lane where Will, taking the author's curtain call at the new First Night, managed to restrain himself from referring again to what might have been. But the play ran for six weeks only. Will remained until his death absolutely firm in his view that the first version of *Great Possessions* was the best version. He probably remained equally convinced that the first version would have run at the Duke of York's for more than six weeks.

During these years Will was living in London, sharing lodgings in a house in South Eaton Place with an Eton friend, Jo Grimond, later to be Liberal Member of Parliament and leader of his Party. Grimond left lodgings to be married in 1938 and his place in the ménage was taken by Brian Johnston, one day to be a famous broadcaster, already another devoted friend of Will from Eton and Oxford. Will's life was star-studded with delightful companions

just as it had been at Oxford; and although they often professed
to regard him and his views as eccentric or absurd their affection
lasted throughout his life or theirs. He led an enjoyable social life
in London, in so far as his stage commitments allowed it. He
was popular and entertaining; and argumentative. With women
he was gentle, sensitive, shyly romantic by temperament, wholly
lacking in confidence and maddeningly elusive. Women felt in him
a sort of innocence as well as charmingly entertaining humour;
and were intrigued by it.

He also, of course, delighted in his friends from the world of
the theatre. He enjoyed the contrast between their interests and
obsessions and the social or sporting interests and obsessions
of his friends from Oxford or in London society. He enjoyed
it particularly when he could establish an area that both his
worlds shared – he often found it in racing, which he followed
throughout life as a punter. He regularly fell in love and out again.
He travelled all over Europe and a little of Morocco with another
Oxford friend, George Mercer-Nairne,[3] who did a certain amount
to educate Will from the picture galleries and palaces of the great
cities of the Continent. It was only a certain amount. Life at the
Hirsel had not been dedicated to the visual arts, and on one
occasion Lord Home, asking George Mercer-Nairne whether he
liked pictures, had led him to a dimly lit bedroom passage where
there were some splendid watercolours, barely discernible. Then
– 'There's a particularly nice one in *here*,' he said, drawing his
guest into a bedroom, 'it's over the bed!' In the bed was lying
Lady Home. It was after ten o'clock bedtime.

Will had not, therefore, grown up in an atmosphere of artistic
appreciation, but on these Continental tours his enjoyment of
pictures increased. It was unaffected by fashion. 'Tell me what
you liked most,' George would say after touring a gallery. 'My
favourites were over doors!' Will would answer, unaware that
this was probably the chosen spot for the temporarily out of
favour.

Where Will was there was always laughter. On one occasion
he stayed at the Mercer-Nairne home, Meikleour, to plan a French
tour. The proposal was to visit Rheims, in particular to see the
stained glass in the Cathedral. But 'let's change it,' George said,
'let's go to Paris instead!'

Thus it was decided, and Will left. Half an hour later the

3. Later Marquess of Lansdowne.

telephone rang at Meikleour. It was Collingwood, the splendid Hirsel butler, and after he and George had had a friendly chat about family matters –

'Lord Home would like to speak to you.'

Then, after hearing the little snatch of singing which accompanied Will's father almost everywhere:

'George?'

'Yes, Lord Home.'

'I'm so glad you're taking Wilks to the Continent. I hear you're going to Rheims to look at the stained glass.'

It seemed simpler to dissemble, loth though George was to deceive.

'Yes, Lord Home.'

'Now mind, George – No f...ing! Nothing like that!' But at that moment (unsurprisingly, for never would Will's father have spoken in those terms) George heard a giggle which betrayed Will's presence in a call-box by the road home. His mimicry could deceive, at least for a short while.

Will's actor's salary, his tiny allowance and a little from *Great Possessions*, kept him alive. And during 1939 he wrote another play, *Passing By*. Centring on a clergyman's daughter who wanted a divorce, it was produced by Noel Howlett at the 'Q' theatre (Jack de Leon) in early 1940. It played to packed houses and there were high hopes of reaching the West End in May. That lay in the future. For Will, in 1939, life was more or less impecunious but almost entirely enjoyable. There were, however, shadows.

Will had played no role in politics at the University, although the Thirties were a highly political era. Inevitably, however, arguments about politics and particularly about international affairs were often passionate at South Eaton Place. Will talked and thought a lot about political matters. His father had taken little part but his elder brother, Alec Dunglass, was Member of Parliament for Lanark from 1931 and Parliamentary Private Secretary to Neville Chamberlain from 1935. The Lambtons were often active in politics (both Liberal and Tory). Will had a mind and a conscience, and some aspects both of society and the international scene disturbed him. The disturbance led to politics.

Personal tastes also played their part. There is theatre in politics and Will found that side of it compulsively attractive. He had sufficiently overcome shyness to stand and perform

before an audience; he felt that both his urge to speak his mind
on issues he cared about and his relish for drama might indicate
a destiny in Parliament. It was an understandable feeling and he
gave vent to it frequently in the coming years. The one member
of the family whose destiny already *had* led him to Parliament,
Will's elder brother, Alec, was very clear that this was a bad idea,
and his view never changed – was, indeed, fortified by all that lay
ahead. 'Politics,' he said, late in life, 'was certainly the wrong profession for William!' And he added, 'William disliked authority.
Resentment at authority nagged him.' Authority, Party discipline,
must be necessary to the orderly conduct of parliamentary life in
a democracy. Will had little time for it.

Will, however, was not reticent or hesitant in airing his views.
He had already taken something of a line in opposition to the
more unimaginative prejudices of his class in *Great Possessions*.
He would continue, in his writing, to try to deflate the smug and
the self-righteous. Above all, he minded about the issues of peace
and war. This would dominate the next decade of his life.

In 1933 Adolf Hitler had become Chancellor of Germany, soon
thereafter assuming dictatorial powers on the death of the aged
President, Field Marshal von Hindenburg. From 1934 onwards
the governments of Europe, sometimes incredulous, sometimes
complacently refusing to credit the worst, sometimes simply
cowardly, considered, month by month, the question 'What is
he going to do next?' Germany had suddenly become – some
said 'again become' – a rogue elephant in European affairs. The
provisions of the Treaty of Versailles, imposed on Germany after
the defeat of 1918, were one by one reversed by Hitler. Soon the
German Army was increased by decree to a planned strength of
300,000, rather than the 100,000 ruled by the Treaty. The German air force – banned by Versailles – was reconstituted in 1935,
and in March 1936 German troops marched into the Rhineland,
which had been 'demilitarised' under the Treaty. In March 1938
Hitler manoeuvred the Austrian government into inviting German
troops to enter Austria, and an *Anschluss* (peacefully and to a
large extent popularly) took place between the two countries.
Henceforth Austria would be part of the Greater German Reich.

To none of these developments did the governments of Britain
and France – the two principal guarantors of Versailles – offer
the sort of opposition which might have reversed the trend. To
most people outside Germany it was clear that Germany was now
controlled by a powerful will, and the instruments of that will –

28

the German people and the German armed forces – were willing, indeed enthusiastic instruments. It was equally clear that the populations of Britain and France had not the slightest desire to risk their lives or their prosperity (fragile in any case, just recovering from a great depression) in military adventures or threats designed – for what? For the enforcement of Versailles, which large numbers of people had come to feel was anyway a settlement draconian and unjust? For the demilitarisation of the Rhineland – an integral part of Germany? For the continuing enforced separation of Germany from Austria – an Austria which was itself a hopelessly uneconomic rump of the Austro-Hungarian Empire, dismembered under the same Treaty and surely needing incorporation into some larger and more viable entity? The idea of threatening war for such causes would have been thought ludicrous by large majorities in the western democracies, which, nevertheless, observed Hitler's actions, and to a large extent his domestic policies, with unease.

Yet even here the picture was hazy. The western world was experiencing economic hardship and a good deal of social unrest. Hitler's more appalling crimes lay well in the future – it was known that Nazi race policy was discriminatory and bullying, but it was also known that in Germany unemployment appeared to have been largely eliminated and that national morale had been enormously improved. The European nations still felt themselves to be suffering from the traumas of the war and only slowly emerging from a 'post-war' period. Now that post-war period, under an optimistic reading, was being restored to normality and Germany restored to health. People said that the domestic excesses of the Nazis were largely due to the state of near civil war which had marked the end of the Weimar Republic. They said that given increased confidence at home, and treated again with a trust which had been withdrawn since that day when the German army had crashed into Belgium in August 1914, Germany would mellow. Talk of war was surely unthinkable. German rearmament simply reflected the natural desire of a great nation to stand level with neighbours, a matter of international self-respect.

Will, unsurprisingly, stood with what was probably at that time the majority in such matters. Not only did his nature revolt from the idea of war on grounds of humanity, but his passionate determination to see more than one side of an argument made him distrustful of simplistic condemnations. Will therefore listened with sympathy to the voices in England and elsewhere which contended that Germany had, on the whole, had a rough deal from the Peace; and that in seeking to wipe the slate clean Hitler not only had most of his country but a good deal of right on his side. Out of curiosity he went with two friends to the Nazi *Parteitag* at Nuremberg in September 1936, and found it theatrically impressive and confirmatory of his own feelings – here were people who had discovered something and someone to be enthusiastic about. Why should that be a cause of hostility?

There was, however, much war talk in Europe at that time and Will thought it nonsense. The way ahead must be the way of negotiation and compromise. It appeared that, to Hitler, the frontiers imposed at Versailles were unjust. Well, Will felt, why not discuss them? Above all, show readiness to be magnanimous. Hitler might or might not, for instance, hope one day to recover former German colonies (in fact this played a negligible part in his aspirations). Was that so deplorable, Will suggested? 'My friends informed me . . .' he wrote, 'that the Empire which we had secured in admittedly reprehensible circumstances was now a free and living entity around the British crown . . . If the reward of building an empire through piracy and astuteness . . . was an empire such as ours, then how much more understandable did the aspirations of more piratical though infinitely less astute twentieth-century empire-builders become . . . Every empire-builder, from Napoleon to Hitler and Mussolini, even Stalin if you like, was treading in the path we had trodden.'[4] Humbug lay behind much condemnation, Will reckoned. Motes and beams in the eye. He therefore opposed other voices – initially a minority but increasing in number as the months of 1938 passed – which said that talk of compromise and negotiation was self-deception, that Hitler was apparently bent on war, and only armed strength would deter him. Will rejected this and continued to reject it. 'Anybody can be negotiated with,' he wrote, 'if he sees hope of getting at least something that he wants and something to which he feels he is entitled.'[5]

The difficulty, of course, was that the something to which Hitler felt entitled was always something to which somebody else also felt entitled; and Hitler, at least, was demonstrably prepared to give effect to his feelings with force. Nor were the crises of the Thirties caused by competition for colonies, nor could they be solved by a little handwringing on Britain's part,

4. *Half-Term Report.*
5. idem.

by the restoration (for instance) of the peoples of Tanganyika – once German East Africa – to German rule. Hitler wanted to challenge the post-war settlement in Europe, and to do so he needed a revision of frontiers in Germany's favour. As a start.

Will wrote that the course of international action he had always believed in was for an imperial power 'to keep [its] own Empire and permit others to keep theirs. This involves permitting others to have such strategic points, comparable to those one has oneself, as they may regard as being essential to their own security.' If we insisted on retaining Gibraltar, what was immoral about the German claim to Danzig? The argument may have an element of even-handedness but it had virtually no relevance to the stresses in Europe in 1938 or 1939. Hitler admired the British Empire. His eyes were on Czechoslovakia and Poland. And they were not Britain's to bestow.

The crux came in September 1938.

Czechoslovakia, carved out of the Austro-Hungarian Imperial provinces of Bohemia, Slovakia and Moravia, was geographically central and politically democratic. It contained a large German population in the Sudetenland, on the Czech western border. The German party in the Sudetenland agitated for secession and incorporation into the Reich. There were claims (with little foundation) that the German minorities were treated badly by the government in Prague. Hitler rattled his sabre.

The relationship between Prague and Paris was thought to be close. On the chessboard of Europe Czechoslovakia, on Germany's south-eastern border, was a significant piece. There were modern arms factories, and the Czech army was large. The diminution – let alone the extinction – of Czechoslovakia meant something like a death-blow to the Versailles settlement: that, indeed, was one of its prime attractions for Hitler. And the extinction of Czechoslovakia would have a considerable effect on the balance of military power in Europe. In Germany's favour.

But there were the Sudeten Germans, rallying and marching in support of their claim to join their fellow Germans just across the frontier, in the Reich. And one of President Wilson's points of principle in 1918 (which, the Germans sourly averred, had then been neglected by the victorious Allies in the final settlement) was the right of peoples to self-determination. There was no doubt where the Sudetenland people were determined to be; and no doubt that they were German.

31

Britain and France – and other powers, including at this time Italy – could not simply accept a fundamental change to the map of Europe by German diktat. Hitler made angry speeches and organised indignant rallies. There was serious talk of mobilisation and war. Everyone supposed that war with Germany (still imagined to be a second-rate military power, not yet fully recovered from the debacle of 1918) would mean massive air raids on England, if nothing else. It was this that the British Government chiefly dreaded – with, as it later transpired, little reason since the German bomber force had not been built up by summer 1938 to the sort of strength which could have done anything like the damage feared. As negotiations were mooted, postponed, repeated, trenches were dug and sandbags were filled all over the south of England.

Neville Chamberlain, attended by his Parliamentary Private Secretary, Will's brother Alec Dunglass (wearing one of Will's shirts as he'd run short, Will always happily related), flew to see Hitler on two occasions and ultimately brought back a settlement – rapturously welcomed at the time and since excoriated as a betrayal – generally known as 'Munich'. Will, unsurprisingly, was among those rapturously welcoming. He felt that Chamberlain had had the courage to reach out for peace by negotiation. If peace now eluded the world, he felt, it would certainly not be our fault – Chamberlain had attempted all. Will offered his services to the Homes' local Territorial Regiment, the Lanarkshire Yeomanry, an offer courteously recorded but not taken up.

Writing of the months between the Munich agreement and the German invasion of Poland which led to the Second World War, Will referred to the Chamberlain policy as having been 'wrecked by the time that emergency arose'. He 'was definitely no longer in the mood to volunteer for anything', when war finally came. It was a curious analysis. The event which wrecked Chamberlain's foreign policy – and, on the whole, the people of Britain recognised the fact – was the German occupation of the rest of Czechoslovakia at the end of March 1939. This – by a Hitler who had declared after Munich that he had no more territorial ambitions in Europe – was perceived as a barefaced reneging on a word. Henceforth talk of negotiation increasingly sounded hollow, as the spotlight switched to Poland.

Will shifted his aim. He fastened on the guarantee given by Britain and France to Poland and argued to himself and others that the establishment of a Polish corridor, including

Danzig, which cut off East Prussia from the Reich had always contained the seeds of war (probably a true, certainly a defensible proposition); and argued further that Western policy aiming at and offering a generous revision of the whole settlement of Versailles might cut the ground from under Hitler's feet. Hitler might – Will was not convinced of it – actually want war but surely the German people didn't; and yet they considered him to be their champion and their voice, because of the intransigent refusal of Britain and France to see the world a little more as it appeared to Germany. Thus Will. He wrote a poem satirising the British guarantee of Poland.

> 'But everybody likes the war, 'cos nobody attacks.
> But what good comes of it at last?' Quoth big Lord Halifax,
> 'Why that I cannot tell' said he,
> But 'Twas a British guarantee.'

Germany was not the only disturber of the peace. In April 1939 Will was invited to stay for a week at the British Embassy in Rome by the Ambassador, Lord Perth, who was at the end of his time there. Will stayed three weeks and then, with a friend and honorary attaché, Michael Lyle, drove the Ambassador's magnificent car – and the Ambassador's spaniel – back to England, managing at Calais to run over the bicycle of a French gendarme. Will had been giving his views on peace and war while in Rome – a difficult time, since the Italians had just invaded Albania, an act which Count Ciano, the Italian Foreign Minister, had specifically assured Lord Perth would not take place, and which led to a furious interview.

Will set out in August 1939 with a friend, Peter Beresford-Peirse, now a clergyman, to visit Germany and to talk, where they could, to 'ordinary Germans' – to discover their reactions to the possibility of war over Danzig, over the Polish corridor. The international sky was very dark that summer. Predictably they discovered little, although met with individual kindness and courtesy. They returned home to find mobilisation already under way. On 1 September the German army invaded Poland.

'It was not in my hatred of war,' Will wrote, 'that I differed from the main body of my fellow-countrymen. It was because of my conviction that war made things worse rather than better that we parted company.'

That was one way of putting it. Will really parted company

from most of his fellow-countrymen in his belief that there could be a basis for negotiation with Hitler. He clung to specific questions like colonies (a non-issue) or the Polish corridor (a real issue, but pretext rather than substance). By narrowing the question thus he could persuade himself that there were actually bargaining chips which could be used, that it was possible at that juncture to treat with Hitler. Most of his friends rejected such a line. To them, and by then to most of Britain, Hitler was not only wholly untrustworthy. He wanted war. He wanted to eliminate Poland. He had wider ambitions, too. If this were so it was impossible to argue that 'war made things worse'. The choice must be between fighting and surrender. Nor, with the knowledge of historical hindsight, were most of Will's friends wrong.

Will never accepted this. To him war was so inhumane and detestable an activity that there must always, or almost always, be a discoverable basis on which human beings on both or all sides could explore ways of averting it. He never held the strict pacifist line that the taking of life, whether in war or not, is so immoral that submission and suffering is to be preferred, but he clung to the belief that rational creatures, if they try hard enough, can surely devise a political solution to a political problem, however intractable – given goodwill, and acceptance that to die and to kill are not reasonable ways to prosecute an argument.

Once the war actually came Will switched his attack to arguing for coherent and defined war aims; objects which might yet – might, indeed, at any time – provide a basis for negotiation. He firmly believed that there were still people in Germany (had he not met friendly and apparently peaceable Germans, dreading the idea of war?) who, given assurance that legitimate German aspirations could be discussed with their 'enemies', would prefer to sit down and argue rather than stand up and shoot. He had met Adam von Trott at the Astors' home at Cliveden during that summer of 1939 and been fascinated by hearing the passion and sincerity with which von Trott (already known to be vigorously opposed to the Nazis on moral grounds) argued for understanding of the German case at that time. And Will had been – naively – discouraged by witnessing Lord Halifax, the British Foreign Secretary and a fellow-guest, remarking across the dinner table: 'Yes, fascinating problem.' It is unlikely that the Foreign Secretary intended to be drawn far on such an occasion, and discussions with 'anti-Nazi' Germans could not be matters of improvisation; but to Will it typified what he chose to regard as the casual insensitivity of the British Minister to what seemed a life and death issue for the other. With such pictures in his mind Will could not believe in a fight to the death with Germany. And surely the way to leave at least ajar the door to peace was to formulate war aims. Matters, he thought, should never have come so far. It had been avoidable.

Will tended, with regrettable over-simplification, to blame 'the politicians' for failing to bring imagination to the task of stopping wars – indeed for causing wars and all the ills of the world. He wrote:

> The politician, I'm afraid,
> When all the evidence is weighed,
> Is looked upon with passive hate
> By most of the electorate.

And also: 'When the world is run by power politics and power politicians, it is power rather than politics that prompts their actions.' This was facile, soap-box stuff and less than generous in one, normally generous to a fault, who spent a good deal of life attempting to become a politician himself.

In all this Will was generally characterised as wrongheaded and naive. As time went on and as the war which had started became increasingly bloody, and increasingly generated hatred, it was certainly regarded as naive to suppose that it could have been avoided, or to deny – as Will denied – belief that Hitler had always wanted it. Will could not easily imagine any human being actually wanting war, as opposed, perhaps, to the fruits of war. He could not conceive a ruler believing in the purgative benefits for his people of struggle and conquest – ends in themselves. Nor could he enter into the mind of one who regarded some races and peoples as so alien as not to deserve the ordinary treatment of human beings. Such attitudes were so far from the easy magnanimity which characterised Will that he failed to believe they could exist. It was easier for him to believe that his 'own side' were, as so often, obtuse about the feelings of foreigners and were allowing lack of sympathy to poison judgement, to demonise.

Will certainly refused to demonise; and he disliked evidence (not impossible, in wartime, to reject as 'propaganda', for there was, of course, plenty on offer) which pointed towards the justice of demonisation. Not only in politics but in life in all its aspects he found difficulty in believing in the reality of evil. He sought excuses for even the most obdurate evil-doer, and it not only weakened the force of some of his drama (since it reduced his

35

range) but it distorted his opinions on public events. Generosity overcame clarity of perception. Magnanimity fought truth. He resisted – refused to accept – evidence that men and women can, quite simply, be wicked. The source of this characteristic was neither foolishness nor moral cowardice – Will was not foolish, and he was the reverse of a moral coward. This turning away from the unpalatable stemmed mainly from his sensitivity, his vulnerability. He loathed contemplating the cruelty and suffering which war, for instance, inevitably produces; thus he could not bear to think of people doing the things which war demands, or which war is designed to avenge. Critics would remark that this tenderness was not matched by an equal sensitivity to the ills which war was ostensibly being waged to correct or defy; but at every stage in life Will was apt to show reluctance to listen to points he did not like, points which could upset his convictions – or preconceptions.

Will's desire that the Allied governments should formulate specific war aims was also dismissed by most people as naive or impracticable, although in this there were some voices in support of his view for a considerable time and the case arguably had sound political as well as moral rationale. For most, however – at least after a little time – there could be no aim short of outright victory: no basis of negotiation with Hitler could be contemplated. It naturally followed that when, at a later date, the Allies gave voice to a policy of demanding 'unconditional surrender', Will saw this as confirming all his fears about the brutal mindlessness war brings to policy.

This lay in the future. In 1938 and 1939 Will's analysis of international politics may have been rooted in flawed philo- sophical – even flawed theological – ground. It may have been superficial and emotional. It was almost certainly impracticable. The basic emotions, however – a hatred of war and a strong desire to see both sides of a question – were honourable and unchanging parts of him. It may be said that Will's views on politics were unsurprising and unimportant – that gifted dramatists, like gifted actors and artists generally, have a frequent record of ignorance and absurdity when touching such matters. In Will's case, how- ever, those who dismiss his judgement as facile and uninformed should in fairness recall the moral courage it took to question a war regarded by the great majority of his countrymen, his friends and his family as wholly justified.

Filled with disquiet by the course of events and his own

quirky sense of loneliness, Will listened to the British Prime Minister broadcasting to the nation on 3 September 1939. Since the German troops invading Poland had not been halted and withdrawn as the British ultimatum demanded, Britain was at war with Germany.

Most of Will's intimate circle probably regarded him with tolerant affection, at least at first, as holding unorthodox and maverick opinions for the sake of it, as an amateur of rebellion who enjoyed being different, liked posture and showing off, but certainly wouldn't allow it to affect his conduct in any serious way now that the crunch was arriving. They were wrong.

CHAPTER III

'Rebel under Arms'

Since most people in 1939 imagined that war would mean immediate and large-scale bombing of British cities, Will joined the London Fire Service – had joined it, in fact, immediately before war was declared and periodically reported for duty in regulation blue and helmet, axe at his side. Most of his friends were now in the uniform of one of the Armed Forces.

There then came the curious period, lasting eight months, referred to as 'The Phoney War'. As between Germany and the western powers, Britain and France, nothing seemed to happen. Large numbers of men had been mobilised and in France a considerable French army and a very small British army occupied defensive positions, dug trenches, or manned (in the French case) the hugely sophisticated Maginot Line with its underground tunnels, concrete fortifications, electricity and so forth. And waited. There were sneak intrusions of lone aircraft. There was patrol activity at sea. There were no bombing raids. War, in the sense in which people had expected it, went on elsewhere: the Germans swiftly and brutally defeated Poland and occupied the western parts of that unhappy country in collusion with the Soviets, who marched, by agreement with Germany, into the eastern parts and subjected the Poles to a savage regime of murder, deportations and forced Bolshevisation. The Soviets also occupied the three Baltic states with strong forces and carried out wholesale 'liquidations' and transportation to Siberia of large numbers of the population thought likely to oppose Communism. Soviet Russia then launched a war against Finland, without warning or justification, and – after a heroic Finnish defence – imposed a peace of victory in March 1940. But as far as the British and French were concerned war for the most part meant inactivity and boredom. For the London Fire Service there was as yet nothing out of the ordinary to do.

Will felt frustrated. With his idiosyncratic views on the war he felt involved – barely but perceptibly involved – in an undertaking he had thought lamentable and avoidable and now found time-wasting and tedious. He longed for some self-expression, however abortive. He resigned from the Fire Service and offered his services as a journalist to the Board of the Imperial Policy Group, an enterprise led by Kenneth de Courcy which produced a news-sheet on current affairs. Will had decided, after reading the news-sheet, that he might find there congenial or semi-congenial spirits with views not too far from his own. He was taken on, at £3 per week.

Will found Kenneth de Courcy a source of a good deal of amusement. The 'Review of World Affairs' which the Group published was regarded with mixed feelings by the world of officialdom. De Courcy dramatised himself as a figure of international intrigue, exceptionally well-informed and influential. Some of his contacts took him at his own valuation; some were deeply suspicious; others simply laughed. He was somewhat in love with what has been called the conspiracy theory of history and politics, and he liked above all things to appear in the know, privileged, ahead of the game. Occasionally, as must generally happen, he hit the target. Whether hitting it or missing it wildly he was not beloved by the Foreign Office. Will chuckled a good deal but on the whole enjoyed his employer's fascinated absorption in the 'reports' he collected from all over the world including, allegedly, from Germany itself, his discussion of them and his forecasts of future trends. This appeared, to Will, at least different from the parroting of patriotic cries which he found so irritating and so mindless. Some – probably most – 'well-informed' citizens might dismiss the projections of the 'Review' as exaggerated, sometimes absurd, even the result of feeding by enemy disinformation. Will could later ask how farsighted did the conventional wisdom itself prove to be in the end.

Will took a trip with de Courcy in January 1940. They went first to Paris, where (somehow) a secret report by General Weygand on the morale of the French army was obtained and studied – depressing reading by any standards. They then went to Rome by train (Italy still being neutral) where de Courcy had numerous contacts; and thence to Venice by air, where the plan was to catch the Orient Express to Sofia (Bulgaria also being neutral).

Tickets for each stage had been booked in London, but when the travellers reached Rome airport they found that their booking to Venice was on a Lufthansa plane staging at Venice but flying on to Munich.

Will had throughout life a pathological fear of flying but he enjoyed the irony of the situation. The German officials looked at his and de Courcy's British tickets with amusement. When a German crew member walked down the gangway and turned a lever above their seats Will muttered, 'He's opening a trap door.' But the German heard him and in passable English said, 'No, I am turning it to "hot" – it is cold over the mountains.' And Will, of course, found in the simple incident fleeting evidence of how unnatural was hatred based on nationality, how everything could be settled between peoples were it not – as he wrote, absurdly – for 'power politics'. To Will all nations of the world were full of human beings as genial and ready to agree as himself, if only one could discover them.

Tour completed, Will returned with de Courcy to London, to find that *Passing By* was about to be put on, with a first-class cast, Noel Howlett himself playing a key part as well as producing. After a few weeks at the 'Q' it was transferred to the Embassy Theatre in early May. There was optimism about the West End run.

Then, on 10 May, the great German offensive in the West began.

From this moment forward Will's country was engaged not in phoney but in total war. The German campaign in France and Belgium soon culminated in brilliant victory. The British army was evacuated from the mainland of Europe. The French concluded an armistice. Everybody expected that the Wehrmacht would next attempt the invasion of Britain. Churchill, Prime Minister since that same 10 May on which the Germans had begun their campaign, made clear that there was no question of any negotiated peace. Britain, if necessary alone, would fight on until victory, however improbable victory at this moment appeared. Throughout the country the troops who had been rescued from France, together with the men already under training and the new intakes, formed the core of what would quite soon become a very large army whose first task was defence of the homeland. Armaments – some purchased from the United States – started to arrive. The battle of the Atlantic was joined; and in the sky the actions soon to be called 'The Battle of Britain' began. Britain was and felt under siege. It was an alarming, defiant, stimulating time.

It did not stimulate Will. He had formed the idea that Churchill was a statesman who, whatever his talents and qualities, actually relished war and preferred by a very long chalk a martial to a pacific pose. Will thus – even in an atmosphere where the Prime Minister was being almost universally exalted as the golden-tongued champion of the embattled nation – chose to believe that Churchill's temperament and attitude to politics were themselves an obstacle to peace; that peace might even now be a possibility if Britain formulated defensible war aims (which might, indeed should, include readiness to discuss Britain's own overseas strategic possessions such as Gibraltar). Will was encouraged rather than outraged by the news from France after the capitulation; news of a French government concluding what seemed a not dishonourable peace with the conquering Germans, based on recognition that the conquerors had a self-evident right to garrison and rule militarily part of France so long as Britain 'persisted' in hostility to Germany and thus threatened the French coast. To Will this – however perversely in the eyes of most of his fellow-countrymen – implied 'negotiation', implied not shame but a readiness to talk, treat, bargain; rather than kill.

All this, of course, was a long way from British governmental policy, and from the spirit which was being nourished at home. Here the expectation was of invasion, and a fight to the death to defeat it. In July, Will (aged 28 and now due) received his call-up papers, directing him to report to the Buffs, an ancient and distinguished East Kent regiment, for military training. Inevitably he felt compelled to write to the Labour Exchange (in charge of call-up) explaining that he was in favour of a negotiated peace, that he opposed indefinite continuation of the war, but that his objections were political rather than religious or otherwise classifiable as 'conscientious'. He was not, within the meaning of the Act, a conscientious objector and would therefore report as ordered since no category of political objectors existed; and he would do his best as a soldier. There is no record of a response by the Labour Exchange, which had plenty to occupy it at the time. Will's position, however, was rational, whether misguided or not; and he maintained it throughout the following years. He felt sure that the future would see the death of many of his most loved friends. He wrote a play (never produced) entitled *The Little Victims*, to stress the point. And then reported as ordered.

But there was indeed danger of enemy invasion, and there is not the smallest reason to suppose that if that had actually happened Will would have in the least faltered. The issue would have been

41

plain, the reaction physical, primitive and justified. When he had been in the army under training for two months there was, in September 1940, the greatest invasion 'scare' of that or any year. Will, with his squad of fellow-recruits, was called out. It was, he wrote,

> The only occasion in the whole war when I felt at peace with myself . . . I spent the night in a ditch and, the following day, I lay in a wood with a Bren-gun trained on a bridge over which delivery vans and farm carts passed in placid disregard of any rumours of invasion that the military might have heard. During that twenty-four hours I knew that feeling of patriotism which had hitherto eluded me. I felt that urge to defend my beloved homeland which, up till that time, I had always criticised for sticking out its neck much farther than a homeland should. I felt that now – if the Germans were really going to invade my country – here was a cause for which to fight in which my conscience would be utterly at rest.
> But nothing happened.[1]

In a sense the passage completes the picture of Will at that controversial time and is necessary to it. He was sincerely patriotic, in the truest sense; he loved his country and was prepared to die for it if it was really endangered. But he believed – and, with considerable courage, made no secret whatsoever of the belief – that the Government of his country had made and would continue to make inadequate efforts to find a basis on which the war could be ended. He thought that the general hysteria which war and fear engender was blunting both sensibilities and reason, leading to excessive demonising of the enemy and to refusal to contemplate paths to peace.

Will was almost entirely devoid of partisan ideological passion. He often, and sincerely, declared that he believed in democracy; but he regarded it as self-evident that there are other systems and that certain peoples at certain periods in their history may be better served (perhaps temporarily, perhaps not) by alternatives. He certainly did not conceive of democracy as a sacred cause, justifying a crusade, something to impose on others; and he was sceptical of many of the attitudes which democratic politicians almost universally find necessary to adopt from time to time – the false bonhomie, the double standard which ascribes all failings to the opposition party, the noisy sort of patriotism which

1. *Half-Term Report.*

wraps itself in the flag and berates the foreigner. Will's attitude to the war was in no sense impelled by ideology. Although rooted in morality, it was not, strictly, religious.

Nor was Will the sort of character who falls in love with other nations and can see no good in his own. Indeed, despite his readiness to chastise his fellow-Britons for too often failing to put themselves mentally in the shoes of others, he was himself archetypically British, not gifted as a linguist, not comfortably at ease with foreigners, happiest with the jokes, the conventions, the recollections of his own people: of those he knew best. Will's attitude was, as he invariably argued, exclusively political. He likened it to that of Charles Fox, a genial patriot who nevertheless challenged the brilliant, pervasive, patriotic war oratory of William Pitt. He did not take much account – the inconsistency was significant – of the fact that Fox, when Foreign Secretary in the Coalition Ministry, himself came reluctantly to see that peace with Napoleon unbeaten was impossible. Will simply thought it bad for a country to hear no voice of opposition, even (indeed especially) opposition to so dynamic a crusading champion as Churchill. Waging war, Will said in many fora, is essentially a policy. As such, in a free society, it should be able to be challenged. He challenged it.

To challenge so powerful a consensus as there was in Britain for the prosecution of the war between 1940 and 1944 was unpopular. Perhaps especially among Will's own contemporaries, of similar background and traditions, it sometimes led to the cold shoulder, avoidance, rudeness. Will did not enjoy this more than anyone would – he was a congenial, sociable, sensitive human being who liked his fellow human beings and liked to be liked. His attitude could irritate, embarrass and alienate at such a time. To many it was near-treasonable. To most it was and remains wrong-headed. Beyond question, however, it was brave.

Will's time in the ranks of the British Army between July and November 1940 was surprisingly happy. His dramatist's eye always sustained him, sometimes in the most unpromising situations. He could not do other than see people as characters, their situations, personalities and language as ripe for theatrical reportage, and this was certainly so among the private soldiers of the Buffs, although he confessed that the vocabulary of some precluded (in those days) much chance of commercial exploitation! He relished the sharpness of wit and the vigour of language he

found in the near-caricature figures among the warrant and non-
commissioned officers; and he liked, and chuckled about from a
suitable distance, the senior officers although he regarded some
of the rest as humourless. Will – his companions in the ranks
called him Bill – was perfectly content to do his subordinate
duties, to drill, clean his equipment, march out on exercises and
prepare to repel a German invasion of England. Everybody liked
him and he could always make them laugh. He was made a Lance-
Corporal.

He was happy because, as he found, his life was essentially
uncomplicated. Physically it was hard but there were no choices,
no intellectual agonisings, no pressure on conscience. His mates
were, like most soldiers of those days, well to the left of centre in
such politics as were desultorily discussed, but were, by and large,
almost entirely uninterested in the war to save civilisation in which
they were engaged, except to curse it as a bloody waste of time.
Their disenchantment included the Prime Minister, Churchill,
popular though he generally was. There was, Will discovered
– perhaps finding a little what he wanted to find – no great
zeal for the cause. If the f –ing Jerries came there'd have to be a
fight but they probably wouldn't. Roll on peace! Roll on demob!
Will's reasoning was no doubt more sophisticated, but he found
this atmosphere restful. He was, in a sense, uninvolved and there
were of course occasional regimental concerts at which he could
give a little popular rein to his talents.

This short period of his life ended when Will was selected
for training as an officer and sent to No. 161 Officer Cadet
Training Unit (OCTU) in the former Royal Military College
premises at Sandhurst. He has been criticised for allowing his
name to be put forward for a commission, implying as it did more
responsible involvement than his disapproving detachment from
the war made appropriate; and the criticism needs an answer.
Will's answer[2] was that since he had acquiesced in call-up after
explaining his position, and had said that he would 'do his best'
as a soldier, he should not object to one category of service as
opposed to another; and the authorities appeared to think that
'doing his best' now implied becoming a commissioned officer
so that there was no particular call for him to refuse.

This may be defensible. It was certainly arguable that Will
was an intelligent, quick-witted and educated man, Britain was

2. In *Half-Term Report.*

expecting what might be the most critical battle of its long existence, and the Army needed officers. Despite Will's very open scepticism about the war nobody was likely to take his views particularly seriously. People of his kind were absolutely bound to fall into line and do their utmost when it came to the push, whatever silly ideas they liked ventilating off-duty. Of course (official reasoning would run) Douglas-Home ought to be an officer. By compliance he acquiesced.

Another consideration must have influenced Will, consciously or not. The war was likely to go on some time. However much he deplored the situation which had led to the danger, Will was as ready as anyone to defend the country. Military service was now his lot. Cheerfully companionable though life was in the ranks he not only felt the prick of conscience – could he be doing more with his talents if danger was real? – but felt, too, the entirely natural desire to spend more time with more people (in this case, commissioned officers) who could talk and discuss at a more intelligent level, although he always refused to accept that he might find them, or some of them, more congenial. Whatever the motive, Will agreed that his name might go forward as a candidate for a commission.

It was a mistake. Commissioned rank implied responsibility. Will, when declining to become a 'conscientious' objector, had said that he 'would do his best'. It was not 'doing his best' to accept the rank and responsibilities of leadership while simultaneously (and openly) challenging the rationale for the war. 'Doing his best' would have implied silence. Will was unprepared for that, and the ensuing tragedy was of his own making. He accepted a commission and soon made clear that he reckoned it helped him towards getting a platform for the airing of contentious views. Some found that hard to forgive. He called the volume of his wartime letters he published in 1985 *Sins of Commission*, a good title. The first sin was his own for accepting a commission at all.

Major-General William Home (second son of Cospatrick, eleventh Earl) commanded the Grenadier Guards between 1886 and 1889. Will's great-uncle, he died in 1916; but the connection was enough for Will to be proposed as a likely candidate for that regiment, where family ties counted a good deal. Because candidates for commissions (after service in the ranks, and recommendation) were allocated to OCTUs in accordance with the regiments they might join, and because candidates for the Brigade of Guards went to 161 OCTU, Sandhurst, Will was posted there – as a potential Grenadier.

He wrote later that he was unhappy there. He wrote that he had been at peace in the ranks of the Buffs because he had been sent there by an impersonal military machine and had done his best without intellectual effort or choice. Now he felt that as a candidate for a regiment of Foot Guards he had become, in some sense, a volunteer; and he didn't want to be a volunteer. There was little of logic in this, but it is comprehensible that Will, a reluctant soldier, only felt at inward peace if he was sent somewhere rather than seeking to go; if he was denied choice rather than offered it.

He soon made it pretty clear that he felt out of place. The Colonels commanding Guards regiments made periodic visits to Sandhurst to see how their candidates were getting on. On these occasions each cadet-candidate had to march up to the Colonel in question – immaculate in gleaming boots, breeches and Sam Browne belt, topped by a regimental forage cap; and entitled, by some historic quirk, 'The Lieutenant-Colonel' although in rank a full colonel – salute, state name, and await response if any. Sometimes there would be a near-affable enquiry as to the regimental connection. Sometimes there would be a hard stare. Sometimes there would be nothing. On the first visit of the Lieutenant-Colonel commanding Grenadiers, Will, with others, paraded and reported. The Lieutenant-Colonel, like all his peers, was a veteran of the First World War, had commanded a battalion in it. He was grizzled and formidable.

'I believe your uncle commanded the Regiment, Home?'

'This or the Coldstream, I believe, Sir,' said Will, 'I can never remember which.' Rivalry between the regiments of Foot Guards was always sharp and Will's reply was not what was expected from a candidate mustard-keen on joining. The Lieutenant-Colonel swiftly made clear that he found Will's attitude un-endearing. So did many of the instructors, the majority of whom were also officers of the Brigade of Guards. Some of them, like Jimmy Lane Fox of the Grenadiers, were old friends of Will from Eton or Oxford days, and by and large they regarded him with affectionate tolerance. Some of them – notably his company commander, Victor Blundell-Hollinshead – Blundell of the Scots Guards – became firm friends despite having patience tested a good deal. Some of them found Will insupportable. For

Will, of course, often got rid of his inner stress by affecting cynicism about his surroundings (and his superiors), sometimes to a near-intolerable degree. He was reported and punished frequently.

Among his fellow cadets, however, Will was extremely popular. He made some lasting friends. He was affable, funny and generous-hearted. He took an interest in the lives and background of each, the more unusual the better. He loved finding, as he did here and there, a fellow devotee of the theatre and wrote and organised the final Company theatrical performance before passing-out, which is still remembered by a few who were there. Richard Longman, also a Grenadier candidate in the same Company, was to act in Will's first post-war play, *Now Barabbas*: Simon Phipps, later Bishop of Lincoln, was himself most gifted, theatrically. Robin Fyfe, a glorious and romantic eccentric who had served briefly in the Indian Army, would sit on the floor in the Sandhurst canteen dressed in Pathan dress and reading bawdily from Burton's translation of *The Arabian Nights* until the sirens went and the alarms sounded for another air raid – these and many others became lifelong friends of Will. Nobody could be with him for long without laughing.

But nobody could be with him for long without finding grounds for dispute. Will was still intransigent in his opposition to the war, in his belief that peace might have been attained had Britain, in particular, been more accommodating; and in this he found few fellow spirits. His firm scepticism about the war undoubtedly affected the enthusiasm he was able to show and led to poor reports on his performance – it could not be otherwise and he did not particularly wish it otherwise. He also, very naturally, found jarring the comparative zeal of fellow cadets, the majority of whom were pretty well straight from public schools or university and were at Sandhurst, barely fledged, and keen to join in this extraordinary adult game called war. Losses hurt him as they always would. When cadets in his Company were killed by a stray German bomb on Sandhurst, Will wrote home: 'Most depressing . . . it really makes one wonder whether any useful solution can be achieved by blowing people to pieces who've done nothing to deserve it. And if we insist on going on with the war until Germany is beaten and then occupying the country I can't believe we'll be very welcome guests.' There followed some unadmiring comments on Churchill. This was not the stuff of enthusiastic leadership. Nor was it very profound. It came, however, from Will's heart. His 'world-view' was as simplistic as it was to most people perverse: he referred in the same letter to 'America and Russia both interested in looking after themselves, by sheltering behind us and Germany respectively', which was a peculiar judgement of the two great neutrals as they then were. Will was, as usual, inwardly raging about his country's involvement in a war which was by now killing large numbers of people – many of them British civilians – and which could, he still made himself believe, be halted by statesmanship.

Without surprise Will learned that he had been turned down by the Grenadiers; indeed he pre-empted rejection by writing to the Regimental Adjutant that he did not wish to join. When fresh choice of regiment was put to him he thought of the regiment in which he had served happily in the ranks. He wrote to the Commanding Officer, who replied (with a good many justified inward misgivings) that if Will would keep off politics, which he, the Colonel, detested and which bored him, he would be prepared to accept him as an officer. His former comrades in the ranks were startled, but it happened. Will became a Second Lieutenant in the Buffs.

From almost his first day as an officer Will, while doing his duty perfectly efficiently, again immersed himself in worrying at the political situation; worrying at his own conscience.

His battalion, 7th Buffs, were stationed in South Devon. The Army's first task was still the repulsion of invasion. The summer of 1941 was particularly marked for Will by two events.

First, on 11 May, Rudolf Hess, Hitler's deputy (although not as close to the Führer in time of war as previously), flew himself in a Luftwaffe aeroplane to Scotland, baled out and managed to have himself taken to see the Duke of Hamilton, at that time commanding a fighter-aircraft sector nearby. It appeared that Hess regarded himself as on some sort of unauthorised mission (or authorised: the truth of the matter was obscure and subject of much speculation until the war was over, and even beyond).

Churchill and the British Cabinet soon satisfied themselves that Hess, being wholly deluded about the state of opinion in Britain, was of no importance. Hess sincerely admired Britain. He had, it appeared, felt that if the British could be convinced of Hitler's genuine desire for friendship with Britain and that if a war-mongering coterie of false counsellors in London could be replaced as government by men who wanted peace in Europe and its united defence against Bolshevism, great advantage could accrue and much blood be saved. The air war and the U-boat battles in the Atlantic – both of which, Hess averred, were causing Hitler a good deal of pain – would be over. Britain would, with her Empire, remain great and untroubled. Hess claimed to be acting as an independent agent and without the knowledge of the German government – to which, of course, his expedition was embarrassing. He had hoped to find, and convey hope to, a significant section of British public opinion opposed, as he imagined, to the war and keen to end the suffering which the air raids in particular had brought. He had, ignorant in this as in much, presumed that if he could get his message to the King (the Duke of Hamilton had seemed a likely intermediary, a senior nobleman with an exalted office at court) the matter could be carried forward.

By the general public, of course, the substance of this was not known, but guessed – on the whole pretty accurately guessed, particularly when the second climactic event of the summer occurred: on 22 June the Germans invaded the Soviet Union with 140 divisions – Operation Barbarossa. Henceforth the war would assume a wholly different political character. With hindsight people said (and Stalin affected to believe) that Hess's mission had been intended, *inter alia*, to gain at least the tacit support of Britain for this enormous enterprise.

There was plenty of distrust of the Soviets in Britain, especially since the brutal and unprovoked Russian campaign against Finland in the winter of 1939–40. Among the political left, on the other hand, there was a considerable surge of sympathy for Russia, an ideological empathy which had been willy-nilly and reluctantly suppressed during the period of German–Soviet rapprochement and the joint dismemberment of Poland. Stalin had sent Hitler messages of congratulation on the German victory over France and Britain in 1940: now this could be forgotten and the image of the heroic Soviet ally cultivated. Membership of the Communist Party of Great Britain began to swell; and it seemed not illogical to imagine that Hitler – using Hess as a non-attributable envoy – had hoped to sound out British attitudes before his great adventure in the east. Without success.

To Will – whose views at the time were not markedly different in essentials from those claimed by Hess – the Hess arrival spelled hope. Hess, Will supposed, had arrived with feelers for peace, and German public dissociation from him was a rational ploy to gain acceptability for him. 'I expect he's here with a peace plan,' Will wrote to his parents, 'and that Hitler warned him he'd disown him, otherwise nobody would listen. I think the war will be over very shortly!' And had Will known more detail of Hess's actual propositions – including the return to Germany by Britain of colonies taken in 1918 – he would have applauded. He had always and consistently advocated such measures of restitution for Versailles, and he would have regarded Hess's assurances of Hitler's goodwill as at least plausible. Above all, Will leapt hungrily on news of Hess's arrival as likely indication that a peace party existed in Germany; and, if so, surely it should be encouraged by the knowledge that there was something to hope for from similarly minded people in Britain? Will wrote after the war:

> My heart felt buoyant, as it had not felt since 1939. It seemed to me –
> 1. That Germany (Nazis and anti-Nazis combined) had tired of the war and had come to ask for peace terms.
> or 2. That there had been a split in Germany and that a powerful section of German opinion had sent Rudolf Hess to treat with the British Government.
> In either event it seemed to me that the end of the war was in sight.[3]

Will, therefore, anxiously awaited some announcement from the Government. When none came he felt passionate disappointment. He thought it a malign example of the dictatorial powers being exercised by Churchill. A 'peace offer' was, in Will's wishfully thinking mind, being concealed from Parliament and public, and there seemed no voice of opposition to prove the matter: no Fox to challenge Churchill's Pitt. Instead, thought and said Will, opposition to Churchill – and, in this case, opposition to Churchill's rejection of any thought of compromise, negotiation, peace – was regarded as unpatriotic at best and treasonable at worst. Why, Will asked, should earnest pursuit of peace, successful or not, be less patriotic than earnest prosecution of war? And on one point Will was unwavering, a point which might have surprised some. After the war – touchingly, perhaps paradoxically but wholly convincingly – he wrote: 'Throughout the war I never once argued the political case from any angle but that of the victor. It never occurred to me, for one single second, that we could poss-

3. *Half-Term Report.*

ibly be defeated, and for that reason it never occurred to me that the moment was not always ripe for a production of war aims.'

Whatever Will's motivation it was not defeatism. Nor was it ever lack of patriotism. It was – simply and indeed simplistically – conviction that the war could be ended by negotiation; and rejection of the idea that negotiation with Hitler was in real terms impossible.

Yet it was, to the British Government and the majority of the British people, indeed impossible in the summer of 1941, the time of Hess's visit, because it would have appeared the gesture of a threatened nation, almost at last gasp, holding in the hand few cards of negotiation; and it was similarly, although for different reasons, impossible after that summer when the entire strategic situation was altered by the invasion of Russia and, in December 1941, altered again by Japanese aggression and by the German declaration of war on the United States. In the world war in which Britain was involved after the end of 1941 she was largely dependent upon the actions and attitudes of allies. Will's ideas about British generosity to Germany, about returning colonies and so forth, had little relevance in the awful context of coalition warfare, of world war.

As to the great question of the hour, the alliance with the Soviet Union, Will was on rather firmer ground when he wrote that after the German attack

> ... Mr Churchill went straight to the microphone and wel-comed Russia as an Ally. Though not disputing either the desirability of or the necessity for this action I could not help noticing the contrast between Mr Churchill's past and present attitude towards his new-found friend. [The press] in the matter of a few hours, switched from a diatribe against Russia which had reached a climax in the Russo-Finnish war to eulogies of Russia which tended to create, in the mind of the bewildered reader, the impression that Lords Beaverbrook, Rothermere, Camrose and Kemsley had been among the original instigators of the Lenin revolution ...
>
> It was this cynicism which finally dispelled from my mind any lingering doubts that the war against Germany might really be against aggression, dictatorship, secret police, anti-religion and so on and so forth ... It seemed to me, thinking logically ... that if war was indeed against such things (and even if it was I still deplored it because I do not think such things can be eradi-cated by war) to fight against dictatorship in one country with

51

a dictator from another country as an ally, however necessary
or expedient, was absurd.[4]

Will, therefore, took the grand alliance of United Kingdom,
Soviet Union – and, soon, United States – as evidence that in
ideological or moral terms the war was certainly no crusade, no
high-minded endeavour to oppose wrong with right. There were
wrongs – and, indeed, rights – everywhere. And if the real cause
of the Western Allies was the pursuit of a more favourable balance
of world power, a smashing of Hitler's Reich so that the 'democratic' West would emerge secure and strong, Will wrote that he
presumed the smashing of German power would inevitably lead
to a confrontation with Soviet power. This line of argument was
somewhat more plausible than ideas about instant negotiation
with Hitler. And it led Will to a continuing preoccupation: the
belief that there must be sanely argued and attainable war aims,
setting the objects and with luck limiting the scale and duration of
a war which was now claiming ever vaster sacrifice of human lives.
The human lives lost would increasingly affect him personally as
time went on. Penrose ('Pen') Tennyson, who had been 'the first
person to like Will for himself', was killed in an air crash on active
service in July 1941. A film director, he had married the actress
Nora Pilbeam, and joined the Royal Naval Volunteer Reserve. His
death hit Will hard.

Meanwhile Will soldiered on at Kingsbridge in Devon, his
heart alienated from what he was engaged in, finding a little
distraction in occasional amateur theatrical activity, Battalion
concerts and so forth. 'I'm doing two Noël Coward sketches . . .
with an actress called Margaret Radclyffe who . . . is now a Wren
at Dartmouth,' he wrote home. He dined and talked with Cyril
Maude, who lived near Dartmouth, about the great days of the
Victorian theatre in which Maude had shone – 'He talked about
Henry Irving as though he'd stayed with him last weekend.' But
Will could find no inner peace.

It was in February 1942 that Will read in the newspapers
that a by-election was to be held in the Cathcart Division of
Glasgow.

The battalion – 7th Buffs, now to be redesignated '141 Regiment, Royal Armoured Corps (The Buffs)' – had in November
1941 been converted from infantry to tanks; Churchill tanks,

4. *Half-Term Report.*

slow-moving monsters designed for cooperation with infantry. They had moved from Devonshire to Eastbourne in Sussex. In Eastbourne, therefore, Will marched before his commanding officer, Colonel Reid, and applied for leave to stand as a candidate in the forthcoming by-election. He wished to present himself as an Independent. His view was that since all political parties (except the Independent Labour Party, the ILP) had joined the Government in the Coalition, anybody who – like Will – wished to oppose the policy of the Government (or some of it) had no option but to stand as an Independent. His brother Alec, experienced in politics, advised him that it was foolish, but to Will, believing as he did, it was the path of integrity if one were minded to tread a political path at all.

The King's Regulations for the Army were framed in pretty uncompromising language:

> No officer or soldier may issue an address to electors or in any other manner publicly announce himself or herself, or allow himself or herself to be publicly announced as a candidate for any constituency for the election to the Parliaments . . . until he or she has retired, resigned or been discharged . . .

There was, however, a wartime waiver which not only allowed temporary resignation in order to stand, but ensured instant reinstatement after the election; and, of course, a significant number of members of the House of Commons held commissions on the reserve, were serving in the active forces and attended the House when they could, generally wearing uniform. Will's application, therefore, was to resign his commission, temporarily, for this political purpose; and Army Council Instructions specified that such applications, subject no doubt to the exigencies of the Service, should be forwarded and would normally be approved. Colonel Reid, therefore, forwarded Will's application. 'He told me,' Will wrote later, 'that any man who went, voluntarily, from the clean, healthy atmosphere of the army into a sink of degradation inhabited by windbags, mountebanks, shirkers and confidence-men should have himself examined by the medical officer as a matter of public duty. With this diatribe I broadly agreed.'

Will at first found some difficulty in getting sufficient support (at least twelve electors) for his nomination paper; and without that no official application for Army approval could have been made. Will, however, went up to Cathcart with a few days' leave, discovered that there was some dissidence in the local Conservative Association, obtained an influential and energetic Conservative dissident as sponsor and mentor, prepared an election address and authorised an announcement to the press. He returned to his regiment; he had now burned his boats, and his application could formally be submitted. He again travelled to Glasgow and the fighting of his first election.

Will's meetings – there were only three days of campaigning – were packed. Press comment was kind. Jimmy Maxton, a veteran of the ILP rooted in 'Red Clydeside', spoke about Will generously, shook his hand and praised his courage. The deputy chairman of the local Conservatives spoke for him. On the other hand Walter Elliot, a senior figure from the Government side, denounced him and all Independents. Will loved every minute of it. There were four candidates – the Government's man (a Unionist), a Scottish Nationalist, and a candidate from the ILP. And Will.

When the poll was counted Will found that he had come second to the Coalition candidate, and well ahead of the ILP and the Nationalist. Three thousand electors of Cathcart had voted for him. He felt hugely elated. He had been entirely frank during the campaign about his views. He had known they were unpopular and most unlikely to prevail but he had expounded them to packed public meetings and he had not been lynched. His central themes, to be repeated on many future occasions, were the necessity for a Parliamentary Opposition even – perhaps especially – in time of war, in order to challenge the conventional wisdom of the Coalition, to challenge the consensus; the necessity for war aims to be formulated, so that all the world, and particularly all the warring nations, could know what Britain was or was not fighting for; and the necessity for open minds in government so that no reasonable opportunity for bringing the war to an acceptable end should be neglected. These, and particularly the last, were not very palatable views in the atmosphere of 1942. Nevertheless Will's father met the Chief Constable of Glasgow during the following month.

'Lord Home, was that one of your sons who stood here in the by-election?'

'It was.' Will's father had by no means approved Will's activities.

'My men,' said the Chief Constable, 'were solidly behind him!'

Will, after Cathcart, felt significantly less lonely.

Recalled immediately to military duty Will was told by a

disapproving Colonel Reid that he, anyway, would have voted for him. And a few weeks later Will learned that the Conservative Member of Parliament for Windsor had died. Once again a by-election was pending.

CHAPTER IV

Riding for a Fall

At Windsor, Will – once more granted leave for the purpose in May 1942 by a long-suffering Colonel Reid and a resigned Army Council, hoist with the petard of their own Instructions – again stood as an Independent. He had offered himself as a Conservative – 'if you will respect my independent views' – an offer not taken up. The Coalition candidate was a Conservative, backed, as throughout the war, by the party machines of all three main parties; and it proved to be Charles Mott-Radclyffe, a serving officer in the Rifle Brigade and a veteran of the campaign in Greece, where he had been wounded. Mott-Radclyffe, an entertaining raconteur and a convivial, intelligent man, had been a near-contemporary in the same house as Will at Eton. Polling day was to be 30 June.

Mott-Radclyffe, as was his duty, proclaimed the virtues of the Coalition, the necessity in wartime for all to unite, and the irrelevance of Independents to the war effort which was surely the prime object of politics at such a moment. Will, as usual, was irritated by the natural propensity of Coalition candidates to wrap themselves in the flag of patriotism, as if only those who unreservedly supported Churchill and his ministry had a proper claim to be called patriots. He felt, justly, that an Independent was up against a formidable machine; every voter in Windsor received a personal letter from Anthony Eden, the Foreign Secretary, and all Party leaders, including Churchill, signed letters to all constituents. The official Conservative Party naturally worked hard for Mott-Radclyffe. Labour, rather primly, refused to give Mott-Radclyffe 'organisational support', but deplored the candidature of Will. When the vote was counted in Windsor Town Hall, however, Will had scored nearly 7,000 votes to Mott-Radclyffe's total of something over 9,000; a remarkably respectable result in such a constituency. There were, inevitably, some spoilt papers, shown to both candidates by the returning officer. The first had written across it in red ink, 'F... the pair of you'!

In the uneven course of Will's electoral battles Windsor was creditable, in that he scored highly and scored against a firmly Conservative establishment in a Conservative heartland. The very fact of the Coalition candidate being challenged was depicted as outrageous. At the Conservative committee meeting at which Mott-Radclyffe was selected, the candidate said: 'Independent candidates are virtually, but perhaps unconsciously, Fifth Columnists: they have no policy, no loyalty. They merely stand for themselves and say what they like ... I hope you will do your best to return me with such a big majority that no Independent may ever again show his nose in Windsor!' At the same meeting the chairman, Lord Fitzalan, and various officers of the Conservative Association, urged Mott-Radclyffe to 'go all out for the Independent' – 'Give him no quarter'! Windsor was referred to, with tones of indignation, as 'a Conservative constituency'. Will's intervention was cheek.

Will rather relished the proprietorial note struck by his opponents. It underlined his thesis that, because of war and the existence of coalition, democracy and opposition had died. He replied vigorously to the accusation of having no policy: 'I rely on my Election address' (cost stood by Lord Home, disapproving but loyal). Will, appealing to instinct rather than evidence, argued that party candidates (and Coalition candidates) would follow party dictates whatever their minds or consciences said. He argued for independence, and 'the right to criticise constructively'. He spoke against 'Time-servers and Yes-men'.

This was popular, knockabout stuff and Will certainly made an excellent impression at the huge number of meetings, large and small, he addressed. He went everywhere, and was extremely welcome. Calling in at a village dance in Bray he was instantly invited to make a short speech and was warmly applauded. A good many people enjoyed the sense of letting off steam and attacking the Government. The Coalition candidate had told them that this was rocking the boat, but many found rocking the boat an agreeable sensation. And Will's irreverent humour and gift for repartee gave them something to laugh about.

Windsor, however, was not a particular feather in Will's cap, although he polled well. His election address – probably influenced a good deal by his agent, a Liberal of the old school – was an unimpressive mishmash of well-meaning platitudes: 'Greater equality'; 'Elimination of Red Tape'; 'overhaul of Government Supply organisations' (what Will knew about these or what he was supposed to mean must remain speculative); 'Works Councils'; 'Post-war planning'; 'Support of agriculture'. These were thin, generalising slogans and gave all too much credence to his opponents' accusations of absence of policy – it is hard to believe that his list of virtuous-sounding cries was composed with much depth of thought. But these cries were adequate for an electorate which wanted, for quite different reasons, to give the Administration a kick on the backside.

For the war was not going well. In North Africa, Rommel's Panzerarmee had just inflicted its most resounding defeat on the British Army at Gazala, and was now standing on the frontier of Egypt. Tobruk, a symbol of British determination to turn the German tide, had fallen. There were recriminations in Parliament. This was not in the least a mood which Will felt genuinely inclined to exploit but it existed and it undoubtedly played a part in his very creditable vote. And, electioneering being what it is, he did exploit it. A slogan was coined – 'Vote for Douglas-Home and no more Tobruks!' This was humbug.

Will encountered a difficulty at Windsor. Independent candidates – and the few Independent Members of Parliament – came in many different shapes and sizes. Some – in the Windsor election notably Mr W. J. Brown, MP – were opposing the Coalition and speaking for Will because they thought the Government half-hearted in its prosecution of the war, and in particular in its plans for an early Second Front in Europe, to take German heat off Russia. This cry – supported vigorously by a combination of the political Left and Lord Beaverbrook's newspapers – was anathema to the Government and their military advisers for hard, practical reasons; and it was anathema to Will because it represented a point of view diametrically opposed to his own. He thus found that independence in politics is unlikely to be, of itself, a unifying and rallying cry, and he found it necessary to dissociate himself from some of his most vocal supporters.

Above all, however, Will made little noise at Windsor about his profounder thoughts on the war, and the necessity for a clear view of its objects. He probably touched on these a good deal in questions and answers, in talking off the cuff, but they certainly played no part in his election address or more formal speeches; and this to some extent undercut his later claim of consistency – he was consistent, but in public not very ostentatiously so.

He was probably advised that the way to win votes in a place like Windsor was not to sound too conciliatory. The result was that Will spoke up for 'vigorous prosecution of the war . . . total efficiency . . . total victory'. 'No more Tobruks!' He referred to himself as 'an ardent supporter of the Prime Minister' (although he qualified this a little by saying he supported Churchill 'as Prime Minister, but not as a dictator' – an unreasonable slur on a man who, whatever his faults, showed invariable courtesy to the House of Commons). His only reference to international affairs was in a plea for a 'World Federation of Liberty and Freedom'. He calmed worries that he might be lukewarm about the alliance with the Soviet Union (dear to the Left) by saying that Britain might learn much from Russia, and Russia from Britain. Of course, he said, we should 'keep our British Empire' (dear to the Right) while allaying suspicions that this might be selfish by joining the aforesaid World Federation.

Compared to Will's brave if foolish speeches for peace by negotiation or for definition of war aims this was milk and water stuff, sops thrown in as many directions as possible and deeply unimpressive. His only substantive point which came from the heart and undoubtedly found some response was his argument that in war, as in peace, good government needs vocal opposition in a democracy; and that all political wisdom is not to be found in the catchwords of party machines or those too obedient to them. This, combined with the temporarily shaky reputation of the Government, no doubt led to a lot of Will's support; his opponent's call for unity was made to sound the call of a man putting loyalty above intelligence. This – and probably this alone – gave Will's campaign the strength it undoubtedly had; this, together with the wit and attraction of his personality.

The contest produced for Will another problem which period-ically recurred. Mott-Radclyffe had known him a long time. He needed to persuade the voters, among other things, that Will was not in any way a politician, that his views were the views of an entertainer, a man of humour and charm but not an *homme serieux*. The point was made by others. A distinguished Con-servative, Jim Thomas, told an audience (Will was in it) that Douglas-Home was a nice fellow but no politician. Another prominent Coalition supporter told an audience that it did not matter how seductive and charming the Independent candidate was, they must not be led astray by his good looks. And so on.

The attempt to write him down in that way was probably not particularly successful. Will reflected afterwards that so much concentration on the adversary gave him advertisement and may have been counter-productive. Nevertheless it was probably the case that his infectious humour, his gift for repartee and paradox, could raise laughs but could also lead to trivialising any message. He never entirely solved this difficulty; and it must be true that to support a convincing exposition of policy wit needs to be balanced by profundity of argument and cannot replace it. In this Will often failed – there might be sense in some, if not all, of what he believed and expounded but his touch was too light. At Windsor, furthermore, Mott-Radclyffe was surely helped by the lack of substance in Will's message as expressed. The most deeply felt parts of it were not much in evidence. His support derived from the general public mood.

Will thought his opponent's supporters – not Mott-Radclyffe himself – played dirty at Windsor. He gave the press a headline: 'Frustrated Independent expresses indignation'. He thought that they had sought to mislead the voters with irrelevancies, that they had cheated, for instance had announced to meetings that he had telephoned and couldn't attend so that the audience dispersed and Will arrived to an empty hall. In his speech after the poll he gave vent to his feelings – while adding that 'my opponent behaved extremely well!' Windsor exhausted Will. His performance there does not add to his later claims to consistency, except at the margins; but it taught him a good deal, he was determined to stand somewhere again, and as far as it went his attempt had scored high.

Throughout these extraordinary adventures Will did his military duty without enthusiasm but with adequate competence. He had said that as a soldier, albeit regretting the circumstances which had made him one, he would do his best; and in his actual performance of duties something not wholly unlike his best was what, so far, he did. He was made Signals Officer and did the job with considerable efficiency. Because he was inherently lovable his comrades loved him, although they often found his views exasperating. He was extremely popular with all ranks. Will's scepticism about the war was, however, an undoubted fly in the ointment of military zeal and his ready wit seldom improved matters. 'Brilliant but sarcastic and lighthearted', ran one report. In truth Will was the reverse of lighthearted, but his disaffection from his country's policy found frequent outlet in flippancy, and flippancy is not popular in the army. Will, furthermore, had the reputation (one which continued in later phases of life) of seeming to refuse to understand a point if he didn't want to take it in. He was obstinate. He could appear blinkered.

Nevertheless Will was promoted to temporary Captain after less than two years' service; and within the small family of his regiment he was by now a 'character' and accepted as such. His humour made him something of a licensed jester. He was naturally in demand, just as at Sandhurst, when theatrical gifts were needed, producing *Cinderella* as the battalion Christmas pantomime at the end of 1942, with Colonel Reid starring as one of the Ugly Sisters. But within himself Will found a sense of darkness, present or impending. The fourth Home brother, Edward, was by now a prisoner of the Japanese. The youngest, George, would be lost on flying training in Canada in June 1943.

It is difficult for a man to go on indefinitely with serving in a disciplined environment while simultaneously making clear how intensely he disapproves of the cause, the *raison d'être* of the service. By the spring of 1943 the cause itself was prospering. The dangerous days of threatened invasion were over. Although the Battle of the Atlantic had reached a critical point the North African campaign had been won. The tide had turned in Russia. One great German army had surrendered in Tunisia and another in the shattered ruins of Stalingrad. When Will had stood at Windsor the Government had been in trouble: now it was riding high.

Yet Will wrote home in March, 'I have come to the conclusion that the war has outrun its usefulness if it ever had any ... the complete disarmament and surrender of the Nazi nations and their consequent humiliation and setback to national pride will ensure another war in 20 years!' It was predictable that he found especially odious the Allies' declaration that they would fight until receiving the unconditional surrender of the enemy, a declaration made at the Casablanca conference in January 1943.

With the sense that the Allies were now moving inexorably towards victory but that it looked like only being achieved after a great deal more blood had been shed, Will felt even more depressed about Allied policy. He had argued for the possibility of negotiation when the Germans had been in the ascendant, cock-a-hoop and calling the tune. It had been difficult – and to most people absurdly implausible – but he had done so. He had supported (unconvincingly) calls for 'more vigorous prosecution of the war' when, in the summer of 1942, the British were taking knocks in North Africa. Now, when it was obvious that the Allies held almost all the cards, it was, Will chose to believe, almost within their grasp to offer an honourable peace. Instead they had announced their determination on total victory, on the crushing humiliation of the enemy. Why should any patriotic German, Will asked, accept this, whatever his view of Hitler? Was Allied policy not inevitably lengthening the war and the suffering as well as precluding the possibility of a generous and durable peace thereafter? Disapproval of the call for unconditional surrender gave Will something he had lacked for a while – a clear cry and cause.

It would be impossible to imagine a viewpoint more different from the implacable policies agreed between the great Allied powers. Britain had endured a good deal in the war and desire for retribution was in the air. The Soviet Union had suffered horribly and savage vengeance was the determined aim of its peoples. The United States had so far suffered little at home but the American people resented what seemed the unforgivable and evil aggressions which had forced them to send young men thousands of miles to die in the quarrels of others or which had destroyed their fleet at anchor at Pearl Harbor without preliminaries. The crimes of the Germans – not yet fully known – seemed to make any thought of premature peace intolerable. Feeling against the Japanese was equally bitter. In Britain such sentiments united political left and right, regardless of their implications. Will was riding for a fall.

Will's battalion – they were now quartered at Eastwell Park, north of Ashford, in Kent – received a visit from the Prime Minister early in 1943. 'He gave a short talk,' Will wrote, 'evidently designed to raise the morale of the troops, though definitely lowering mine.' Military life was concentrated on preparing for the great adventure of the war, the Allied invasion of north-west Europe which it was now clear was unlikely before the following year. In Russia the last major German offensive, at Kursk, failed in July 1943 and in the same month Anglo-American forces landed in Sicily, marking the return to Europe of Germany's western opponents. In Germany itself, almost nightly, great Anglo-American bomber forces were bringing ever-increasing destruction to the cities. By summer 1943, the Battle of the Atlantic was won, and the U-boat threat defeated. At Eastwell Park Will, unhappy, trained radio operators and looked for woods in which he might shoot pigeons. And brooded.

1943 dragged on. Will again applied for leave to stand at a by-election at St Albans – he was determined to oppose, publicly, the official position on 'unconditional surrender'. He knew he had no hope of winning but he desperately wanted to give the matter an airing. Army approval, however, arrived too late: he wrote several letters to the local press, saying what he would have said publicly in a by-election, but he did not stand. Will's next political foray came in March the following year, 1944, at Clay Cross in Derbyshire.

Clay Cross was a solidly Labour seat. Will felt time slipping away. He knew that once the invasion, the 'Second Front', began there could be little chance – and perhaps little propriety – of leaving battle to fight elections. He thought, entirely mistakenly, that a traditionally Labour electorate might incline to his views; he was standing as an 'Atlantic Charter' candidate.

The Atlantic Charter had been agreed at a meeting between Churchill and Roosevelt in August 1941, before the United States was at war. It was a joint declaration committing Britain and America to certain admirable principles: the self-determination of peoples as to territorial boundaries; free trade and economic collaboration; the rights of men to choose their own forms of government; the freedom of the seas and the security of frontiers. These principles were, it was soon perceived, unlikely to be applied in territories occupied by the Soviet ally.[1] In February 1944, furthermore, Churchill told the House of Commons that the term 'unconditional surrender' meant that the Allies would not feel in any way bound by undertakings or obligations vis-à-vis a defeated enemy. The victors, he said, would have a free hand. There would be no question of the provisions of the Atlantic Charter applying to Germany.

To Will this was confirmation, yet again, of what he regarded as inexcusable double standards. If the clauses of the Charter had really represented political principles and ideals, how could it be defensible to say that they only applied to nations which had fought on the winning side? And what hope – here Will was

---

1. Many, if not most, of the provisions of such agreements as that made by Churchill and Roosevelt with Stalin at Yalta were, of course, in flagrant disregard of the Atlantic Charter, shifting boundaries in an inhuman way wholly regardless of the desires of populations. But exalted declarations are generally subordinated to realpolitik, and thus it was in the Second World War.

pursuing a theme he had followed since the beginning – had Germans opposed to Hitler and desiring what was good, if their enemies made clear that, whatever their conduct, Germany was beyond the pale?

The electors of Clay Cross had little patience with such sentiments. They were primarily interested in local matters; the Labour man was 'their' man and backed the Coalition: to oppose him was blasphemous. As to foreign policy, which was Will's only interest and platform, to them, or many of them, the Germans were devils to a man, the Russians were virtuous heroes who had been inadequately supported (for nefarious reasons) by the capitalist nations, and talk about the Atlantic Charter was meaningless waffle, designed to help the Germans get away with it. Will was mobbed by hissing crowds of youngsters carrying red flags. He lost his deposit. He had, in a speech after the count, said that he would now return to the army to fight in a war he no longer considered just. These words were reported in the press.

It was April 1944. In Will's battalion the commanding officer, Colonel Reid, a Regular, had gone to another appointment in the previous July and his place had been taken by a distinguished Scottish Rugby International, Colonel Waddell, an eminent stockbroker in civilian life, dynamic, energetic and reputedly determined to cut out from the battalion any dead wood. Will had supposed that he, above all men, would be regarded as dead wood of a particularly cancerous type but Colonel Waddell had instead (and, Will said, most mistakenly) made him battalion adjutant, an appointment which he held for only three weeks.

He was, in fact, a perfectly efficient adjutant, the chief executive officer of the battalion, and some thought Colonel Waddell's replacing of him mistaken. There was little personal sympathy between Waddell and Will. The previous commanding officer, Colonel Reid, had been a somewhat old-fashioned disciplinarian, a regular officer of high principles who had had a good many misgivings about Will but found him essentially good-hearted and had liked him. Waddell was a different sort of person; but one, nevertheless, who did much for the regiment's fitness for war and was generally regarded as a most capable and inspiring commander. He knew Will's father – Lord Home was widely loved in Scotland – and he assuredly regarded Lord Home's third son as a perplexing and potentially troublesome subordinate but one to whom he would extend what forbearance he could.

Inevitably Will, although still going through the outward forms

of 'doing his best' as he had undertaken, became the more alienated from his duty the greater the enthusiasm of his superiors;
the enthusiasm jarred. It was clear that the crunch was coming.
The battalion's tanks were now 'flame-throwers', called 'crocodiles', designed to project fire and flame at a range of up to
eighty yards into defended strongpoints and fortifications. Will
– perhaps illogically and emotionally – felt this a particularly
barbaric development: but he was, of course, in a mood to feel
something like that about any development.

For him the war had almost run its course; he had always
thought it avoidable, it had widened and deepened and led to
the enormous slaughter now happening on several fronts as
well as in Germany. He had paid lip-service to its vigorous
prosecution when things were going badly but now it was going
triumphantly well, in strategic terms. Yet nobody had found, or
desired to find, any sensible way to end it; his Government was
hell-bent on prosecuting it until the enemy was utterly destroyed.
Danger to Britain, in the sense of invasion, had long disappeared;
and now Will, himself, was about to play some insignificant but
reluctant part in the continuing tragedy. And had not yet made
a really sounding protest.

And there was the additional matter of war crimes.

There were four main strands in Will's rebellious thinking.
Often combined and overlapping in his argument, they were
separable; and they were of differing validity.

First there was the belief, held from the beginning, that the
war could have been prevented by more intelligent diplomacy; and
that, once it had begun, it could have been ended by Britain with
some imaginative proposals to Germany, even after the defeat of
1940. The rationale for this belief of Will's was entirely political.
He was making a personal political judgement, and although in
his writings he tended to mask it with diatribes against 'politicians' or 'power politics', to mask it behind a generalised (and
sincere) hatred of war, the truth was that the judgement, when
dissected, was highly suspect. It rested, for the most part, on
inadequate information and on a false analysis both of Hitler's
mentality and of the psychology of the British people. The only
moment when peace – of a kind – could have been concluded
by Britain after September 1939 was in the summer of 1940 and
on Hitler's terms. However conciliatory the British Government
at the time, it is highly improbable that a peace policy would

have been supported by the people; and after the German air raids of 1940 and 1941 it is impossible. Thereafter Britain was involved – with energy and enthusiasm – in coalition warfare, and any British arguments for peace by negotiation would have been brushed aside as irrelevant.

There was a subsidiary element in this strand of Will's thought, the belief that a sound starting point for negotiation would be an undertaking to revise the provisions of the Treaty of Versailles on the one hand, and on the other to treat with some sort of equivalence the British possession of an Empire and the German desire for one. Why, Will often asked, should the British have been dismissive about German claims to Danzig (a German city) for instance, while hanging on to Gibraltar, manifestly a strategically advantageous outpost which happened to be in someone else's country? Will persisted in regarding Imperial possessions as some sort of burglar's swag, with a very hypocritical burglar denouncing the burglaries or aspiring burglaries of others. This actually did little justice to the German claim to Danzig, which was ethnic rather than strategic, historical not military, but Will was seldom troubled by inexactitudes when hunting a telling analogy.

Arguments for 'revising Versailles' had little but academic interest after 1940. Hitler had done the revising. As to Empire and the 'burglar's swag' argument, it failed on every count except the one of inducing in the British a little historical humility. In practical terms, by now, the Empire arguably represented anyway a disadvantage for a hard-pressed Britain, demanding far more (especially in the maritime resources needed to defend it and maintain communication with it) than could possibly be contributed by it. Nor would self-abnegation about Empire have been in the least impressive to Hitler – Hitler rather admired the British Empire and what he supposed (mistakenly) was Britain's ruthless rapacity. Will read the signs wrong, preferring to see only an example of double standards and British humbug.

Second, there was Will's regret that the parliamentary coalition of the major parties was unchallenged, and his belief that the lack of continuing and organised opposition in Parliament was bad for democracy and bad for Britain. This could be advanced as an abstract thesis, and it was congenial to Will's temperament which was argumentative, radical and rebellious. It was, however, a view coloured not primarily by his distrust of the principle of coalition, but by his disagreement with the enthusiastic prosecution of the war which this particular Coalition had been formed to carry on. For Will the Coalition meant that politics had become a matter of cheering on one's own side – and a belief that one's own side should include every elector in Britain, whose sole preoccupation should be how to win the war. To him this was repugnant, and he could voice his repugnance by an appeal to history and to principle; Britain, it has been said, abhors coalitions. The point was essentially political, and to the majority, without question, the demise of 'party politics' before the greater cause of national emergency and national unity was good rather than bad. Will, anyway, probably over-estimated the interest of the British in politics. This 'opposition' point was, however, periodically popular when the Coalition Government was, for whatever reasons, temporarily under a cloud.

Third – and particularly relevant when it was perfectly clear that the war was going on and would be fought to something like a finish – was the matter of War Aims. Here Will was on firmer ground, both politically and morally. He asked for clear definition of what Britain (but of course it had to be not only Britain) was fighting for. Churchill had given his own defiant answer in the early days, when Britain was in danger and alone. The aim, the only aim, was victory, and elimination of the brutality which Nazism represented. Will questioned whether that was enough. Should there not be an attempt to formulate specific objects? Specific arrangements and concessions, however far-fetched such might seem in the climate of war? And would not the formulation of such aims at least offer a glimmer of hope that an enemy might one day see his way to discuss them, even accept them or some of them, and thus save lives and suffering?

To be clear about why and for what a nation is fighting is rational. War is a political act. Clausewitz called it the pursuit of policy by additional means and that is precisely what it is. It is not a killing match, a mindless exercise in slaughter and destruction. To be morally defensible it must have definable and attainable objects. In his plea for definition of Allied war aims Will had Clausewitz, at least, on his side. In the Second World War the plea would not – and, of course, Will knew that it would not – receive much endorsement. To Western governments[2] it was

2. The distinction is relevant. Of the Allied nations at war Stalin had the clearest war aims, understood Clausewitz, and kept his mind, free of sentiment, pity or illusion, on the primacy of politics.

enough that the war was to defeat evil (or one manifestation of evil). The Atlantic Charter and suchlike represented aspirations, perhaps, but it would be premature to formulate concrete aims. It would also be politically impracticable – and increasingly embarrassing. In publicly pressing for specific definition of war aims Will was touching a sensitive nerve and his cry was a good one. It was also certain to get nowhere.

It was the issue of war aims, however, which brought Will most sharply against the policy of 'unconditional surrender'. He argued that to demand from an enemy not simply the cession of territory (which might or might not be just), not simply the abandonment of fruits of earlier victories, not simply recompense and restitution for injuries inflicted, but the *unconditional* surrender to the victor's will and whim without any prior definition of what would be demanded – this, to Will, was an irrational recipe for war indefinitely prolonged and for the alienation of every patriotic German. In this – very defensible – proposition Will at times exaggerated and went somewhat off the rails. The demand for 'unconditional surrender', applied to the German Reich Government. It constituted a statement of policy. Will sometimes wrote and argued as if it applied to individual German commanders and soldiers 'who are convinced' (he wrote from France in July) 'that if they surrender they will be shot'. If that were so (and in view of the large numbers who surrendered one can say that it was not so) it had a bearing on the Geneva Convention, on the treatment of prisoners. It had no relevance to the 'unconditional surrender' policy. The latter – here Will was on good ground – undoubtedly fortified the general patriotic resolution of the German soldier, implying as it did that there was no hope for the German Reich. It did not, however, imply a policy about acceptance of surrender in the field different from that always and everywhere applying. Surrender in the field is always unconditional. This confusion of Will's would one day be significant.

The fourth, and as it ultimately turned out the most crucial, strand in Will's thinking was the matter of double standards. He had always instinctively revolted against these, in the ordinary domestic contexts of life. He had always detested the attitude of mind which demands from others reactions wholly different from those accepted as natural in oneself. He had consistently loathed humbug. Now this surfaced against the enormous background of the war; and particularly in the question of war crimes.

The Allies, in several very public declarations and in wording negotiated between themselves, had made clear that after victory the perpetrators of atrocity in the enemy's ranks, whether of Party or armed forces, would be tried and punished for their crimes. They further made clear that there could be no simple defence of pleading enforced obedience to superior orders, even if those orders were, according to the enemies' code, legal. There was to be no hiding place behind authority. Otherwise, it was argued, the only guilty human being would turn out to be Adolf Hitler, from whom all authority in the German Reich ultimately flowed. Underlings too, as well as those who transmitted orders, were to be hunted down. And thus it should be for the Japanese and every enemy.

Will found the implications of this to be odious humbug, and in this strand of his thinking was on the best ground of all. First, there was a tacit assumption that only the enemy committed war crimes – not put in words but generally understood. This, of course, was to Will unacceptable nonsense. War crimes were committed as a matter of course on the Eastern Front, by both sides and with every circumstance of barbarity, a fact which was widely known. Furthermore – although Will did not personally encounter it – there were plenty of examples of, for instance, the shooting of prisoners by certain British and American units, particularly Waffen SS prisoners, sometimes regarded as so brutal as to deserve no mercy; a completely untenable as well as illegal and immoral view. A blind eye was often turned; nobody's record was impeccable; and it was ludicrous to suppose that only the enemy's was flawed. And what about, Will asked, unnecessary casualties inflicted on non-combatants?

But beyond the obvious one-sidedness of the business, Will queried the Allies' policy on the issue of obedience as a defence. The Allies seemed to be saying (indeed were saying) that the only proper course open to a German subordinate, given an order whose discharge he believed immoral, was disobedience. Disobedience whatever the personal hazard. Disobedience whatever the legal code under which the subordinate was serving and whatever the tradition of discipline he had been brought up to observe; the order, furthermore, might be strictly speaking correct, but the subordinate must be responsible for exercising private judgement on its morality. Disobedience, to avoid the penalty the victor would otherwise exact.

To Will this was not only unrealistic – for years he and his fellow countrymen had been taught how ruthless was Nazi enforcement of obedience as well as how draconian were the systems of the German Wehrmacht. It was also, surely, an example of a double standard, or very likely to be. Would a British officer or soldier, Will asked, deciding to defy an order he deemed immoral, be allowed to plead the primacy of conscience and escape punishment? That was what we were demanding of the enemy. Will would, ultimately, receive an answer.

One strand of thinking, popular with many, altogether passed Will by. It was the argument that the conduct of the Nazi regime was so infamous that war had to be waged to the bitter end in order utterly to destroy it; nothing else would do. Will could not come to terms with that way of thinking. He thought it narrow, prejudiced and unconvincing. Wartime propaganda, he believed, painted black and white too starkly. Will – it was a constant facet – could not easily believe in wickedness; folly, hypocrisy, greed, vanity, but not real wickedness. This lacuna was the obverse of his generosity and instinctive charity towards all men.

This desire to believe that, at heart, people sympathised with people, that people could find a basis for shared laughter and enjoyment if only self-seeking politicians and others didn't get in the way – this genial warmth could lead to failure in understanding of how humanity reacts, especially in war. In his sympathetic and well-crafted play about the German wartime occupation of the Channel Islands, *The Dame of Sark* (1974), Will asked the real Dame Hathaway of Sark to comment on the accuracy of the typescript. The Dame was content, save one comment. Will had finished the last act (after the island's liberation) with the death from a mine in the harbour of the agreeable young German soldier, Muller, whom the Dame has befriended. When told by a British officer of it the Dame (according to Will's script) said, grieving, 'It goes on, Colonel Graham, it goes on! When will it ever stop?' Dame Hathaway, commenting, told him that it was indeed true that she heard at that moment of a German soldier's death, and, she wrote, 'I was NOT in the least sorry! and I said so!' Will recounted this, typically, with a self-deprecatory chuckle. The exchange, however, shows in William both the sympathy and the illusion. And both persisted.

Throughout these times Will, inevitably, was extremely lonely. He loved his family but he knew that to them his stance was wrongheaded, troublesome and largely inexplicable. He loved his old friends but he knew that to most of them, too, he was being silly. To them, or most of them, there were rights and wrongs in

70

any issue but the war had to be fought, by and large we were in the right, and to rock the boat was unlikely to shorten the business. A good many people (including some in his battalion) shared at least some of Will's views about unconditional surrender but few, even of these, would have subscribed to his belief that negotiations with Hitler's Germany had been possible. Nor, with the benefit of hindsight, is it likely that many would change their minds.

Some felt more vehemently hostile. On the other hand a few – a very few – trusted their affection sufficiently to try to understand despite their disapproval. Jakie Astor sent a cheque for £150, writing that he supposed Clay Cross and its lost deposit had pretty well cleaned Will out (it had), but that Will deserved credit for sticking up for his views even if they were, as the donor suspected, bloody stupid. On the whole, however, Will was isolated, unsupported, alone. A man who kept emotion tightly within himself, he was probably often close to breakdown. The demands of living a disciplined life of service – and anticipation of the coming demands of battle – can be near-intolerable unless courage and endurance are fortified by a sense that the task is worthy and right. Will lacked it. Such a situation can lead to a certain paranoia.

Will was not paranoid, but his private antipathy to much of the public role he had to play increasingly irked him and he felt that the pressures inside him would have to burst into some more dramatic protest than he had yet achieved with his by-election efforts. He felt morally detached from his country and its army at what was obviously a critical moment in the life of each.

For by now the whole vast panoply of invasion was ready. Will was now serving with his brigade's 'Forward Delivery Squadron', a reserve of replacement tanks under brigade control. With this squadron he moved to Aldershot, ready for the great day. On 5 June he took out to dinner a young ATS officer, Mary Churchill, and when he saw her home to her barracks they heard overhead the roar of huge numbers of aircraft – 'The fulfilment,' as Will wrote gloomily, 'of her father's policy.' Next day, 6 June, he wrote home with an uninterested facetiousness which many would find odious: 'I hear on the wireless that the Second Front has begun! I suppose the day will come when I shall attend it!'

For some that day had already come. A significant number of 7th Buffs, now 141 Regiment RAC, took part in the actual

D-Day assault. On 19 June, after writing a characteristic letter home which ended 'When are these peace terms coming along?', 269 Forward Delivery Squadron, Will with it, landed in France.

For the next eleven weeks there was an awful inevitability about what happened to Will. Nothing deflected it. He was not killed. He was not wounded. The varying demand for the regiment's 'Crocodiles', specialist weapons, meant that squadrons and troops were generally separated, supporting different brigades, allocated as the course of the Normandy fighting dictated. Will was kept in reserve most of the time, or allotted some sort of liaison duties. Colonel Waddell had come to terms with the problem he personified. Will took every opportunity, while still in England, to make his feelings clear but his Commanding Officer – charitably if inaccurately – professed to believe that Will would see things quite differently when actually in the theatre of operations.

In France, after a few weeks had gone by, Will applied in writing to resign his commission. He said he was perfectly happy to drive a tank or serve in some subordinate capacity; it was the sense that his commission implied some responsibility in a policy he detested which he couldn't stand. The dilemma had, of course, been there from the beginning. He had been wrong to accept a commission, feeling as he did; and now he knew it. He had contemplated applying earlier but imagined it might be construed as a simple attempt to avoid battle. Now the battle of Normandy was under way it seemed possible to try again. The application to resign was, understandably, ignored. People had other things to do. And commissions, in wartime, were not to be resigned voluntarily without extended procedural complications. Such resignation, in either peace or war, can never be claimed as a right; a fact specifically stated under Military Law.

Will found a little relief in poetry:

> Dumb must we fight, like beasts in silence, hating.
> Our minds, our souls encased in bands of steel,
> Our heavy hearts o'erlaid with armour plating
> So that we cannot feel.

The 'war aims' issue angered him. 'It is criminal,' he wrote home on 12 July, 'not to a) give them our terms and b) make sure that they know they will be treated justly', and to his sister Rachel, he wrote, 'Our propaganda here is futile or non-existent.' When news came of the July plot to assassinate Hitler, Will saw in it evidence that to at least some in positions of responsibility in Germany the time for peace was overdue. In this he was right, although wrong in not realising that to most of those brave conspirators nothing could be done unless Hitler personally was removed. Will had never appreciated this, because he had never appreciated the true nature of the Nazi regime. He wrote, on 23 July, 'If only they [the Allies] would give an ounce of encouragement to the German generals instead of calling them rude names they could close down the war in a week', and this was certainly mistaken. Will wholly misunderstood how isolated were those members of the German opposition who were prepared to act, and he also misunderstood the loyalty inspired in the German majority by Hitler. He insufficiently appreciated that this loyalty – which in an earlier context he had generally refused to condemn, saying (with some reason), 'Plenty of us would have felt the same' – was a near-insuperable impediment to any peace short of victory.

Nevertheless Will's instinctive feeling for Germans trapped by an intolerable moral dilemma was honourable. He remembered his pre-war meeting with Adam von Trott. Had he known of it he would have been appalled by the British Foreign Office line at this time, which was dismissive of any exploration of 'peace feelers', from whatever quarter, in Germany. It was supposed that those initiating them could almost certainly not 'deliver'; and was also presumed that they must, perhaps unknowingly, be acting under covert Nazi inspiration. Nothing must be done to impede or confuse the march towards unconditional surrender. Will's completely uninformed guesses as to the line officialdom was taking in all this were by no means wide of the mark. His feelings that the mind of the enemy was being misjudged led him to apply for a job in the directorate of Psychological Warfare, but it came to nothing.

The fighting in Normandy continued. He noted, with his usual reactions to all nature, the beauty of the countryside and the particular birds observed. He remarked the extraordinary youth of some of the German prisoners, some little more than children. And humour could surface: 'We have a tame young magpie in the Mess,' he wrote on 5 July, 'which gazes into space like a bishop trying to remember the text of his sermon.' He had amiable skirmishes with a brother officer, squadron second-in-command, whom he had always accused of making off with his, Will's, underclothes, ex-laundry. 'Still wearing my panties – he says you are not to worry, quoting the old saying "He that hath two pairs of pants let him give to him that hath none!" To which I reply "and from him that hath none shall be taken away even that which he hath!" '

He observed, with some relish, that propaganda had misled us about the sufferings of the French civilian population – the farmers were apparently doing pretty well and German occupation did not seem to have been particularly rigorous (or, he might have added, particularly unpopular). What was certainly unpopular – and made Will wretched – was the fearful casualty bill among the French civilians from Allied bombing. At this stage of the war, with total Allied air superiority and a certain reluctance to accept more casualties to ground forces than absolutely necessary, objectives tended to be 'softened up' by extensive aerial bombardment and a good deal of it hit the French more than the Germans. Will witnessed the huge air raid on Caen in July, the continuous roar of exploding bombs from the shattered city for hours on end, and he hated it. He was also, inevitably but by no means unjustly, alert to further examples of 'double standards':

> I counted no less than twenty-three shattered [German] ambulances on a five mile stretch. No doubt the ink-firing canon back in London would have said they were carrying troops, yet I failed to understand how a pilot were to ascertain whether an ambulance were carrying troops or not. And if the only solution were to shoot at those ambulances then I could not understand why such a solution should be condemned in the Germans and condoned in ourselves!

Will had just read an article by a clergyman in the British press haranguing the Germans for not respecting the Red Cross. He accepted that mistakes are made in war. What was intolerable was the assumption that they are only culpable when made by the other side.

In August he tried to enlist the support of his uncle Claud Lambton in seeking candidature in a by-election at Berwick. He was sharply rebuffed and accused (unfairly) of inconsistency. His attempt to stand (at Clay Cross) as an 'Atlantic Charter' candidate was thrown at him. 'Is it not a sad commentary on the distortion of the human mind,' Will wrote back (he was very fond of his uncle) 'that I, the only man in three continents to stick up for a solemn declaration made by three so-called statesmen, and since overthrown by them – should be told I have finished my political career?'

By the middle of August the battle of Normandy was over. A

large part of the German army had been trapped, with enormous slaughter, near Falaise and the Allies at last began the great pursuit which would take them to Paris and Brussels, liberate a large part of the Low Countries and bring the British and American armies to the frontiers of Germany itself. Meanwhile the Germans left garrisons in the Channel ports, with orders to withstand siege. The absence of a major usable port was hampering the Allied advance – Cherbourg had fallen on 27 June but its installations were so thoroughly wrecked by the Germans before surrender that it was some time before it became useful. Most supplies were still coming in over beaches, using the provisional arrangements devised for the early post-D Day phase of campaign. Calais, Boulogne, Dieppe and Le Havre were still in German hands. There was a further and important consideration. The 'V' weapon sites, from which a ferocious bombardment of British cities was being undertaken, were on or near the Channel coast. It was urgent for the Allies, and particularly for the British, to clear it.

The clearance of the coast – the advance of the left wing of Eisenhower's huge force – was entrusted to the First Canadian Army, which had one Canadian and one British Corps under command. Each of the Channel ports was invested during the first ten days of September, while the Second British Army took Brussels and advanced to the Dutch border.

Le Havre, the nearest of the ports to what had been the Normandy beachhead, was held by some 11,000 German troops commanded by a Colonel Wildermuth. 1st British Corps crossed the Seine near Rouen and moved towards Le Havre along the right bank of the river on 2 September. It was clear that the place itself would be a hard nut to crack and an assault was planned, preceded by fire from the formidable 15-inch guns of warships as well as an extensive aerial bombardment. Dieppe had already fallen, on 1 September, and within five days the Canadian Corps had surrounded Boulogne, Calais and Dunkirk.

But on 23 August, a fortnight before 1st British Corps, the Buffs, and Will, arrived before the great defended port of Le Havre, Will had written a letter to the *Maidenhead Advertiser*. Extracts were published on 30 August:

> As regards the situation in the world today, I am profoundly worried. The Atlantic Charter has been cynically cast aside. Instead the negative demand for unconditional surrender stiffens the German resistance and hamstrings any opposition to Nazi rule.

It seems that Allied statesmen intend to win a victory by force alone. Their alleged desire is to teach the Germans that force does not pay. In fact their action will merely teach the Germans that force, when backed by unlimited resources, pays hand over fist . . .

I maintain that commonsense, statesmanship and Christianity alike demand the production of peace terms now. If our leaders' terms are just, where is the danger in producing them? If they are not just, why should men die to impose them on the enemy?

Will's letter continued by saying that he (and, incidentally, many officers and men in the forces) felt so strongly that he had applied to resign his commission. He could not ask men to fight for motives political leaders would not publicise. He had, he said, no stomach for a war of annihilation. 'We were told that this struggle was against Nazism. Now it appears that it is to be against patriotism – that quality which in everybody but a German or a Japanese is said to be a virtue.' And so on. It was a frank and powerful letter. In it Will made clear that he did not expect much support.

A cutting of the *Maidenhead Advertiser*'s 30 August edition was sent to Colonel Waddell early in September. Will's application to resign had, for the moment, been left pending; there was a war to fight. Communications with the press 'on military subjects', however – a category from which Will's letter could hardly be excepted – were forbidden to members of the Armed Forces under the King's Regulations. In the case of one who had frequently (with permission granted) engaged in direct political activity during the war, this particular ordinance clearly had to be interpreted with judgement, but, equally clearly, Will had – as a serving officer – laid before the British public a personal denunciation of British Government policy in the most important (and military) department of policy: the waging of the war.

'You shouldn't do it, Home,' said Colonel Waddell. In all the circumstances it was a restrained remark.

But later on the same day, 6 September, in the Headquarters Squadron Mess of which Will was a member, another officer, whose job was Intelligence, tackled him with the words, 'There's something happened up your street.' He told Will that the German officer commanding in Le Havre had asked for a truce under which civilians could be evacuated. The Germans were presumably in no doubt of what was coming. The request, said

Will's informant, had been refused. There was not time.

Will said that he understood the attack was not due for three days. A shrug of the shoulders told him all he thought he wanted to know. Later the same evening he received orders for his own part in the coming operations – to act as liaison officer with one of the 'Crocodile' squadrons. Will reported to that squadron next morning, 7 September. All was quiet. Nothing, Will thought, to impede the move from the city of every civilian who wanted to come. And no urgency.

That evening – and still no battle – Will told the squadron commander to whose command he was attached that he intended to return to Regimental Headquarters next morning, and formally to refuse to take part in the battle.

That is exactly what he did. On 8 September Will saw Colonel Waddell and said that he could, in conscience, take no part in the assault on Le Havre. He repeated this refusal in front of the regimental second-in-command, who was summoned. He knew that to some people he would seem simply to be evading duty out of fear, but on that score his conscience was clear. He had, he knew, consistently explained that to take part in battle – and face its risks – demands confidence that the cause is just, and the planned conduct of battle legitimate. He lacked that confidence. He was ordered back to the Echelon – the supply vehicles of the squadron.

He was not placed in close arrest – an officer in arrest requires an escort of commissioned rank and Colonel Waddell could not make one available. The Colonel undoubtedly hoped that the matter could be quietly dealt with, without legal proceedings. Will, despite his obvious need to have made an explicit protest, hoped so too. He wrote home on the same day that he committed the 'offence':

> I have refused an order to go and attack Le Havre . . . I do hope you won't be upset. Probably there will be no trouble about it – on the other hand I might be court-martialled and dismissed the Service.
>
> You have always been very tolerant about my point of view and, after all, it's the only consistent end to my useless Army career. It's entirely their own fault for keeping me in it. I've made repeated requests to Waddell to let me go and he wouldn't. I applied to resign my commission when I saw how the 'unconditional surrender' racket was causing unnecessary

casualties and he held up the application. However he's very friendly – as is everybody.

And Will continued the letter by denouncing the refusal to allow the German commander to evacuate civilians, denouncing the unnecessary futility of attacking Le Havre at all, and denouncing the coming infliction of civilian casualties by bombing.[3] He also wrote to Colonel Waddell apologising for making such a nuisance of himself but saying how inevitable it had been that some such crisis of conscience would at some time come. Two days later he wrote home that he doubted if he would be tried by court martial, because his earlier application to resign his commission had been held up.

The battle of Le Havre took place. The port fell. And a week later – the war having moved on, and Will with it – he wrote of having applied to go into Boulogne (now itself under siege) to see the German commander. 'Sat in my jeep,' wrote Will, 'with newly washed white pants to serve as a white flag, but permission didn't come!' Will still felt that despite having refused to obey an order, he might pursue his improbable peace-making under some sort of licence.

He also wrote yet another letter to the *Maidenhead Advertiser*. It would be published on 27 September.

There exists in the army a procedure for the summary disposal of some charges against an officer, a procedure by which senior officers – Brigade, Divisional commanders – may, within competences established by regulation, deal with the matter summarily. Will was not, for the time being, formally charged – when a soldier of any rank is charged with a serious offence which may lead to court martial the first proceeding is the taking of a written summary of the evidence including (if he wishes) a statement by the accused. This was not yet done. It was clearly hoped that the case against Douglas-Home could be dealt with quietly, summarily – but informally.

'I saw the Brigadier this morning,' wrote Will to his parents on 21 September. 'He is a very nice man. He said, "I have the greatest respect for anybody who sticks up for their views." ' The interview left Will with the impression that some other military employment, perhaps looking after prisoners of war, would be

---

3. About 3,000, by some counts, in the event.

found for him. It seemed as if the business was to be allowed to blow over, grave though the offence had been – deliberately so, and by Will's volition. But he had made his protest, his challenge. On 17 September he had written that he felt happy for the first time for four years.

The next move was for Will to appear before his Divisional Commander, General Hobart. Hobart commanded the 79th Division, which contained all the 'specialised armour' – including the 'Crocodiles' – wherever deployed. By now the Allies' advance was rapid. The British and Americans had occupied much of Holland and attempted to cross the Rhine at Arnhem. The war had closed up to the frontiers of Germany.

The *Maidenhead Advertiser* had received a large number of letters commenting on Will's first letter of 23 August. These, published in the edition of 6 September, were predictably hostile. Correspondents referred to 'the perfidy of Germany'; 'a record of atrocities to remind them that they were dealing with a generation of sub-human Germans'; 'a man-eating tiger [which] if allowed to live must at least be kept behind bars'; 'the strongest, foulest and most brutal tyranny that ever threatened humanity.' 'Annihilation,' wrote one reader, 'seems the only way to deal with such brutes.' The paper, restrainedly, observed that subscribers to the *Advertiser* seemed to support the 'unconditional surrender' policy. It had reminded its readership of Will's 1942 candidature for Windsor. Now he seemed to have few friends.

Will's second, September, letter, had been written before he had the chance to see the violent press correspondence aroused by his first, but he had heard of it and returned to the charge. Attacking the 'tired old men' who played power politics with the lives of the young, he described them as those who 'demand that we should fight regardless of our private beliefs and in the same breath condemn German officers and men for doing likewise.' He continued:

> I have definitely refused to fight. When ordered to attack Le Havre I refused to do so because, rightly or wrongly, I could not bring myself to take part in an operation against troops who admittedly did not want to fight but whose commander refused to accept unconditional surrender!

Will then referred to the German commander's offer to evacuate civilians, 'which offer was refused'.

This German general [*sic*], who was captured and wounded,

79

still refused to accept unconditional surrender. I heard him
described . . . as a crazy, obstinate, fanatical lunatic. I cannot
help wondering what decoration would have been pinned by a
grateful monarch on that German's breast had fate decreed that
he assume the role of a British officer, commanding a British
garrison . . .

He ended his letter by saying that he expected as a result of
this correspondence to be the 'most hated man in England –
not, however, by the forces'. This letter was published on 27
September and was reported nationally.

In its next edition, on 4 October, the *Maidenhead Advertiser*
referred to the considerable publicity attracted in the national
press: 'The original letter has been placed at the disposal of
the War Office.' The *Advertiser* said that a number of letters
had been received, some making bitter attacks on Will. 'Others
commend the courage he has shown in giving public expression
to his convictions, and support his views.' Will was not utterly
alone. By then things had moved.

Will's regiment was near Calais when he received orders to
report to Divisional Headquarters, at Ghent, on 29 September.
When he arrived on the previous evening, an officer in the mess
where he was lodged told him that his photograph was in all the
British papers. The national press had headlined Will's letter to
the *Maidenhead Advertiser* published on the previous day, and
the BBC News Service had reported the whole story of his refusal
to obey an order and the reasons he was professing. Next morning, not yet having been brought before the General, Will found
that an officer of the Buffs had been sent by the regiment to
escort him back in close arrest.

There could now be no question of dealing with matters
summarily or quietly. Instead they moved formally and fast. Will
was charged. On 2 October a Summary of Evidence was taken in
his presence by an officer of the Judge Advocate General's department – the branch, staffed by legally qualified men, responsible
for legal advice to courts martial and to commanders exercising
judicial powers; the branch which produced prosecuting officers
and officers to take summaries of evidence in cases of difficulty or
sensitivity. The Summary of Evidence was a necessary preliminary
to trial by court martial. Will, after due warning, was enabled to
make a statement which was recorded in the Summary for use

at a court martial if one took place; and in his statement he reiterated the views he had advanced so often. He concluded with the words: 'I am therefore prepared·... to stand my trial on the issue of whether the conscience of the individual comes before the orders of the State when the individual believes those orders to be wrong.'

On the following day, 3 October, a Field General Court Martial was convened by General Hobart to try Lieutenant the Hon. W. Douglas-Home under Section 9(2) of the Army Act, for 'When on active service disobeying a lawful command given by his superior officer in that he, in the field, on 8th September 1944 did not proceed to C Squadron 141 Regiment RAC (The Buffs) and act as liaison officer in the battle of Le Havre, when ordered to do so by Lieutenant-Colonel H. Waddell, commanding.'

On 4 October the Court assembled and proceedings began. For exactly four years, with obstinate sincerity, with a heavy heart, with what unwisdom or otherwise opinions will differ, but with undeniable courage, Will had been riding for this fall.

PART II
1944–1967

CHAPTER V
Counter-attack

Will conducted his own defence at the trial. He never pretended, then or later, that he had not committed, and deliberately committed, a serious offence. He had willed his nemesis and it came in a room in a château near Ghent, in Belgium.

Will's plea was 'Not guilty' for a technical reason. A plea of 'guilty' would have precluded the calling of any evidence save that of character. Will wished to call, or rather to give, evidence. He also wished to hear the prosecution's case stated (a plea of guilty would have denied him that) and to elicit from the chief prosecution witness acknowledgement that he, Will, had earlier made his views clear. He also wanted to make his statement as evidence and not simply in mitigation of punishment after a plea of guilty. He intended to plead extenuating circumstances. He had prepared this statement in writing, had it typed and brought it to court.

The evidence for the prosecution was formal: Colonel Waddell; Major Duffy, commander of the squadron with which Will had been ordered to liaise; Major Mills, the second-in-command, who had witnessed Will's refusal to obey the order; and Captain Storrar, who had been present at the taking of the summary of evidence and noted Will, after warning, making his statement; this statement, too, was produced.

Will only put one point in cross-examination. From Colonel Waddell he asked confirmation that he had frequently discussed his anxieties and put them to him in both interviews and letters. The point was agreed, and when Will asked if it were true that – perhaps because of his lightness of touch in expression, for which he apologised – these views had not been taken very seriously, Colonel Waddell replied that he had certainly believed Will's views would not be the same in the theatre of operations as those he had expressed in England.

Will called no witnesses for the defence and introduced his

own written statement with a short speech. In this he suggested that his state of mind – produced, as he accepted, by primarily political rather than moral factors – had made it impossible for him, with good conscience, to have taken part in the battle of Le Havre. The written statement ran to some 4,000 words and covered the extended arguments against the prolongation of the war with which the reader is familiar. The prosecuting officer, Major MacDonald from the Judge Advocate General's branch, put only three questions. Did Will suggest that he had not understood what he was doing? Answer, No. Had Will been in full possession of his mental faculties? Answer, Yes. Had he understood that he was disobeying a lawful command? Answer, Yes. The prosecuting officer then reminded the court that it was not for them to pronounce on what Will's motives had been, nor on whether they had been good or bad. The only question for the court, he said, was whether or not Will had disobeyed a lawful command. And that he had never attempted to deny. The prosecution at a court martial has an obligation to bring before the court any circumstance which might be helpful to the accused, even if he (especially if defending himself) has not called evidence to that effect. It was certainly not Will's view at the time that it had in the least failed in this duty.

The Judge Advocate, Major Nield, then summed up, as Will was later to put it, 'fairly, concisely and calmly'. He dealt with Will's plea that his mental condition constituted an extenuating circumstance within the meaning of the Act and advised the court that 'mental inability' to comply with an order must mean some disease of the mind resulting in failure to understand. In this case it did not apply. As to Will's own statement, the Judge Advocate commented that while there might be no reason to doubt anything the accused had said, the court had only to decide the legal issues. The circumstances submitted by the prosecution had been, in effect, admitted. It could not be concerned with the righteousness or otherwise of political or ethical views advanced by the accused.

The court – a Brigadier, a Lieutenant-Colonel and three Majors – was closed for consideration of the finding at five minutes past four in the afternoon of 4 October 1944. Five minutes later it was opened again for the finding to be announced. Guilty as charged. After another Major in the regiment had been called to give evidence as to character and had spoken up for Will, the court was closed for consideration of sentence. Proceedings were accurately reported, without comment, in, among other papers, the *Maidenhead Advertiser*.

The sentence of a court martial is not announced until it has been confirmed by the appropriate authority, in this case the Commander-in-Chief of the 21st Army Group. Eight days later the sentence – 'to be cashiered and to suffer one year's imprisonment with hard labour' – was confirmed by Field Marshal Sir Bernard Montgomery, and on the morning of 15 October it was promulgated and Will informed. 'It might have been much, much worse. Please don't let it upset you,' he wrote home, 'don't look upon it as a disgrace. There is no disgrace in breaking the law in what one believes to be a good cause, provided one is prepared to pay the penalty by which the law is upheld – as it must be.' It was a good, brave letter.

By then Will's battalion had reached Holland, Will with it pending final decision. To others at this time he appeared in good spirits, cheerful and at peace with himself. It is understandable. The sentence of cashiering – or dismissal, a milder version of the same penalty – is mandatory before a commissioned officer can be condemned to imprisonment. Will for a long time referred to the cashiering, with the stigma he thought attached, as an optional extra. He referred, in a letter from prison, to the Army Council's rejection of his petition and 'insistence on cashiering'. 'A little hard to be thrown out in disgrace,' he wrote, 'having tried to be relieved of one's Commission without success.' He mistook the point. If the sentence were to be of imprisonment at all (which, although it hurt, he did not so much dispute) he had, under the Army Act and the law, to be deprived of commissioned rank beforehand. The Army Council had no discretion.

Many aspects of this grievous business were uncertain, and would remain so for a long time, ultimately to re-emerge for investigation and discussion late in Will's life. To what extent was he correctly informed about the German Commander's request? Had such a request in fact been made and rejected, or did Will snatch at a report and use it as the pretext for a protest which had long been simmering inside him? To what extent did humanitarian factors – concern for the French victims of the bombardment – feature in his decision (as would one day be presumed) or was that decision primarily based, as his words at the time implied, on the essentially political factor that he considered the demand for unconditional surrender to be unnecessarily prolonging the war – a tenable proposition but hardly one for a junior regimental officer? To what extent could the bombing, or the refusal to agree a truce, be objectively regarded as a war crime? To what extent, if it were, could the crime imply responsibility in junior officers entirely unconnected with it and simply doing their duty in another part of the field? And were any of these questions realistically to be taken into any sort of account in the circumstances of a trial in the field in mid-campaign, 1944?

These and other matters would one day receive extended attention in a very different climate of opinion. One most regrettable consequence of Will's actions was that Colonel Waddell was removed from command. Although he was subsequently promoted, this was a hard pill to swallow for a competent, ambitious man, a natural achiever. He had done his utmost to protect Will from the results of his own actions; and he felt bitter about it – understandably. Will wrote later that he regretted this aspect. He was right to do so and it may be thought a pity that his regret was not more emphatic. Waddell, furthermore, demonstratively refrained from speaking against Will thereafter although he was at least once heard to observe that he had made a mistake in having him court-martialled, rather than shooting him on the spot!

Meanwhile, on 23 October, Will was admitted a prisoner at Wormwood Scrubs. He was now a civilian.

There thus began a very different phase of Will's life. It was a phase which started in darkness but was soon to reach sunlight and success. From his first day in prison his letters home were vigorous, amused and entertaining. 'Not one man in a hundred keeps his sense of humour in prison,' Will wrote later. He qualified.

The experience was, inevitably, a very upsetting one. Will had always known that sooner or later his attitudes would lead to something like this, he had brought it on himself, but when it came it was naturally a shock. Will, despite his assumed flippancy, was a serious and fastidious man and the routines of prison, the inspection for venereal disease, the dirt, the hunger and above all the remorseless lack of privacy were intensely disagreeable. The atmosphere of suppressed violence (or unsuppressed; he wrote of witnessing a prisoner beaten near insensible by his fellows, the warders looking on without interfering) was deeply unpleasant. Visitors found him understandably low in spirits. He was very, very lonely. Nevertheless he showed the utmost resilience. He submitted a petition to the Home Secretary, which he was advised might have the same effect as an appeal (there was no appeal from the finding or sentence of a court martial); it got nowhere. He wrote facetious and complaining letters, knowing that they had to be read by the prison authorities. He told his parents how much he was learning, such as how to open a Yale lock with a button and a piece of string. He gave directions about friends to be contacted, mostly with light-hearted messages. He reiterated, tirelessly, the points which had led him to make his stand: 'I refuse to be labelled and put aside as a crank. I could be just as good a soldier as the Duke of Marlborough (past not present) but I am not a soldier and I entirely disapprove of the modern Duke of Marlborough's war. It is my object to teach people, however inadequately, that soldiers have minds of their own.'

Will's resilience, of course, derived mainly from his courage, which never dimmed. It also owed much to the friendliness with which he had continued to be treated in the army after sentence. Of the officers and soldiers of the Buffs he wrote that nobody was anything but kind – 'not one man had an unpleasant word to say.' He knew that some of his friends and acquaintances, perhaps especially those who had lost friends and relatives in the war, would have difficulty in accepting him, but he didn't come across them in Wormwood Scrubs and his letters (strictly rationed) from his family were affectionate and supportive, quietly tolerating what he had done for conscience while still wholly disapproving.

Yet probably the greatest help to Will at this time, and the strongest spur to his resilience, was that he felt inwardly at peace. His nerves were, at first, in a poor state and the high points in the solitary struggle he had been conducting throughout the war kept on returning to torment his mind. Nevertheless he knew, now, that he had made his protest, made it publicly and suffered for it. He had broken every rule by not only refusing an order but by publicising the action in a letter to the press, and he had done so deliberately. He had lanced a boil, and whether his behaviour had been wrong-headed and disloyal as most contended, or conscientious throughout as he believed himself, it was behind him and he felt wholly unapologetic about it. He was no longer in a false position – one accepted for too long by himself, as he admitted. He had no painful and daily need to reconcile the duty to which he was bound with the duty imposed by conscience. He was a prisoner but he was free. The inner relief was great; the future must be better.

Will felt, unsurprisingly, that his private battle was by no means over. It could only be fought at the political level and his letters had plenty of references to the possibility of finding some constituency for which to stand when he emerged from prison. His parents' hearts are unlikely to have been rejoiced by this prospect but Will's announced intentions were another evidence of resilience. The prison library was good and he was reading a great deal – lives of distinguished statesmen for the most part, as well as the whole of the Bible – and politics past and present were much in his mind as they always had been.

Will enjoyed the drama of the political battle in a democracy and he had, of course, firm and idiosyncratic views on foreign policy, views deriving much from his generosity of feeling, and owing a good deal, also, to ignorance. Certainly no ideologue, he was eternally an idealist. He continued to give the family stern lectures in his letters on the evils of having demanded unconditional surrender. The prospect of a General Election after the war's end had Will hoping (fruitlessly) for nomination somewhere as a Liberal. Since he was allergic to the idea of party discipline, disliking all authority, party and party programmes meant little to him. He simply wanted a platform from which he could say what he thought. No party could have accommodated Will for long. That was the insurmountable bar to him as a politician, although it may have said much for him as a man.

But there was another, and increasing, aid to Will's endurance of prison. At the beginning of December 1944 he was transferred from Wormwood Scrubs to Wakefield 'Open' prison in Yorkshire. And a play was forming in his mind. It would not be written in prison – the regulations forbade it. In a later play, *Contempt of Court*, Will had a retrospective dig at the system, making a barrister say to the stage judge:

> They were sent to Wormwood Scrubs, from which enlightened prison they emerged this morning. My Lord, I deliberately use the word 'enlightened' because these days a prisoner may write a diary or a book or a play, which was not always the case.

That was nearly forty years on: Will never forgot these things.

Instead, Will's theatrical gifts found expression at Wakefield, as in the Army, in the production of a Christmas pantomime, *Babes in the Wood*, and letters home were full of requests for various articles of clothing for use in it. There was also, in April, an Easter concert devised by him. After the Governor had approved the programme, however, Will inserted a special item, 'The Dance of the Seven Mailbags' (the prisoners were often employed in sewing these unglamorous articles). The curtain rose on Will swathed in seven of them. He then swayed and rotated in a parody of every parody of every eastern dancer, shedding mailbags in turn until finally, to a musical crescendo, he threw aside the last and turned to take the wild applause of the prison population, staff and prisoners alike, wearing only some scarlet knickers belonging to the chief warder's wife. Will was reprimanded for adding this unauthorised concert item, but the reprimand certainly covered amusement. For the prisoners, of course, Will – as usual – was an irreplaceable character. And all the time he was absorbing material – human types, characters, turns of speech, situations – which would emerge in his first serious play since the war; in some ways the most serious he ever wrote.

Will wrote, to the permitted maximum, letters to the family. He was indomitably cheerful. 'I don't think there's anyone here you know,' he wrote to his sister Rachel from Wakefield, also asking her to send a 'complete Burns' to the chaplain at Wakefield for 'my friend from Scotland'. As the time of release approached he was apprehensive. 'Let me know any people who regard my last activity with acute distaste,' he wrote (also to Rachel). 'It is essential to know who will cut me after this. Somebody remarked the other day, "You'll get your punishment worse when you get out of here!" ' He knew that to some the way he had thought was incomprehensible and the way he had behaved disgraceful. He expected this. He had counted the cost.

The routine at Wakefield mercifully included plenty of hard work in the open air – Will had found the physical inactivity at Wormwood Scrubs almost the worst of its aspects. Now he generally felt well. There were some true friends who visited Will in prison, on the few occasions when the regulations allowed visits. Will was hurt that, as he thought, not many wrote him a line, although he always realised that some did not feel inclined. When discharged, however, he found a pile of mail he had not been allowed to receive; for such was the system. Lord and Lady Home came, as did his eldest brother Alec, after (with some difficulty) getting the Home Secretary's permission. The visit was made curious for Will – and recollected with invariable hilarity thereafter – because Will had grown a black beard and his appearance caused Alec first to dissolve in helpless laughter and then, from sheer astonishment, to find greater ease in talking almost entirely to the supervising warder. Will's father – entirely in character – felt that he had to end his own visit by calling on the Governor, to thank him, as it were, for his hospitality to the family.

On 6 June 1945 Will was discharged. Peace in Europe was a month old. The German war was over. Will travelled first to London for a few days to investigate (without success) the prospect of a candidature in the forthcoming General Election; Parliament had been dissolved in the immediate aftermath of victory. He had found at least one relation cold towards him, although he had met one or two old friends, including a brother-officer from the Buffs and his former batman, now discharged, who were wholly agreeable. Will's nerves were raw at the prospect of meeting people. He had a clear conscience but his experiences had given him a sense of rejection; he felt a strong need for demonstrative acceptance, for signs that he could again be, as he had been, a man whose society it was proper – even fashionable – to seek rather than shun. His shyness – buried, almost, since Ludgrove days – was in evidence with all but a few intimates; and it was indeed true that for some time there were people who regarded the action of disobedience in wartime, disobedience of perfectly routine orders to take a perfectly routine part in battle, as unpardonable. They did not want Will's company; and some of them never relented. For his part Will was remembered for never bearing a grudge.

Then Will decided to go home. It cannot have been easy, despite his parents' affection. It was going to be a different sort of home-coming from any previous. He described it clearly.[1] Lord Home's chauffeur met the train. 'Morning, Mr William. Well on time this morning.'

Breakfast with parents and sister Bridget. Lord Home discussing roe-deer seen from the drawing room windows. The state of salmon in the Tweed. Family news – Alec was conducting his election campaign in his constituency, South Lanark, and Lord William Scott, sister Rachel's husband, in Roxburgh and Selkirk. Edward was missing in South-East Asia, where the war was still going on.

Will was nervy, somewhat dreading encounters with familiars, relations even – perhaps relations particularly. But when they

1. *Mr Home Pronounced Hume*, Collins, 1979.

appeared their good sense and robustness soon had the desired effect. His Uncle Claud Lambton, Will remembered, wanted 'to know everything: why I had not been shot? Why I had been sent to a civil prison? . . . had I met a lot of murderers? what was the food like? could one drink or smoke? would I be asking any new-found friends to stay at Hirsel or would they be coming uninvited through the sky-light at night?'

And so forth. 'How's the gaolbird looking, Collingwood?' was the final shot, to the Hirsel butler. 'Well, Captain Claud,' was the answer. Will began to return to life. Life outside. And there was work to be done.

Now Barabbas was written in ten days of that summer of 1945, in a wood near the Hirsel while Will was at home. It is the first and perhaps the only one of Will's plays to be written fully and uninhibitedly from the heart and with emotion undimmed by reticence. Others, plays such as *The Dame of Sark* and *The Kingfisher* are full of 'heart' and were written with more experience and technical skill. *The Bad Soldier Smith* has heart – it is purely and unashamedly autobiographical. Others again, late plays like *The Lord's Lieutenant* and *David and Jonathan*, attempted a theme of emotional intensity with only partial success; in these plays Will was writing without as deep an involvement of his own feelings, and it shows. But *Now Barabbas* was composed when Will, whatever the indomitability and humour he had shown, was raw from the experiences of prison. That, too, shows and gives the play its especial strength and poignancy.

Now Barabbas is set in a prison like Wakefield, with ten prisoners, led by a senior, a 'stroke', sharing a mess. Will's time at Wakefield, from December 1944 until June 1945, had provided the material. His observation was always acute, his ear for dialogue exceptionally sharp. The play is concerned with the depiction and interplay of a number of wholly credible characters, all 'inside' for reasons which are only hinted at, if that. There is the Irish 'stroke', Paddy, a rebel and a Nationalist, convicted of exactly what we do not know. There is Anderson, the 'big, black, lugubrious negro', with a ready line in repartee. There is Spencer, the pretentious and thieving poseur with unconvincing talk of his (clearly fictitious) past as an officer in the Royal Air Force; Medworth, the elderly and insinuating homosexual, and Richards the younger, absurder, and also homosexual caricature.

There are the irrepressible wags: Brown, the bigamist; Smith, the witty young tough. There is Roberts, the near-innocent.

There are the warders, 'screws': King, good-natured despite himself; Jackson, harsh but not without wit. There is the Governor, tough, experienced, humorous, fair and wholly aware of the characters of his charges. There is the Chaplain – Will had made trusting friends with the Wakefield prison chaplain, a vivid and sincere preacher. The atmosphere and dialogue presented by *Now Barabbas* are wholly convincing. The play is moving, often funny, fair-minded and persuasive. It does not preach. It conveys restrained and comprehending authenticity.

And there is Tufnell. Tufnell is a murderer. He has been sentenced to death and is awaiting confirmation or commutation of sentence. Will he or will he not swing?

Tufnell was played in the London production by Richard Longman, a friend of Will from when they were in the same company as cadets at Sandhurst, a professional actor who had been captured in Italy and a prisoner until the end of the war. Tufnell's is a strong and emotional part. When told by the Governor that the law is to take its course he breaks down hysterically, with violent attacks on the chaplain who has comforted and befriended him (Will had held long talks with the chaplain at Wormwood Scrubs, a much-liked Welshman, about the latter's experiences of executions). The fate of Tufnell and the sympathy engaged for him are vivid dramatic experiences. The touched-in, understated anxieties, bitternesses and quarrels of the other prisoners bring them to memorable life. And the humour never jars.

If the first bombshell to burst over the household at the Hirsel in 1944 and 1945 was the court martial and sentence to a year's imprisonment with hard labour of the third Douglas-Home son, the next was almost as traumatic. In July 1945 the results of the General Election came in, spread over an unusually long period because of the need to collect the votes of servicemen abroad. Collingwood appeared in the drawing room after luncheon one day while Will was still at home. His face was grim. He addressed Will's father.

'He's lost, my lord.'

'Who's lost what?'

'Lord Dunglass, my lord – he's lost South Lanark!'

All over the country traditional Conservative seats were tumbling in a landslide not seen since the beginning of the century. Mr Attlee was sent for by the King and invited to form a Labour administration, most of whose senior members had of course served in the Coalition Government, as had Attlee himself as Churchill's deputy. There was, however, a general sense of doom. Red revolution must be the prescription of the incomers, to judge from the rhetoric of the election. The eminently respectable and patriotic Clement Attlee was supposed to be a British Robespierre, and among Conservative families and voters the dismissal of Churchill – until yesterday the apparent hero of the entire nation – was incomprehensible and unforgivable.

To Will it was both comprehensible and forgivable. He had felt out of it during the campaign, having missed his chances (as he saw it) of getting a nomination, for whatever party. He sympathised with his brother but still felt wholly estranged from what had been the policies of Churchill's government (and of most of Attlee's colleagues as well as Attlee himself). He had enjoyed the actual course of the election, the sporting element, the excitement of results, the sense of change – he always enjoyed elections. He had watched, with a chuckle, how Alec's defeat seemed to be taken far harder by Collingwood than by Lord and Lady Home. In three weeks Will had completed his second post-war play.

The Chiltern Hundreds was the first of a number of plays in which Will drew on the quirks of his immediate family; 'he had little imagination,' some of them remarked with a touch of irritation, 'he simply wrote about us!' The setting – Lister Castle – provides the Earl of Lister with opportunities to pot rabbits spotted through the French windows while his long-suffering Countess tackles the domestic problems of the now comparatively servant-less age. Only comparatively – Beecham, the butler and mastermind of all, has been at the castle a long time and has the family under fairly good control; loyally, correctly and often surprisingly. To this ménage the loss of his Commons seat in the General Election by the eldest son of the house, Lord Pym, comes without particular shock – it is just one of those things, and his successful Socialist opponent will, as a matter of form, be invited to stay. Lord Lister is Lord-Lieutenant and the invitation will be *de rigueur*. Only Beecham refuses to adjust. The origin of the plot lay in Collingwood's announcement to the Home family, 'He's lost, my Lord!' Will developed it splendidly from there, and he gave the principal male characters – Lister, Beecham and the victorious Labour member, Cleghorn – some superb lines. Nor were Lady

Lister and Lord Lister's sister, Lady Caroline (carried off happily by Cleghorn), far behind. Inevitably the new MP and the Listers get on admirably. Cleghorn, at their first dinner, is immaculate in a dinner jacket, his hosts in their usual shabby informality.

LORD LISTER: I want my evening clothes tomorrow, Beecham.
BEECHAM: If your lordship recollects, you gave them to the game-keeper last year.
LORD LISTER: Well, dash it, he won't want 'em every night.
BEECHAM: No, no, my lord. Your lordship gave them to him with a view to scaring off the pigeons from the plums.

So Tony, Lord Pym, has no seat and no job. And Beecham is utterly distraught.

LORD LISTER: The bath water was cold today.
BEECHAM: I'm sorry to hear that, my lord.
LORD LISTER: It's not your sympathy I want – that doesn't heat the bath water. The fire must be kept in, at night. It isn't much to ask. Whose job is it?
BEECHAM: It should be the oddjob man's, my lord, but as we don't employ one the responsibility devolves on me ... I'm afraid the boiler slipped my mind last night, my lord. The day's events had served to drive domestic details of that nature from my head.
LORD LISTER: What day's events? What happened yesterday?
BEECHAM: According to the papers the Electorate conspired to bring the Socialists to power, my lord.
LORD LISTER: Oh, that! Well, what the devil's that got to do with you?
BEECHAM: I feel the matter very strongly, as I told your lordship yesterday.
LORD LISTER: Daresay you do. That's no excuse for going round and sabotaging everything ...

June, Tony's ambitious American fiancée, feels that Tony and his like are accepting events with too little of the spirit of resistance – as does Beecham. But Lord Lister has no desire to let politics intrude where there are more serious concerns.

JUNE (to Lady Lister): Good morning, Moll. (To Lord Lister) Good morning, Joe.
LORD LISTER: What's that?
JUNE: I said 'Good morning, Joe.'
LORD LISTER: Ah yes. I've set a snare.
JUNE: You have? What for?
LORD LISTER: Oh, rabbits, chiefly. It's a rabbit snare, you know.
LADY LISTER: Joe, do stop talking about rabbits.

LORD LISTER (hurt): Why? They interest me.

LADY LISTER: Yes, dear. I'm slowly learning that. So long as you've got your beastly rabbits you don't mind if Tony starves.

LORD LISTER: What? Tony hungry? Have another piece of toast. You're worse than Beecham, Moll. You ought to take a sedative.

LADY LISTER: I sometimes wonder if I didn't take one when I married you . . .

Will – it recurred often – greatly enjoyed setting the fun against an electoral background. Lord Pym changes party, to the disgust of Beecham.

BEECHAM: I don't like turncoats, my lord.

PYM: . . . you voted for me as a Tory, so it shows you think I ought to be in Parliament. I've chosen the best vehicle, that's all.

BEECHAM: Talking of vehicles, the tumbril had at least a certain dignity, my lord.

The Chiltern Hundreds contains farce, but in it Will held up a mirror to the puzzled insouciance with which his parents' class and generation were, on the whole, facing the new circumstances of a war-weary, impoverished Britain and a would-be egalitarian Labour government. He did so with kindness and with no touch of bitterness – no play is friendlier to all parties, and when politics and politicians are mocked it is with an infectious chuckle. Will had recovered his sense of fun. Horace Walpole wrote, 'My great ambition is not to grow cross,' and Will echoed him. His good humour was at the root of both his character and his art: by the time he had finished *The Chiltern Hundreds* he had taken the first steps back to true health. That November and December, at Douglas, he was shooting almost every day.

Will now found somewhere to live in London – two rooms in the house of a charming dentist, a fellow inmate of Wormwood Scrubs confined for running over someone in the wartime black-out, having drink taken. In London, Will started to make contact with his earlier world. It was not always easy. His prime task, however, was to persuade some theatrical management of the merits of *Now Barabbas* and *The Chiltern Hundreds*.

In February 1947, *Now Barabbas* was produced by O'Brien, Linnit and Dunfee at the Boltons Theatre in Kensington, with Colin Chandler directing. After a month the play transferred to the Vaudeville, in the West End, and ran for a further four months. By then it had been overtaken by *The Chiltern Hundreds*, produced by the same management.

The reviews of *Now Barabbas* were all that Will could wish. 'A play I'll always remember . . . William Douglas Home has with great courage written more than a play' (*London Calling*). 'Scorchingly vivid' (*Cavalcade*). 'Indelibly stamped on my mind is the play's atmosphere of timelessness in a dead world' (*Daily Mail*). A few reviews pointed to a certain sentimentality, but all praised the sharpness of the characterisation, and the acting certainly underlined the sense of realism, that 'suspension of disbelief' theatre should induce. 'The play is so realistically written,' one critic found, 'that it makes us feel we have shared that experience.' Harold Hobson, henceforth a perceptive and admiring observer of Will's talents, wrote of him as 'rich in promise and achievement'. James Agate, testy doyen of critics, had a censorious (but constructive) point to make about Tufnell's execution:

> If ever a playwright missed his chance for a fine ending it was this author in this piece . . . It is nearing eight o'clock and the doomed man has heard the steeple 'sprinkle the quarters on the morning town'. And into the minds of some in the audience tonight must have come recollection of Houseman's great lines:
>
> > Strapped, noosed, nighing his hour,
> > he stood and counted them and cursed his luck;
> > and then the clock collected in the tower
> > Its strength, and struck
>
> The gaolor removes his cap. Was ever opportunity so missed?[2]

Many will disagree. Will's treatment of the moment was severely understated, with the prison 'coming to life' again after the clock strikes, and it was a most effective treatment. But Agate's review showed serious, and interested, comment. It would be a long time before Will would hear that sort of voice again. Penal reform was a continuing interest of his; he was particularly concerned to emphasise the ill consequences of confining the young and vulnerable with hardened old lags. He had seen it. When Roy Jenkins was Home Secretary he asked Will to serve on the parole board for Parkhurst Prison, a task he performed conscientiously, and with loathing.

Somerset Maugham wrote to Will that *Now Barabbas* would

2. James Agate, *Ego 9*, George Harrap, 1948.

have and deserve a *succès d'estime* but that *The Chiltern Hundreds* would succeed at the box office. And so it did – Will's first triumph. Will, with the promise shown in *Now Barabbas*, was likened to Galsworthy. The critics were disappointed that after the emotionally charged *Barabbas* Will had written (as the *Sunday Graphic* put it) an 'utterly conventional light comedy', but others wrote of his having reminded audiences that there is 'fun in politics', and although the *New Yorker* was later to describe the plot loftily as 'intricate, childlike and annoying' it had the grace to call the play 'pure P. G. Wodehouse'. Now, if not then, high praise.

With a superb cast headed by A. E. Matthews and Michael Shepley, *The Chiltern Hundreds* ran and ran. Will made occasional speeches from the stage, including one on an anniversary of the opening when he said that so long as a Labour government was in office he intended to write comedies to cheer people up. It was almost as if he was mending fences with the Leader of the Opposition, Winston Churchill.

Helped considerably by *The Chiltern Hundreds*, for the next three or four years Will lived a prosperous and fashionable life in London. He carried through life an unabashed ignorance about money. He enjoyed spending it, he enjoyed even more giving it away, being generous with it, but as a subject finance bored him miserably and he found discussion of his own or other people's money distasteful. He was entirely robust – the well-honed resilience – if times were hard as they sometimes were. He seldom complained (except about taxation, the rudiments of which he never made the smallest attempt to understand). He treated both abundance and shortage of money as something of a joke.

Transient prosperity now gave him an old Bentley and a flat in Down Street, and the 'fashionable' aspect of life was surprisingly important to him for a while. He was in demand in society. The past was past and this mattered to him more than might be supposed. The scars of 1944 may have been self-inflicted and their source cauterised but they never ceased to itch. Will, despite his confidence in his own conscience, had often felt an outcast, bravely though he had laughed the feeling away. Acceptance was welcome. Self-confidence was still fragile.

Outwardly, however, Will had recovered. He was the successful playwright with a host of friends in several worlds. He was – and he always was – immensely kind. A friend, especially a friend in difficulties, was invariably looked after by

Will, accepted his flowing hospitality, made to feel welcome and important. Thanks embarrassed him. To help people – quietly, with a joke, or anonymously – was his nature. Inwardly, however, there was a good deal of loneliness and insecurity. His nerves were still in poor condition. It would take more than revived popularity among his friends, smart or otherwise, to drive the shadows away.

The popularity was very real. Will was an irresistible companion and the mention of his name was enough to bring a smile in most quarters. Although some of his male friends and acquaintances would take time to forgive what they regarded as incomprehensible behaviour, women found him enchanting. In many ways he preferred the company of women to that of men. 'Men's talk' bored him. If men sat over their glasses and cigars after a dinner party he tended to slip away. But he dived into the life of dances (although he cared little for dancing), gatherings in country houses for race meetings, sport, laughter and flirtation. He loved entertaining pretty girls, taking them out to the theatre, to dinner. In a curious way he discovered and enjoyed a second youth. At heart serious, he had a way, which some found exasperating, of masking a serious point behind a witticism, of turning a criticism or probing question with a flight into gentle mockery – or self-mockery. Even people who loved him complained that they had never got through the curtain of flippancy, the screen of beautifully told anecdotes, with punchlines crafted and timing impeccable. With an inscrutable (and exceptionally handsome) face and sphinx-like expression, in a deadpan voice emitting only sometimes an infectious giggle, Will could give the impression of absolute resistance to the smallest baring of the inner self.

The impression was largely accurate. Will firmly protected his privacy of emotion. Still 'shy' in a sense he had not really outgrown he feared the pains as well as the embarrassments of personal disclosure, and he never indulged it. He was averse to displays of physical endearment (a family as well as a personal characteristic); essentially non-tactile.

Nevertheless Will inwardly craved affection, and his susceptibility was such that he often at this time (as when young) supposed himself in love or let others suppose it. He once described himself as like a kettle which boiled over too quickly. While he was the reverse of sexually aggressive, he could move from instant attraction to what he thought might be deep feeling with confusing speed – and certainly confusing and bewildering the girl concerned; the suddenness of his declarations could resemble the sequences in some of his plays. But then he would shrink from commitment, dreading rejection. The personality projected was elusive to the point of being maddening, especially to anyone genuinely attracted. The escapes from emotion into laughter in his plays mirrored an aspect of his own life.

This was inhibition. The walls he built around himself, carried their own stresses and would not always be good for his health. He gave himself, on the other hand, some hard training in exposure by periodically taking a part in one of his own plays, giving an actor a rest. He did this for a fortnight as Lord Pym in *The Chiltern Hundreds*; he would do it in other plays later. RADA proved its enduring value to Will and performance on stage refreshed his roots as a playwright. But he wore armour, and the barrier it made between him and the arrows of the world could also sometimes inhibit his convincing dramatic expression – though not his understanding – of the raw emotions of others.

A successful playwright, however, needs continuing success, and in practical, commercial terms this was always to be a problem for Will. Enormously prolific, he wrote too many second-rate plays. His real successes were spaced overlong. He wrote two pieces during these years. One of them, *Ambassador Extraordinary*, was produced by Linnit and Dunfee in 1948 and in London was loudly booed by the gallery. In it Will scratched again at the sore of his earlier political preoccupations. Britain and a fictional Mauretania are about to go to war over the latter's pretensions to some strategically desirable piece of territory, the Chah Peninsular. The Foreign Secretary, Sir Hartley Harris, is a conventional, not unsympathetic politician, his wife a 'men-are-so-silly' stereotype, not unlike the Countess of Lister. The Mauretanian Ambassador, Baski, is a 'superior person' from a minor country, a character often drawn by Will and able to voice his views on the double standards established great powers can apply. To this group descends a fantasy figure, an Ambassador from Mars, to impose what Will is suggesting to be sanity. The dialogue echoes much of Will's immediate past argument:

SIR HARTLEY: They mean to have it!
LADY HARRIS: Hartley – does it really matter if they do?
SIR HARTLEY: Of course it does. The principle's involved. We can't have people grabbing other peoples' territory.
LADY HARRIS: But surely it's been done before?

Will

SIR HARTLEY: It's out of date.
LADY HARRIS: It's only out of date when it no longer pays.

This was the 'burglar's swag' approach to Empire, which Will had so often advanced with, his friends and critics suggested, inadequate understanding of historical and political facts. The man from Mars (with superior planetary wisdom) summarises it:

MARS: And so we have decided that the Chahland crisis cannot be resolved in peace because the Mauretanians desire an Empire and the English do not wish the Mauretanians to have an Empire –
SIR HARTLEY: These Mauretanians – backward, unprogressive – are doing –
MARS: Just exactly what you did when you were growing up.
SIR HARTLEY: But when we had grown up, we stopped.
MARS: When you had got enough. All robbers do!

And the Mauretanian Ambassador declaims, 'We Mauretanians will fight to have an Empire on the lines of that which you have had so long.'

There is, as always, good-humoured fun to sugar the pill of some pretty naive political philosophy. The Foreign Secretary tries not to take his medicines:

SIR HARTLEY: The Third World War – the final one – is due to start at any moment now. And I – the man who's working round the world to stop it – have to waste my time while you are playing round with pills.
LADY HARRIS: Now open up and don't be silly, dear. Don't lose your temper with the Mauretanian Ambassador. If you were in his place you'd do exactly what he's doing now. Now lick the spoon.

But there were shouts of 'rubbish' from the gallery. The mixture of farcical subplot and deliberate fantasy with what Will intended as a serious albeit gentle message failed to enchant audiences. Rightly so. Will's political shafts were, most thought, as naive as his story was absurd. Some entertaining dialogue (and not enough of it) could not save the day. For a play to project a persuasive political or moral message as well as to entertain, it must have high quality. Will himself wrote that, to succeed, a play should have good and varied character parts, a strong plot and an unforgettable dénouement. *Ambassador Extraordinary* probably failed to match any of these requirements. Like most gifted

102

performers Will had off days. This was generally acknowledged to be one, although later productions in the provinces went well. And Will, never yielding on such occasions, faced the gallery from the stage: 'Please go on. I like heckling. I hope some people have enjoyed the play. As for the others [he looked up at the gallery] it doesn't much matter. If they don't learn the lesson of compromise taught tonight, in six months' time that gallery won't be here.'

'A brave man', wrote J. C. Trewin in the *Birmingham Post*. Will may not have won the argument but he had not and never would run away.

The play was, however, significant in showing something of Will's continuing preoccupation with certain issues, a preoccupation which trial and prison (and a successful comedy) had not diminished. There was the obsession with double standards – the self-deception with which a person (or a nation) can apply different criteria to another's conduct from those regarded as defensible in his own. There was the question of peace and war – did the fictional quarrel in the play possibly justify threats of force: of killing and destroying? Theologians argue that for a war to be just it must be proportionate to the wrong to be righted. Will agreed, while contending that in too many cases it is not so proportionate. And there was the eternal – and eternally endearing – concern with good humour. Whatever the bitterness of international, or personal, feelings matters can only be helped by a touch of good nature, good manners; a smile. The fact that *Ambassador Extraordinary* proved a pretty inadequate vehicle for these messages did not reduce their importance to Will, disappointing though the upshot was.

In October 1948 Will appeared with a cast of distinguished names – Ronald Squire, Beatrix Lehmann, Sonia Dresdel, Celia Johnson, Cedric Hardwicke and many others – in an all-star matinee performance of Barrie's superb one-act, teasing mystery, *Shall We Join the Ladies?*, at Drury Lane. All the cast were former students of RADA and the matinee, in the presence of the Queen, was to raise funds for rebuilding the Malet Street theatre. The experience was good for Will. He was among the people he most revered. He once wrote a (never performed) second and explanatory Act for *Shall We Join the Ladies?*. His next play, also produced by Linnit and Dunfee, was called *Master of Arts*. It started in September 1949, at the Strand Theatre.

Master of Arts (printed version) carried a dedication by Will to Robin Douglas-Home, his brother Henry's elder son and a gifted, attractive, well-loved nephew, at that time seventeen years old. The play held no political message whatsoever – it was an agreeable comedy, rather in the manner of Ian Hay, set in a public school (clearly, although not explicitly, Eton) with a cast of betting, occasionally tipsy, schoolboys; young housemaster falling for sister; absent-minded ducal parent; ex-actress outspoken Duchess. And a left-wing Cabinet Minister parent, with a more left-wing wife, who enabled Will to get in some shrewd but genial digs at those who criticise fee-paying schools but use them.

Master of Arts was not very successful commercially but it was a good-natured lark, showing Will's skill at construction, with excellently contrived deceptions and unmaskings, well up to the standard of a Lonsdale or a Pinero. Roland Culver, a charming actor, led. Will gave it his particular stamp by showing authority – the housemaster – caught out and blackmailed by a boy into complicity. Will loved what might be called egg-on-the-face humour. And he enjoyed both precocity and impertinence.

RONNIE: [the housemaster, having been shown a tell-tale photograph]:
It's utterly disgraceful. Schoolboys kissing women ten years older than themselves.

ROBIN [errant boy-photographer]:
Why Sir? Disraeli's wife was far older than him.

RONNIE: That's neither here nor there.

ROBIN: I mean, Sir – some men like their women older and some women like their men, well, younger, Sir. Besides, he's going to be a Duke. And dukes are sort of ageless to a woman, Sir.

Since the plot turns on Robin's illicit absence from school at Ascot (a not infrequent occurrence at Eton in Will's time – in fact the curriculum was retimed during Ascot week to make this harder) there is a good deal in the play about racing and betting. And this was increasingly another of Will's preoccupations. He longed to be, and ultimately was, an owner and the fact comes out strong in *Master of Arts*; and he was an inveterate better on the Turf, often punting through the card on every race in an afternoon. He never varied his stake, following a system mathematically incomprehensible to anybody else; and, as with most gamblers, his friends heard something of his winnings, little of his losses (and both were sometimes considerable). *Master of Arts* did not provide very substantial winnings but it kept Will's hand in, it was a relief from political preachment, and it gave him a good deal of fun.

In 1950 Will – some may think astonishingly – was adopted as Conservative candidate for Kirkcaldy, in Fife. The Conservative Party was in opposition, although the Attlee Government was in considerable difficulties, and would, in the event, be beaten in 1951. The local Constituency Association invited Will – cashiered and an ex-convict – to represent them. He found this endearing. Will had generally claimed to be at heart a 'Conservative with independent leanings', one forced into standing as an Independent by disagreements (not themselves anti-Conservative disagreements in any doctrinal sense) with the wartime coalition. Party, however, demands loyalty and a measure of conformity. Will alleged that his record showed no inconsistency, but it was not a record to recommend him to a Conservative Association. Kirkcaldy was broadminded. So – it lay far in the future – was a Liberal Association in South Edinburgh (twice).

Will was not now engaged on any political crusade. There was no 'unconditional surrender' to savage, no absence of war aims to deplore. *Ambassador Extraordinary* had produced a fictional, and unconvincing, construct for Will to attack. At the heart of his Kirkcaldy candidature was a simple desire for the fun of fighting an election. This, of course, had also been there on previous occasions but there had been pain and conscience as well. Now he observed simply a tired and unpopular Labour administration and the chance of a new deal, with the aged Churchill urging a revival of national purpose. Churchill, Will decided, had by 1950 probably shed his ambitions to strike attitudes imitative of his great ancestor. If Churchill – with a magnanimity Will always acknowledged – accepted Will as a follower, Will could probably accept him as a leader.

Unfortunately the Korean War broke out in summer 1950, when the Communist forces of North Korea crossed the frontier into South Korea early on Sunday morning, 25 June. Very soon the North Koreans had almost completely overrun South Korea. The aggression – barefaced and brutal – was considered by the Security Council of the United Nations, an organisation Will was apt not only to defend but somewhat to idealise. The United Nations recommended members to help South Korea (the Soviet Union was boycotting United Nations meetings, in protest at the continued seating of Nationalist China, so could not exercise its Permanent Member veto). The war was on.

Will, therefore, found himself defending the policies of a

Party dedicated (as were the Government) to a new version of Coalition war. General MacArthur had launched a bold counter-offensive with United States forces and had driven the enemy back to the frontier, liberating the capital, Seoul. MacArthur was then authorised to move north of the line – the 38th parallel – between North and South, in order to destroy the North Korean forces and prevent a repetition of the latter's attack. He was forbidden, however, to cross the northern border of North Korea into Manchuria.

The movement of MacArthur's troops into North Korea triggered the entry into the war of very large Communist Chinese forces. Soon the United Nations were represented not only by a considerable American army but by a British Commonwealth Division, as well as Turkish and other troops. The North Koreans undertook a counter-offensive and the United Nations troops withdrew to something like the original line, where a ferocious war of attrition, with fighting comparable to that in Europe in 1914–18, was waged for two years before an uneasy armistice was negotiated. Casualties were enormous and the country, or much of it, was devastated.

During the United Nations counter-offensive there had been a good deal of controversy about the correct strategy and about what risks (including the risks of Soviet intervention and a broadening of the war) might be run. Ultimately MacArthur was dismissed (in April 1951) for his 'hawkish' statements on the situation. The British Labour Party and thus (until late 1951) the British Government were uneasy at MacArthur's views or some of them. The British Conservative Party (still in opposition) were a good deal less so.

It was inevitable that sooner or later Will would find himself parting company from Party leadership in this sort of situation. He decided that Churchill's bellicosity – he had supported the more vigorous prosecution of the war pressed by MacArthur – was an obstacle to peace. At a meeting in Glasgow he said so. Afterwards Will asked the Conservative agent how he thought the meeting had gone. Everybody knew that a general election could not be far away, and the performance of candidates mattered. The agent was philosophical. 'You've got the Communist vote all right,' he said. The Kirkcaldy Association, tactfully and courteously, told Will that they now recognised a mistake. They asked for his resignation and got it.

It was with a certain slightly puzzled relief that Will's friends learned the theme of his next play to be produced. It was to be a love story. Indeed two love stories.

CHAPTER VI

Speckled with Success

Caro-William, written during 1950, was produced in 1952 at the Embassy Theatre in Swiss Cottage, ran for some four months and never reached the West End of London. It is a moving and perceptive play, and showed Will's sensitivity to delicate nuances of character and feeling. To an extent inhibited though he sometimes was in the depiction of emotions, he could certainly understand them; particularly the emotions of a character with whom he could empathise.

In this play Will's theme was historical and it fascinated him. Historical themes are notoriously hard to handle in the theatre. Will, in *The Thistle and the Rose*, in *Caro-William*, as well as in *Betzi* (1965), *The Queen's Highland Servant* (1968), *The Douglas Cause* (1971) and *The Dame of Sark* (1974), handled them with a good deal of aplomb and understanding, as well as excellent taste. None broke box-office records but all are well-crafted, well-researched and entertaining.

The story of *Caro-William* is that of William Lamb, later to be the Prime Minister Lord Melbourne, and his marriage with the fascinating, unstable, impossible Lady Caroline Ponsonby, Caro-William. William Lamb was born at the heart of the Grand Whiggery, that nexus of powerful and wealthy families which ruled England for much of the eighteenth and early nineteenth centuries. Deriving their position from the Protestant settlement which had ushered in the Hanoverian dynasty and replaced a sort of monarchy with a very definite and ruling sort of aristocracy, the Whigs combined lofty political principles – 'civil and religious liberty throughout the world' – with, very often, great possessions and, equally often, disdain for the restraints of personal morality. Because they talked in high, enlightened terms they thought themselves liberal and temperamentally reformist, while constituting, in fact, as proudly exclusive an oligarchy as any nation's political life has ever produced.

Will enjoyed the Whigs, to some extent because he loved the character of Charles James Fox, probably their most attractive historical standard-bearer. He would have denied feeling affinity with their exclusiveness, and although he was tolerant he had no taste for the well-advertised sexual profligacy of many; but he liked their style, their scepticism, their expansiveness, their readiness to gamble, their welcoming of new ideas, their cultivation, their generosity. In William Lamb, Will could find a deeply sympathetic character round whom to build a play, a man who had been schooled by the intensity of his own emotions to conceal them. Like many writers in the genre of historical drama Will was prepared to remake character and remould situation to enable him to make points congenial to him; but he did his homework thoroughly and with insight. His characterisation of William Lamb – he drew a good deal on Lord David Cecil's *The Young Melbourne* – convinces. Will wrote him as calm, tolerant, detached, temperamentally averse from exercising heavy-handed authority whether in political or matrimonial affairs; and he appreciated Lamb's aloofness in emotional matters, maddening though it may have been to one affected. Will savoured detachment like a man savouring a good wine. He intensely disliked the sexually aggressive type of male – not for his sexuality but for his aggression. He loved William Lamb, a civilised, sensuous, intelligent, withdrawn man. And, of course, Will enjoyed the ability to set Lamb's personal drama against the background of politics, always – with racing – a favourite environment.

William Lamb is being opposed in an election by a Tory, Dunscombe, and that in the Melbourne family borough of Hertford:

GEORGE LAMB: [William Lamb's brother]:
    I hope you're going to slate that fellow Dunscombe.
WILLIAM: I hate slating people, George.
GEORGE: But still, it's such dashed cheek to come and stand down here.
WILLIAM: He's got a perfect right to do it, George. One can't expect to get in unopposed for Hertford, just because one lives at Brocket Hall. That's a Tory point of view (and a dashed good one, too).

MRS GEORGE
(to William's father):
    Lord Melbourne, please don't let him talk like that! I never know if he's a Whig or a Tory.

LORD MELBOURNE: Don't believe he knows himself!
WILLIAM (when pressed):

> ... because my creed is compromise I stand up as a
> Whig and propagate my Tory principles.

And when George, imitating a heckler, yells: 'That won't do! a politician's either one thing or another!' William retorts, 'A politician, yes! I quite agree! But I am not a politician. I am a statesman, Sir.'

There were plenty of shades of Windsor and other by-elections here. Shades, too, of Will's annoyance with alleged Conservative dirty tricks at Windsor: 'The Tories'll do anything,' George Lamb says. 'They always have and always will.'

This was in response to the fact that Dunscombe had dragged into the campaign Caroline Lamb's notorious conduct, particularly her passion for Lord Byron which had created scandal, even in Whig circles. Will's play does not handle this passion on stage – it is reported, or is past, and John Gielgud remarked, fairly, 'As so often happens in a historical play the Byron episode, which is the most interesting, is over before the play begins ... there is too much description of reported, backstage action.' It is, however, good, vivid description.

William Lamb refuses to fight and proposes to resign his candidature. When his sister Emily, Lady Cowper, remonstrates, William counters: 'You've always told me tolerance has been my ruin.' And later, excusing his failure to exercise some authority over his wife and her behaviour which is wrecking his life: 'It isn't in my nature, Emily. I couldn't tell poor Caro that she wasn't to do this or that. It's quite impossible for me to be an autocrat.'

EMILY: In that case you should not have married.
WILLIAM: Very possible. Autocracy's opposed to every principle
            that I possess.

There was much of Will in much of this. And the exchanges between William Lamb, determined as he is to remain invulnerable, and the wild, romantic – and ultimately drunken – Caro-William are deeply felt and convincing. Lord Byron, the love of her life as she persuades herself, has gone. William is tolerant and apparently – but only apparently – unhurt. Caro-William finds some outlet in flirtation with the young poet, Edward Bulwer:

CARO-WILLIAM: Love! Why must men always talk of love? As though
                it were a definite condition, like a cold, and to be treated

	with a kiss, thrice daily after meals! (She turns away and takes a drink of brandy.)
BULWER:	Well, isn't that the cure?
CARO-WILLIAM:	The cure! Why do men always want to cure their love? Why can they never leave it in the clouds where it belongs? (refilling her glass)

And when Bulwer asks whether making love is not the thing that keeps all human love alive, Caro-William responds fiercely: 'No, that's what kills it, Edward! That's what kills it dead!' Caro-William is portrayed as repelled by physical love while excessively vulnerable to the sensations of emotion and imagination. It is, however, painfully easy to believe in the love she inspires in William Lamb – and to share it. Will was good at painting the fascination of an impossible – or simply unsuitable – woman. It is also easy to believe in Caro-William's frustrated love for her quiet, admirable, immovable husband.

Psychologically the play is subtle, ambitious and brave. And the conclusion, managing to avoid mawkishness, is skilful and moving. It also shows Will's skill at construction – the historical background and the complexity of the relationships needed clever handling and (*pace* Gielgud) Will managed to convey the necessary information to the audience economically, wittily and without excessive interruption to the flow and pace of the central drama. Will, of course, could not resist playing for one or two easy contemporary laughs: 'A dreadful fellow, Byron!' says George Lamb. 'Why does Harrow always turn out cads?'

Critics and managements, recalling *The Chiltern Hundreds*, always tended to wish Will safely harnessed to comedy, and to regard his essays into serious feeling as alien to his strengths as a writer. Some thought William and Caro insufficiently effective, as cast. 'In the last analysis,' the *Times'* critic wrote, '. . . a failure to establish the personalities of the two principals.' But *Caro-William* was a play with insight. It showed strong and necessarily concealed emotions in its central characters – an effort of subtlety made for the first time in Will's playwriting career. He was thirty-eight.

Also written before 1950, and produced first in Bromley, in September 1952, came *The Bad Samaritan*. The play was, therefore, first staged before *Caro-William*, but did not reach the West

111

End – first, for a short run, at the Criterion and then the Duchess, for a respectable run of some 150 performances – until the summer of 1953. Reviews were mixed, with references to 'clever talk' and 'strong theatrical situations', underpinned by praise for the acting. The play did not make money for Will.

In one sense *The Bad Samaritan* continued the mood captured by Will in *Caro-William* in that it was a story of love between young people, essentially mismatched young people, immature in their feelings and unsure where body ends and heart begins. In another sense it was a different sort of play in that it was contemporary (set, like the comedies, in the immediate aftermath of the war) and based on imagination (in defiance of his relations' strictures) rather than recorded history. It was, for Will, an ambitious play and his most serious since *Now Barabbas*.

The Bad Samaritan deals with a difficult and delicate theme, which could appear superficial, even bathetic, in the hands of a less skilled playwright. Two brothers, Brian and Alan, are the very different sons of a cathedral Dean. Will wrote them as contrasting types and (narrowly) avoided stereotypes. Brian is light-hearted, fun-loving, easily confident with women, mildly dismissive of his parents' religious scruples and practices, of the whole atmosphere of the Cathedral Close in which the play's action takes place. Alan is shy, musical, explicitly a virgin, designed for ordination in the Anglican Church. The two girls – Jane and Veronica – are also written as contrasting types (although both are very pretty). Jane has had an affair with Brian and is in love with him, while knowing he is promiscuous and temperamentally impossible. Veronica (Brian's weekend guest) is a Catholic and an innocent. She and Alan fall in love – with remarkable speed – and into each other's arms and beds, both believing this sinful. Veronica (after only one encounter) later finds herself pregnant. Alan, unaware of this and merely contrite for giving way to a night of passion, goes abroad; gives up thoughts of ordination in the Church of England; becomes a Catholic; and intends to become a Catholic priest, vowed to celibacy. The Dean and his wife (sympathetically depicted by Will, always good at parents) are upset by all this. Ultimately Brian rediscovers his own love for Veronica and marries her, to the general relief of all (except perhaps Jane).

Will's agent was sceptical. 'It has the tremendous advantage of always holding the stage, because there is incessant life in it. At the same time ... arguments between Catholicism and

Protestantism can hardly fit into this kind of manner. *The theme is too big for the boots you have put it into.*[1] It could have been pretentious nonsense, and embarrassing as well. In fact, in Will's hands, it was a sensitive play. There were echoes of Will, or some of Will, in Brian, who says: '. . . I've reached the conclusion that there are only two kinds of people in this world: those who are good enough to think they're wicked and those who are wicked enough to think they're good. I salute the former and mistrust the latter.' And later to the Dean, his father, remonstrating with his son's reluctance to go to church: 'I blame it on the war. For six years I spent Sunday mornings marching up and down. I spent them listening to sergeant-majors demonstrating how to drive a bayonet home in someone else's guts. And how to twist it when it's in . . . I've fired an ordnance piece, at matins time, towards a lot of Germans I had never met. And, possibly, I blew them all to pieces at matins time.' And there was some perceptive characterisation. Jane: 'I'm just a useful antidote to loneliness and Brian, underneath his superficial cheerfulness, is just a lonely and bewildered little boy. He's always searching for a kindred soul. He's out there, searching now . . . Brian is the kind of man who can't exist unless he's loved.'

In Alan, Will drew a portrait of an emotionally immature and over-idealistic person, as much at sea with the interaction of mind, spirit and senses as a schoolboy. He is certainly at sea with Jane, a warm-blooded, warm-hearted, essentially vulnerable young woman, unhappily in love with philandering Brian.

ALAN: Why don't you try to . . . keep him at arm's length?
JANE: Because I love him, Alan.
ALAN: I asked a silly question.
JANE: What do you think he feels?
ALAN: A dreadful trinity: desire and pity and contempt.

Veronica is suddenly (and not very convincingly – although this was credibly conveyed on stage, and a first-class cast were with the play, including Michael Denison, George Relph, Virginia McKenna) smitten with passion for Alan. And then he hates himself, and her, in a raw and almost Victorian spasm of guilt:

ALAN: I can't forgive myself . . . We were wanton.
VERONICA: Love's never wanton.

1. My italics.

113

ALAN: Was it love?

This was the sort of emotional contortion which could have been wholly unconvincing as well as already wholly out of fashion. It was redeemed by Will's fluency of dialogue and construction. His characters lived, to a surprising degree. In his introduction to *The Bad Samaritan*'s printed edition Lionel Hale wrote that Will was a dramatist whose ideas instinctively translated into terms of human conflict and that all his plays showed a writer thinking and feeling instinctively in the idiom of the theatre.

This was surely right, and enabled Will to handle difficult and unpromising themes – usually, if not invariably, with success – within the constraints of a stage and the compressed timespan of a play. The play, Hale wrote, was pre-eminently actable. And Will – as ever, and sometimes to excess – knew how to lighten serious emotion with throwaway lines –

JANE: Your father thinks the Church is something more than a profession.
BRIAN: So do I. I think that it's a racket.

But there was undoubtedly a good deal of self-expression, too, in *The Bad Samaritan*. Will had been in love with Kathleen ('Kick') Kennedy, sister of the future President of the United States, who had married the Duke of Devonshire's heir, had been widowed by his death in action in 1944, and had herself died in a flying accident in 1948. She had been very fond of Will and had visited him in Wakefield Prison. He had contemplated becoming a Catholic at that time. The Dean in Will's play is hurt by his sons, and dismissive. 'They cursed the English Church because we weren't doing what they lacked the strength to do themselves ... Alan rushes off to Rome and joins the Roman Church – more comfortable, of course. He isn't any longer on his own. His individuality, his views on celibacy, cease to be eccentric. He finds safety in a crowd.'

Will probably prized what he called and thought of as his individuality above almost everything. Nevertheless, like most people, he went on searching. And Brian can move quickly from light-heartedness to depression:

BRIAN: ... it makes me see how much there is in life that's sad.
JANE: You've always seen that, haven't you? That's why you joke about it, isn't it?

Precisely so.

Will reckoned that the play had been 'emasculated', as he put it, before opening in London. He had written (and there were performed at Bromley) a prologue and epilogue, which he later described as 'the pivot on which I constructed the play'. These were cut. 'I should never,' he wrote, 'have permitted this. It is always a difficult decision for a playwright to decide whether . . . to stick to his guns. Usually [that] course is wisest in the end.' Will was regarded by managements as obstinate in his reluctance to rewrite his work, although late in life he became somewhat more accommodating. He was convinced that, more often than not, changes to the author's original concept spoiled the play. Thus it was with *The Bad Samaritan*.

Will first met Rachel Brand in the autumn of 1950. She was many years younger than him, an exceptionally beautiful, entertaining and attractive girl, fair, funny and with pronounced likes and dislikes. He fell deeply in love.

Rachel's father, Thomas Brand (later to inherit from his father as Viscount Hampden), was a distinguished merchant banker with a high reputation in the City as one who really understood money. Her mother, born Seely, came from a gifted and sometimes eccentric Nottinghamshire family of enormous charm. Rachel, elder of two daughters, was as treasured as she was popular.

Caro-William and *The Bad Samaritan* had been written but not yet produced. Will, in early 1951, was attending the birth (the second birth: it had previously had a short run at the Boltons where the young Dorothy Tutin, straight from RADA, had made her name in it) of *The Thistle and the Rose*, to be tried out in Liverpool and then move to the Vaudeville in the West End of London. Meanwhile, however, Will had nearly lost his love; nervous, self-doubting, equivocal and unsure of himself, he had suddenly discovered that Rachel had gone to Spain with a small party of cousins – and a young man. He could be decisive, and romantically decisive, if the occasion demanded and it certainly demanded now. He set out – with a companion, Otto Herschan, to give essential moral support – and drove the ancient Bentley to the ferry to France and through France to the Spanish border.

The Bentley when loaded with luggage had absolutely no means of being safe if left alone. Herschan had pointed this out on a previous occasion when Will, en route to Scotland, had simply tied a thread to the car door, led it through a window into the house where he was staying, and attached it to his big toe. It was observed to him that a thread could easily be cut, but he was sure that this was most unlikely and that the improvised security device was foolproof. Now there was little luggage, but there were currency and financial difficulties in driving across Europe without preparatory arrangements and Will did not in the least solve them by paying a visit to the Casino in Biarritz. But he eventually reached Madrid. He and his friend were looking worse than travel-stained but managed to bluff their way into an expensive suite at the Palace Hotel; and set about trying to find where on earth Rachel might be. Spain is a large country and Will had no address.

Despite attempting to get the help of the British Ambassador, Will didn't find her – and he had to return to England for the First Night of *The Thistle and the Rose* at Liverpool. He telephoned Rachel's home and left a message, and when he got to Liverpool he found to his nervous joy an answering message: 'Miss Brand telephoned.' Will kept that scrap of paper in his wallet until the day he died. His desperate trans-European journey had not achieved its immediate object but it may not have been time altogether wasted. Soon after the play opened in London they became engaged.

Will did not greatly look forward to the meeting with his prospective father-in-law. He had had no commercial success in the theatre since *The Chiltern Hundreds*, although *The Thistle and the Rose* was moving to London – at the Boltons theatre it had earned Will, from the *Daily Telegraph* correspondent, a description as 'the most accomplished historical play since *The Rose Without a Thorn* and *Richard of Bordeaux*'. Will, however, was enough a man of the theatre to know that historical plays, perhaps particularly if set in Scotland and presented largely in Scottish vernacular, were likely to have limited staying power in London. *Master of Arts* and *Ambassador Extraordinary* had sunk without trace. *Caro-William* was still in a drawer, with *The Bad Samaritan*. Will lived not extravagantly but without much budgetary calculation; throughout life he was dependent on his own efforts – what he spent he made, but what he made he spent. His takings, furthermore, generally came in gross; and that tended to be how he spent them. Then there was the matter of his past record, of his apparently irresponsible political forays, of the war, of Wormwood Scrubs. He realised that a successful and eminent merchant banker might not regard him as the ideal son-in-law.

116

He visited the Brands at their house, Mill Court, near Alton, and has described his first interview very credibly:

'Well, Sir, this engagement –'

'What engagement?'

Will wrote, 'He was, of course . . . out to capture the initiative, a policy which is, no doubt, instinctive to all Bankers. Having captured it he suddenly spoke. "What's your overdraft?" he said. I told him. "I've known bigger," he replied.' But that night Tommy Brand saw him leave with the words, 'I don't think you'll make her a bad husband.'

During his engagement Will's father, 'the wee Lordie', died. Will had loved him dearly, had depicted him in his writing, whether fictionally or in fact, as the sweetest-natured, the most unswerving and the most understanding of fathers. 'All done by kindness!' Lord Home used to say and mean. Will knew well that he had given his parents much to disturb and distress them as he had pursued his solitary and eccentric courses. They had been loving and staunch. Will missed Lord Home enormously, and so did Scotland.

Will and Rachel were married at St Peter's, Eaton Square, in London on 26 July 1951 – a very large wedding at which (according to some accounts) Brian Johnston, senior usher, instructed his fellow ushers, 'Friends of the bridegroom on the left, bride on the right', and halfway through the influx of congregation had to call out, 'Sorry! Change over!' Will and Rachel first lived at Cranshaws, a house Will had rented in 1950 in the Lammermuir hills. It was a bleak place, but in a beautiful position not far from the Hirsel and with echoes of Will's early years. It was isolated and well-suited to the more ruminative aspects of an author's life. Will's and Rachel's eldest child and only son, James, was born in Edinburgh after travelling from Cranshaws in May 1952. Three daughters – Sarah in 1954, Gian in 1958 and Dinah in 1964 – followed, after the family had moved south.

Will loved his children and his children loved him. Indeed, all children loved him; and for his own family it was a particular pleasure that, because he worked and wrote at home, they saw more of him when growing up than did most children their fathers. He had a particular manner of speaking to the young which distinguished him from all other grown-ups. He tended to refer to them not simply by first name but as Mr (or Master) or Miss. For many of them he found a particular nickname which stuck to them through life. His teasing was always kind.

He treated them with a mock seriousness which never seemed affected or patronising. He could and did talk to them, tell stories to them, ask their opinions and give his own exactly on a level. He rarely condemned. Even more rarely did he show ill-temper. He never modified the tones of his deliberately expressionless voice or the expression of his deliberately deadpan countenance. Children found his companionship irresistible. They found they could always rely on his promises, his word. They sensed, with that infallible instinct most children possess, that they were with one who really felt with them and for them, but who would never seem intrusive nor embarrass with excessive demonstrations. His understanding was almost tangible. Sometimes his imperturbability may have puzzled. Generally it comforted. They teased him, they told stories about him, they brightened when he came into a room. And always children found Will funny as well as unfailingly gentle.

His own children knew that there were certain rules and they respected them. When Will was working in his study in the mornings they never intruded. They knew that he had a meticulously observed routine. One quirk echoed prison. He sharply called out if anybody shut his study door – shut him in. For his part, throughout life, he kept in affectionate touch with them, telephoning, leaving absurd messages if they were out. He left his family in no doubt whatever of how important they were to him; and he also, although the reverse of conventionally strict, left them in no doubt about standards, about right and wrong. It was always understated but always effective.

Will and Rachel moved from Cranshaws in 1952 and spent some time in the Dower House of Jakie Astor at his home, Hatley, in Bedfordshire. Then, in 1953, they bought a house they both knew well – Drayton, near East Meon in Hampshire. Drayton is a delightful house, with a fascinating terraced garden on a south-facing slope and one of the most exquisite small views possible to imagine. There Will and Rachel brought up their family and lived for the next thirty-two years. At Drayton they entertained an enormous host of friends – friends for weekends, for nights, for luncheon, for dinner, a never-ending procession of people of all ages who loved them. Members of both families, brothers, sisters, nephews, nieces, cousins, uncles, neighbours abounded. Will and Rachel never failed them. Will's brother Henry, a frequent visitor, was fond of a dram, sometimes to an imprudent degree, and one day found himself sentenced to thirty days' imprisonment after

At Springhill: Rachel, Alec, Lady Home, Will, Bridget, Henry.

Springhill: Lord Home with Bridget, Henry, Alec,
Rachel and Will (in front).

Will at Springhill, 1916.

Will with his first roebuck, 1924.

Will in 1930.

At Eton, 1930.

Douglas Castle, 1931.

Brian Johnston and Will at The Hirsel, 1934.

Neville Chamberlain at The Hirsel. *(left to right)* Rachel (Will's sister), Alec Dunglass, Lady Home, Robin
(Will's nephew), Neville Chamberlain, Lord Home, Elizabeth Home, Flizabeth Dunglass, Bridget (Will's

Second Lieut. the Hon. William Douglas-Home, Independent candidate for
Cathcart, 1942.

Dorothy Tutin in *The Thistle and the Rose*. (Photograph: John Vickers)

The Thistle and the Rose: tactical planning before Flodden. (Photograph: John Vickers)

Will and Rachel, 26 July 1951.

Anna Massey, *The Reluctant Debutante*, at Drayton, 1956.

In New York for *The Reluctant Debutante*: Cyril Richard, Adrienne Allen and Wilfrid Hyde White, Rachel.

Rachel and Will, returning from Hollywood, 1956.

Change of sex, a dangerous subject? not on your life, as created by William Douglas Home and played by Henry Kendall ...is good for laughs as deep as I have had for a long time

OLD TROOPER
NEWS OF THE WORLD

Aunt Edwina

...nd Rachel behind the scenes at the first night.

Will addressing the audience at the Fortune Theatre.

A. E. Matthews on 'This Is Your Life', May 1958; Will is second from the right.
(Photograph courtesy of the BBC)

e Reluctant Peer: Prime Minister Sir Alec Douglas-Home arrives to see his brother's play, with the producer, Peter Saunders, in July 1964.

Kenneth More after opening a church fête in East Meon.

At the End of the Day: Will, with Marcia Williams and Harold Wilson.

Hathaway, Dame of Sark, on her
ieth birthday in 1974. Will's play
Dame of Sark opened that year.

The Kingfisher: Ralph Richardson, Celia Johnson

Rex Harrison during the filming of *The Kingfisher*, with director Alvin
Rakoff, Lucy Fraser and Allie Rowell.

Chess with Will on the Ile de Ré, 1978.

Drayton.

Will with his grandson Felix at Derry.

Will and Rachel at Drayton.

rian Johnston presenting Will with a
ventieth birthday present, Drayton, 1982.

Will receiving the university tie at the
Centre de langues vivantes in Lille,
1987

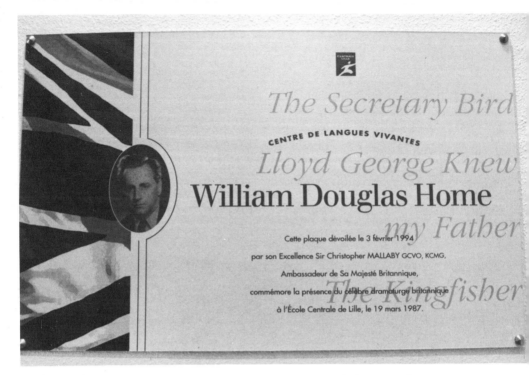

The plaque in Will's honour at the Centre de langues vivantes.

Will at Derry.

a difference of opinion (not his first) with the Perthshire traffic police. Will rallied round at once. Having telephoned Henry to tell him 'the first thirty days are the worst', he spoke to brother Alec.

'I'm going up to visit Henry.'

'You can't. He's not in long enough to be allowed visitors.' But later Will telephoned Alec again, having persevered and travelled north.

'I managed to see Henry!'

'Ah,' said Alec. 'Well, I expect it was Old Boys' Day.'

No house, large or small, offered warmer hospitality than Drayton or exuded more sheer fun. For Will was the most delightful of hosts, unobtrusive, easy, generous and amusing always. At the heart of this lay his huge happiness in his marriage. The fragility of confidence, the hidden unease, the doubts, had dissolved. This came not simply from Rachel's great gifts, competence and charm but from the fact that she wholly shared his professional life. She was an excellent and perceptive critic of his work – and of the producers, directors, actors, actresses who were involved in it; a perceptive and often a more stringent critic than Will. From the first day they constituted a partnership and it was extraordinarily strong. They consulted about plots, constructions, contracts, directors, casts. They shared the agony of First Nights – sore trials to Will, who could barely bring himself to face them and soon an even sorer trial to Rachel. They shared triumphs and they endured disasters together.

From the time of Will's marriage, therefore, there began a sunlit period. There were patches of shadow in it – Will was a hardworking and prolific author and few players score memorably in every innings. But there were high points and for some five years they rewardingly dominated life.

The first of Will's plays to be produced after his marriage had been written before it, and the fact shows clear. *Caro-William* and *The Bad Samaritan*, with their undoubted merits, betray nevertheless an uneasy, dissatisfied author; a certain lack of confidence, mirrored by the leading characters. Managements, however, were convinced – understandably – that Will should again write to his strengths; and that his strengths lay in comedy. Will obliged. Next, in 1954, came *The Manor of Northstead*. Produced by Peter Saunders and directed by Wallace Douglas, this was a straightforward sequel to *The Chiltern Hundreds*, set some nine years later. Some doubted whether the joke could be told a second time; A. E. Matthews (who was persuaded again to play his part as Lord Lister) was sceptical although he proved almost as popular as previously. Instead of Lister Castle, the play is set on a West Highland island. Cleghorn, now a Labour peer, has married Lady Caroline, while a prosperous Beecham, whose guests the Listers are, has rented the island and the fishing.

LORD LISTER: I knew a fellow once who couldn't keep his knees together because he'd got bandy legs – from playing too much polo out in India. Do you know how he got a rupture?
BEECHAM: No, my Lord.
LORD LISTER: By picking up a croquet ball at Ranelagh.
BEECHAM: Indeed, my lord.
LORD LISTER: I can remember it as if it was yesterday ... It's all poppycock saying you can only remember the nice things in life. This fellow was a rotter – Carter-Brown they called him. Quite unbalanced – tried to run away with Molly once. What was I talking about, Beecham?
BEECHAM: Your lordship's conversation ranged from the erstwhile dominions to Ranelagh, my lord.
LORD LISTER: He bent down to put his ball against the other fellow's – and then – by Jove, I can hear him saying it – he said 'By God I've strained my guts'.
BEECHAM: Indeed, my lord.
LORD LISTER: And he had, by Jove. He had a rupture, Beecham.
BEECHAM: Yes, your lordship mentioned it.
LORD LISTER: What do you mean I mentioned it? He's only just bent down.
BEECHAM: You told the story in the flashback style, my lord.

The setting lent itself to a little ornithology.

BEECHAM: Her Ladyship had a turn, my lord.
LORD LISTER: A tern for breakfast – serve her right.

'What's that mean, Willie?' asked Peter Saunders, going through the script with Will. On being told, he said, 'Nobody knows that.' 'Everybody knows that,' Will said. Saunders turned to his secretary. 'What's a tern?'
   'A seabird, Mr Saunders.'
   'Right. Stays in, Willie.'
   It ran on delightfully, giving A. E. Matthews plenty of scope and all the best lines. And in the play there is, of course, a General Election pending so that with a neat inversion of the earlier plot

Cleghorn persuades Mrs Beecham (previously Bessie, the maid) to stand as Socialist candidate for the suddenly available Outer Isles constituency (the member has disappeared), while – with an entertaining parallelism of the kind Will enjoyed – Beecham secretly persuades Lady Cleghorn to stand as the Tory. But the missing MP turns up unexpectedly and the absurdities multiply as the two wives prepare to stand against their (unsuspecting) husbands' parties and principles. *The Manor of Northstead* may have been nonsensical but the plotting was ingenious and the play ran for a year in the West End. *The Chiltern Hundreds* had ended with Beecham, the butler, on the telephone to a newspaper after the dénouement, announcing his decision to resign his newly won Conservative seat:

> I am applying for the Chiltern Hundreds . . . My dear young man, where is your education? To apply for the Chiltern Hundreds is the only means whereby a sitting member may resign his seat – a Parliamentary privilege of which, in my opinion, far too few MPs avail themselves . . . My resignation is a purely personal affair. What is that? What is my policy? My policy is this. It is embodied, always and forever in the phrase – They also serve who only stand and wait.

The closing applause was always loud and sustained. With admirable symmetry Will gave Beecham a comparable closing in *The Manor of Northstead*, although he allowed A. E. Matthews to share it. Young Lord Pym, again goaded by his American wife into standing (as a Liberal), has caused embarrassment to both Government and Opposition by holding the balancing seat, after a tie. To resolve the matter he has been given a peerage.

BEECHAM [into the telephone, to a newspaper]:
> His Lordship has become a peer . . . What's that? What difference does it make? Precisely none, I'm glad to say. *Plus ça change, plus c'est la même chose* . . . you don't know what that means? My dear young man, I thought the Scots were educated . . . I was quoting from a Continental proverb which, when freely translated, means – 'This is where we came in.'

LORD LISTER: And this is where we go out.

The play – although there were plenty of comments in the vein of 'This type of comedy is Mr Home's forte' – was generally judged sufficiently entertaining but a rather pale imitation of *The Chiltern Hundreds*. A. E. Matthews was always popular, and Will loved him. 'Have you seen my play? I'll give you a ticket,' said Will, when another (very disappointing) play was on and he ran into Matthews.

'No. Thanks.'

'I'll come with you.'

'No, thanks. I prefer going to the theatre alone.'

But when Will saw him later he simply remarked, 'By God, I was!'

Although *The Manor of Northstead* did its duty for a year, Will was conscious that no really promising successor was yet in sight. Drayton had been bought and there were two children already in the family. Then, in 1955 (although conceived early in 1953), came *The Reluctant Debutante*, produced by E. P. Clift and his partner, Jack Minster.

Before *The Reluctant Debutante* Will published his first book, *Half-Term Report* (Longmans, Green, 1954). It is the most serious and most seriously written of three books of memoirs he composed.

Half-Term Report covers Will's years at school and at Oxford entertainingly; and, equally entertainingly, recounts his introduction to the theatre, his year at RADA, *Great Possessions*, *Plan for a Hostess*. It is, however, primarily concerned with Will's conscientious struggles and uneasy life in the army. It is an apologia and an explanation. On the last page Will walks out of Wakefield Prison, hoping once again to play some part in political life. It is well titled. A half-term report only tells part of the story, suspends judgement, notes progress. Will, when writing it, had enjoyed a year or two of both success and tranquillity, and although the success was still precarious the tranquillity was assured. Nevertheless his experiences and the pain of them were still raw. Objectivity would increase with the healing and it took many years.

The Reluctant Debutante formed in Will's mind when he was living at Hatley. He had been sitting once in the Brands' flat in London and his young sister-in-law, Tessa, had been badgered by young men on the telephone. To her father's enquiries she generally said, 'You can't want to meet them, Daddy, can you?' She was bored. Will saw the possibilities.

The play not only re-established Will as a writer of social comedy in the first rank but launched a new and brilliant actress. Anna Massey played the debutante whose rejection of suitable young men causes her mother such anxiety. Celia Johnson played the mother to Wilfrid Hyde White's father when the play opened at the Cambridge Theatre, and one critic compared observing those two to the watching of a brilliant singles match at Wimbledon where every stroke is perfect and the rallies continue exactly the most satisfying length of time. Gifted though they were – and both were lifelong friends of Will and Rachel – they needed Will's dialogue and they relished it. Will himself took the Hyde White part for a fortnight later in the run to give the actor a short respite after a minor traffic accident.

The play was set in those already remote-seeming days of the Fifties, when debutantes 'came out', 'did seasons', while their parents escorted them to dances, paid huge sums to give dances themselves and nervously monitored daughters' progress in what was supposed to be a (very inefficient) marriage market. As the curtain went up Sheila and Jimmy Broadbent were breakfasting in their London flat, opening invitations, and Will described later how his heart had nearly stopped at the opening lines:

SHEILA (mother): Lord and Lady Aspath. Who on earth are they?
　　　　　　　. . . Mrs Arthur Milligan. I've never heard of her. What
　　　　　　　is the matter, darling?
JIMMY (father): —

And there was silence. Suddenly the whole theatre heard the distinctive and penetrating Hyde White voice: 'Come on, boy, give me the line, boy!' and the prompter hiss, 'My poached egg!' The Stage Manager had failed to produce a property poached egg for Sheila to enquire, 'What's wrong with it?' and Jimmy to respond, 'I just don't like the way it's looking at me!' (Will had written the opening scene when sent to bed by Rachel with a bad cold.) With no egg Jimmy had dried up before starting. Then the dialogue ran expertly until the end.

SHEILA:	Who's Mrs Arthur Milligan?
JIMMY:	I've never heard of her.
SHEILA:	But darling, what about her husband?
JIMMY:	What about him?
SHEILA:	He's not on the invitation card.
JIMMY:	Perhaps she hasn't got one.
SHEILA:	But she must have one. The daughter's called Belinda.
JIMMY:	That's no proof she's got a husband.
SHEILA:	But she must have had one at some time, Jimmy.

| JIMMY: | Perhaps he's dead. |
| SHEILA: | Oh, what a good idea. I never thought of that. I'll say 'yes, on the understanding that he's dead'. We owe it to our darling Jane. |

And the telephone – Will was sometimes ridiculed by critics for his dependence on telephones but he used them to great effect – was a splendid instrument in Celia Johnson's hands, getting wrong numbers, asking the wrong young man to dinner, affecting old acquaintance with what sounds a suitable young man's mother:

| SHEILA: | ... and we'll have a lovely talk about your mother. By the way, how is she? In the country? How I envy her. Well, do give her Sheila's love. |

and checking in *Who's Who* and finding the mother died before the war:

> ... Jane, it's too, too terrible. He must have thought me mad. I'll have to ring him up again – (At the telephone) ... About your mother. I'm so sorry. Yes, I know she's dead. Yes, yes, I know it was. But I'm so sorry about asking you to give her my love just now. (To Jane) He says he can't because she's dead! (At telephone) I know. That's why I'm so sorry. (Repeating away from the telephone) A long time ago! (At telephone) Yes, David, it was a silly mistake to make. (Away, repeating) She couldn't help it. (At telephone) No *I* made the mistake. When? Well, just now. You know, I talked to you just now.

But she had, of course, been speaking to another young man and so the confusions and absurdities and laughter rolled on as Jane fell in love for the first time with the young man whose (undeserved) reputation was black but whose prospects, unknown to Sheila before final curtain, were ducal (Italian). To read *The Reluctant Debutante* having seen it well performed is to appreciate how effectively Will wrote to his cast's strengths. Celia Johnson's distraught expressions and half-completed sentences, Wilfrid Hyde White's chuckling rejoinders:

| SHEILA: | Oh dear – I've ruined Jane for life. What shall I do? |
| JIMMY: | Fill up your glass, old girl. If horses went to dances they'd be in clover. They sleep standing up. |

Jack Minster directed and his production note, given in full in the published version of the text, said much about the playwright's own skill: '... the less the characters are acted the better. They are real people in a quite real situation and the less effort made the better will it all come off. The play is so full of laughs that some of them are expendable ... Jane Broadbent need not fear to be a little nicely rude. She's young and was of the impression that she did not want any part of the boring business; that it was all going to be a nuisance and no good could come of it. In fact, magic came of it.'

And Anna Massey came of it, wholly entrancing audiences with her wit, charm and sureness of touch in a first performance. As for the two brilliant principals, Celia Johnson was on stage about twice the time of Wilfrid Hyde White. 'Wilfrid,' she once said, 'what do you *do*, what do you *think* about, when you're *off* stage?'

'Oh, lots of things. What I'm going to have for dinner. What I'm going to back at tomorrow's race meeting. That sort of thing.'

'Ah,' said Celia Johnson, 'much the same as you do when you're *on* stage, in fact!' Will enjoyed that.

Will wrote, affectionately mocking and with unquestioned knowledge, of a world in which the sequences of his plot, the dances, the clubs, the shared schooling of the men, the shared prejudices of the women, could be taken for granted by West End audiences in London, and accepted as credible and entertaining by wider audiences as well. Will had too strong a sense of humour to guess that by pitching his stories thus – in Lister Castle, in a Hebridean fishing lodge, in a Chelsea flat taken for the London season – he was, in the eyes of some, making some sort of social statement. Such innocence was not to last.

Will assigned the film rights in *The Reluctant Debutante* to MGM for £50,000 (this, in 1956, equated to perhaps £600,000 in the money of 1995) and obtained a contract to write the script. He felt rich. Foreign rights were sold. The play was doing well in London, a contract had been agreed for an American production – Philadelphia, Boston and New York – and in anticipation of the film MGM undertook to finance a visit to Hollywood by Will and Rachel. Will had never been to America, although Rachel had spent some of the war years there – her father had been Chief Executive of the combined Anglo-American Production and Resources Board in Washington. Prospects seemed exciting. The film, with Rex Harrison, was to be made in France.

With this sense of prosperity Will decided that he could afford to buy a racehorse. Soon after the price of £50,000 was agreed with MGM, Will rang his accountant with what seemed the excellent news. He was appalled at the professional's reaction.

'No racehorse. Please, no racehorse.'

'Why?'

Will, he was told, would be paying large sums in taxes on the sale to MGM for years to come. He was aghast. He was invariably flummoxed by matters of tax. He never wholly absorbed the fact that his takings from plays were paid gross and that there would be a considerable – in those days a very considerable[2] – demand from the Inland Revenue thereafter: a demand which lost little in savagery from being delayed. But not only the shadow of taxation lay over the filming of the *Debutante*.

MGM, despite a warm reception for the stage play in New York, had decided that the film needed a different – and American – scriptwriter. This had been galling and financially most upsetting for Will who, although MGM had honoured their agreement to finance his and Rachel's visit to Hollywood, had seen his contract to write the script cancelled. He had had no part in the filming process. But in the following winter, in Scotland at the Hirsel, he suddenly received a telegram asking if he would be prepared to go to Paris where filming was about to start. Would he write – re-write – the film script?

What had happened was this. Rex Harrison – who had replaced Walter Pidgeon in Wilfrid Hyde White's original part, that of the debutante's father, Jimmy Broadbent – had told MGM that the script (now rewritten in America) wouldn't do. It was, he said, wholly unlike the play he'd seen in London. He wouldn't do the film unless it were changed.

Will was gratified. He rightly appreciated that his position was strong. Filming was already prepared and was due to start in three days. Money had been laid out. If Rex Harrison jibbed, huge sums would have been wasted. When he was told how much MGM were offering for a revised script he found the strength to decline. They must, he said, pay what they had originally offered before cancelling his contract. Not a penny less.

They agreed. Will drove through winter conditions from Scotland to Dover and thence to Dunkirk and Paris in time to start work on scripts at once. He met Rex Harrison – totally determined not to accept the American script – the producer and the

2. The basic rate of income tax at that time was over eight shillings (40p) in the pound, to which, for 'surtax' payers, was added a 50 per cent surcharge – leaving remarkably little of the gross.

director. All were delighted, two days later, with the new scenes Will now gave them. They congratulated him on the speed and expertise with which he'd worked in his hotel.

Will, assessing the situation accurately, had simply brought from England his original playscript. It satisfied. The *Debutante* marked the high point of Will's commercial triumph so far. It ran for more than 750 performances in the West End of London.

In Will's next play produced in London, also at the Cambridge Theatre, *The Iron Duchess* (March 1957), he reverted to pure farce. He also, less happily, reverted to a light-hearted (but half seriously intended) political message, a sermon. The fact that laughs came with the farce served only to underline the simplistic triviality of much of the message. It was something of an echo of *Ambassador Extraordinary* and equally unconvincing. When the politician in Will started to influence the dramatist the play generally suffered.

The setting was standard for Will. Percy Garvald, the Secretary of State for Colonial Affairs, is staying with his pretty and rebellious daughter, Mary, at Cranshaws Castle, home of the Duke and Duchess of Whitadder, parents of Freddie, Lord Cranshaws, Garvald's Parliamentary Private Secretary. There is a crisis in a British island colony, Gimalta, where an independence party have demanded rights of self-determination and announced an ultimatum. Britain, in the person of Garvald, a pompous caricature, threatens firm action – all expressed in reactionary and implausible terms.

The Cranshaws' cook, Mrs Green, also has ideas of independence, however. The Duchess refuses to accept her notice and has her locked in her room:

DUCHESS: Mr Garvald, do you really think that when the status quo is threatened, so to speak, then force is always justified?
GARVALD: I have no doubt of it – no doubt at all.
DUCHESS [to Collins, the butler]:
Ah, Collins, Mrs Green has given in her notice and I've told her that I won't accept it.
COLLINS: So I understand, your Grace.
DUCHESS: So if she tries to leave its up to you to stop her, and use force if necessary, Collins.
(curtain at end of Act 1 Scene 1).

Will enjoyed this sort of parallelism, just as he enjoyed a

rebel-within-the-fold like Mary, attacking Freddie who loves her: 'The way you talked about that wretched little island – so intolerably patronising.'

There were good throwaway lines:

FREDDIE: You evidently didn't hear his [Garvald's] speech.
DUCHESS: I did. It was quite deafening. It even drowned the clicking of my secateurs.

The Duchess, earthy and tolerant, recalls Lady Lister in *The Chiltern Hundreds*, just as Ronald Squire (one of those loyal friends who had visited Will in prison) brought his own imperturbable charm to the Duke, bored with politics and disenchanted with much else except fishing, a living reminiscence of Lord Lister:

DUCHESS: Alfred, what will I do if you're killed?
DUKE: Get on to my insurance company on Monday morning!

And Mary, inevitably, has the last word in any exchanges with her father. The Gimalta independence guerrilla leader is due to be executed:

GARVALD: I don't think you need shed any tears for him, my dear. The man's a traitor and a terrorist.
MARY: Like Washington!

Mrs Green escapes, however, and in a ludicrous dénouement, captured with the Duke's sporting rifle, is spared execution (ordered by the Duchess), thus procuring the pardon of the Gimalta independence leader. And Mrs Green is shown by Will as reverting to happy cook status, having had her fling.

MRS GREEN: I wanted to be free. And now I am I doesn't like it.
GARVALD: Do people really think like that? Good Heavens, if Patros [the rebel leader] thinks like that he might well join the Commonwealth.

Will was too sophisticated to suppose that this sort of nonsense held a genuine message. Nevertheless he was, legitimately, suggesting that Britain as an imperial power sometimes had too little comprehension of how subject peoples might think and feel. He was, obliquely, preaching sensitivity, and it could be argued that at times and in places the sermon had been a fair one. In *The Iron Duchess*, however, there were too few genuine targets for satire, too many Aunt Sallies. Of course the play was intended as fooling, but it betrayed Will's intelligence and he did not do himself justice.

At this time, furthermore, Alec Home was Secretary of State for Commonwealth Relations, a member of first Eden's, then Macmillan's Cabinet. Britain had plenty of problems with security in overseas possessions – Kenya, Cyprus, Suez. The Suez operation itself, a difficult and most divisive issue on which Will felt strongly (and strongly critical of the Government), had taken place a few months earlier, autumn 1956. These problems and crises were real, complex, expensive and challenging. There were no easy solutions and no glib formulae with which to slide the problems away. Will – although expressing a view under the guise of farce – implied a superficiality which was less than he owed himself. People laughed good-naturedly at the farce but could be irritated by the superficiality. For Will obtruded the message. Ludicrous, and funny, though the situations in *The Iron Duchess* were, it was perfectly clear that the author intended the audience to take the point within the fun.

'It's in your power to stop all this,' the Gimalta politician (who had, inevitably, been at New College with Lord Cranshaws, the Parliamentary Private Secretary) says to the Minister, 'by giving us our freedom. Or by allowing the United Nations to take over.' Will tended to idealise the United Nations, showing a good deal of ignorance of its constitution, rules and powers or lack of them. He supposed that the UN could already be envisaged as some sort of independent and disinterested agent, a world police force subject to an equally impartial world authority. In the real world of 1957 such agonising problems as those of Cyprus, with its hostile and intimidatory communities separately backed by an antagonistic Greece and Turkey, were those which exercised the British Government. The desire to hold on to possessions for strategic, let alone economic, reasons played in most cases comparatively little part.

But unabashed self-interest, well larded with hypocrisy, was easier to guy; and Will guyed it. Satire may legitimately be somewhat off target, but if too far off it fails. Friends said, 'What does it matter? Who ever takes William seriously?' Yet at his most serious best Will deserved to be taken seriously, and hoped for it. The times, furthermore, were running against him. He was vulnerable. *The Iron Duchess* was taken off after only sixty-five performances. The last seven years, nevertheless, had been speckled with success.

CHAPTER VII

Swamped by Breakers

In 1956, John Osborne's play *Look Back in Anger* was produced in London.

Although no single theatrical event produced what Will and others called the 'New Wave', the Osborne play was often quoted as catalyst of a movement which needed expression. A good many intelligent theatregoers, and probably more dramatic critics, were becoming irritated by, as they saw it, the blandness and divorce from everyday reality of much that was offered on the stage. The consequence was a vogue for what was (inaccurately) dubbed 'kitchen sink' drama: plays which tackled, in an allegedly down-to-earth and realistic way and in everyday, often coarse, language, the situations, in particular the domestic situations, of real people – by which was generally meant working-class or lower middle-class people. Drawing rooms, let alone Lister or Cranshaws Castle, were out. Peers and debutantes were out. The conventions of society on which Will had chiefly drawn (with a good deal of ribaldry) were out – out, mocked and pilloried as symptomatic of an effete dramatic culture wholly unrelated to the experience and interests of ordinary people: real people.

It was inevitable that the successful playwrights of the immediate past – Rattigan, Douglas Home and others – were not only out of favour but were excoriated by most dramatic critics if managements had the effrontery, in defiance of this fashionable mood, to put on their plays. Will was pilloried the most.[1] Although he was writing busily managers were wary. Seeing clearly the way the wind (the gale) was blowing and sensibly anxious about balance

---

1. This anathema was not entirely shared by Osborne himself, in spite of a reputation for vitriolic abuse a generous man: nor did Will feel anything but admiration in reverse, but the mood, as usual, ran far beyond the gifted few who had to an extent engendered it. If, on the other hand, generalised criticisms of Will's plays (by Osborne or whoever) reached the press, Will invariably – and equally publicly – responded.

sheets, they were rejecting his plays. If one was tried the chorus
of criticism was wholly predictable. First, his play (likened to his
earlier plays, successes in their day but now beyond the critic's
contemporary reach) would be dubbed snobbish, irrelevant, concerned with ludicrous and anachronistic characters acting out
false and superficial situations – whether entertainingly or not
was seldom taken into much consideration. All the social assumptions behind the play's theme would be twisted by a reviewer
to suggest that Will had somehow produced a tract to justify
some aspect of 'the Establishment'. Looked at from a left-wing
viewpoint this was inevitable but it was to miss the point. Will
wrote a play about a Duke (for instance) because he perceived,
accurately, that a Duke involved in a ridiculous situation can be
made to appear slightly more ridiculous than another man in a
similar case. Rank heightens the contrasts endemic in drama. The
perception is at least as old as Shakespeare. But Will also knew
about Dukes, and this, too, stimulated attack.

For the second sneer against Will the playwright was caused
by Will the Earl's son. Often referred to by Kenneth Tynan, the
foremost (and brilliant) exemplar of this wave of criticism, as
'The Honourable William', Will found his plays damned because
their author bore a courtesy title. The inverted snobbery of this,
the injection of class resentment into what should be objective
and artistic judgement, could infuriate Will more than any other
attack. He may have disagreed with but he never resented fair
criticism based on the merits or demerits of a play, but inverted
snob sneers without regard to the play's actual content justi-
fiably provoked him. And Will was combative. He never ignored
a challenge – he never had. He gave examples of the ludicrous
and class-based injustice of some dramatic critics of the day in
his last book (*Old Men Remember*) published in 1991. It referred
to the time when the New Wave broke and after; and the book,
although courteous as Will unfailingly was, showed that his anger
was not dead.

Meanwhile Will went on writing in the way he knew best;
he knew that he could produce witty dialogue actors could use
to brilliant effect, he knew that he could construct dramatic
situations and devise scene endings as skilfully as any. He knew
that he could make people laugh. Audiences, furthermore, were
by no means always as hostile as critics. But to reach audiences
managements needed persuading, and Will understood their cau-
tion although he was suffering – he needed money. Nevertheless

for all the prejudice, as he saw it, of too many dramatic critics, it cannot be denied that some of his plays in this unhappy period (for it lasted several years) were far from being his best. Even his most loyal supporters conceded that some were indifferent, objectively considered. But Will was operating under great pressure, as does any man facing obdurate and seemingly unreasoning hostility.

The third, and most fundamental, reason for Will's fall from favour was a change in underlying mood. More recently, it would be described as a differing perception of 'political correctness'. Will was not politically correct. He could laugh at life, even when much of it was painful. He could and did treat serious things easily, take the sting or the tension out of a situation or an emotion with a line of light-hearted banter. This, whether in writing or in life, was part of his inherent good manners, as well as his inherent delicacy of feeling. The new wave of writing and of writers, on the contrary, were puritanical – not in the sense of avoiding obscenity or blasphemy since in some works these became near obligatory, but in the sense of a deadly seriousness about what was presumed to matter; in large part a deadly seriousness about themselves. Genial good humour, Will's most engaging characteristic, was to be deplored.

The New Wave had, however, only recently broken when Will's next play was produced in 1959. It would have been impossible to conceive a theme more repugnant to the new puritans than the one he chose. Will's play dealt with the phenomenon of a sex-change; of a man of total conventionality, a retired Colonel, a Master of Foxhounds, who becomes a woman. Will, furthermore – and for many unpardonably – handled the theme as uproarious comedy. He made it funny. Retribution arrived fast.

Aunt Edwina began life at Eastbourne and then moved to Bristol, Edinburgh and Dublin before opening at the Fortune Theatre in the West End at the beginning of November 1959. Henry Kendall played the name part of Colonel Edward Ryan, DSO, MFH, 'Aunt Edwina', and Margaretta Scott led as his wife, Cecilia. The cast of ten were excellent and Will always felt grateful to them and proud of them. They preserved high morale and performed valiantly through prolonged batterings. Wallace Douglas directed and the play was produced by Paul Clift and backed by the American Anna Deere Wiman, who had also backed *The Reluctant Debutante*.

Will had high hopes of *Aunt Edwina*. He had written it

in a fortnight, in a hotel bedroom at Gstaad while the family skied. He deliberately made the plot outrageous and incredible – Aunt Edwina/Colonel Ryan makes no concessions to femininity whatsoever and has clearly never felt the slightest ambiguity about her/his sexuality. It has all happened by accident; the Ryans have just returned home (in the opening scene) from a cruise and a trip to America. Their children, David and Rosemary, ignorant of this remarkable development, both intend to get engaged and to break it to their parents. Edward/Edwina is lurking in the garden rather than going with Cecilia into the house to encounter the family:

CECILIA: You must be very brave, dears.
ROSEMARY: What's the matter, Mummy? Do you mean he's ill?
CECILIA: Well . . .
ROSEMARY: Really ill, you mean?
CECILIA: No darling, he's not ill at all.
ROSEMARY: Well then, what's all the fuss about?
CECILIA: Well, darling, the fact is . . . I really don't know how to tell you, but your father . . .
DAVID: Mummy, there's a woman by the goldfish pond.
ROSEMARY: Where? (she runs to French windows) Yes, there she is, Mummy – in a red hat –
CECILIA: Yes, I know, dear. That's what I was going to tell you. That's your father.
DAVID: Don't be funny, Mummy – it's a woman.
CECILIA: I'm not being funny, darling.
ROSEMARY: Mummy, you don't mean that Daddy's –?
CECILIA: Yes, dear, that's exactly what I do mean . . .
DAVID: I thought it only happened in the *Daily Sketch* –
CECILIA: No, dear. It happened in New York.
DAVID: But, Mummy, why?
CECILIA: I don't know, dear. At least I think I do. Do you remember when he thought Seaforth was feeding badly in the cubbing season? Well, I got some pills for Seaforth from the vet and left them in the bathroom and your father took them thinking they were Alka-Seltzer. And I don't think they suited him.

Will, mistakenly, supposed that a subject which could obviously cover a tragic reality if dealt with realistically could be made innocuous and uproarious if handled as farce. Thus Edward/Edwina – a joint Master of Hounds with his wife and only interested in hunting and in his military past – reckons that life can simply go on as before except for the small matter of changed gender. He smokes his pipe, cross-examines his son about the season's hunting and supposes that he can continue with Cecilia the joint Mastership. He is reminded, however, of the Hunt rules which stipulate that at least one Master must be a man. Then David's fiancée's father – American Senator Bendle, excellently drawn by Will, a disconsolate, rich man whose wife long ago left him for a saxophonist – falls for Edwina.

BENDLE: From the moment I saw you, I knew all about you.
EDWINA: Did you really?
BENDLE [much
drink taken]: Sure. I knew you were a lonely soul. And what more did I
            want to know? (Edwina looks apprehensive) Nothing. And
            why? Because I reckon if you take one lonely soul and add
            it to another lonely soul, you get twin souls. Well, did you
            ever hear twin souls were lonely?
EDWINA: No.
BENDLE: And 'no' is right – well, honey? (Edwina avoids his lunge)

Will presumed that the absurdity and the confusions, more redolent of a Ben Travers piece than anything else, surely nullified criticisms of bad taste. He simply refused to believe that an audience's sense of humour could be so defective as to blind it to the joke. And the joke – it is inevitably something of a one-joke play with variations, like *Charley's Aunt*, a classic with which several commentators inevitably compared it – was maintained until the end. The ultimate compatibility of Edward and Cecilia – and the problem of the Mastership – is solved by Cecilia finding herself in similar straits. She returns home after a temporary and unexplained disappearance and finds the house (Edwina's secret having reached the press) besieged by reporters:

ROSEMARY (seeing two figures in the garden):
            It's Uncle Reggie all right. But the other one's a man.
EDWINA: One of those damned reporters.
ROSEMARY: No! It's Mummy, Daddy.

And then:

ROSEMARY: David!
DAVID: What's the matter?
ROSEMARY: Mummy's done a Daddy!

Will wrote alternative openings and endings which turned the entire story into a dream of Rosemary during concussion after a hunting fall, but these did not alter the basic thrust of the play. It was about a (wholly incredible) double sex-change. And it was funny. Will reckoned that, at the least, he could not be accused of turning out another bland drawing-room comedy. A curious fact – perhaps incomprehensible except to those who knew him – was that Will was, within himself, so entirely incapable of genuine bad taste that he had something of a blind spot in the matter.

Before the first production there were warning signs. Will sent the play to both Jack Minster and Wilfrid Hyde White, stalwarts of *The Reluctant Debutante*. Minster was uncertain. Hyde White was unequivocal in his rejection: 'You'll never get away with it, dear boy.' Will showed it to Roland Culver, who not only refused to take the part but told Will he hoped nobody else would. Meanwhile Minster had sent *Aunt Edwina* to Robert Coote, who was leaving the role of Colonel Pickering in *My Fair Lady* at Drury Lane. Coote's refusal included words like 'disgusting'. Will was up against it. There was undoubtedly a problem.

But Clift, nevertheless, put it on. And at the opening night in Eastbourne, to Will's enormous relief, the first great laugh came as it should, to greet Cecilia's 'That's your father'. The whole evening went excellently, laughter often holding up the action. Local paper reviews were good and the theatre was, for that week, full to capacity. The following week at Bristol was also most encouraging, the leading local critic referring not only to 'great funniness' but to 'tactful treatment and impeccable taste'. *Aunt Edwina* then moved to the Edinburgh Lyceum, her penultimate staging post. A tour was then planned in Dublin; and then London.

A year or two previously Will had been enrolled by Jo Grimond, leader of the Liberal Party, as Liberal parliamentary candidate for South Edinburgh. He had always found the possibility of Parliament hard to resist, Jo Grimond was an old friend with whom he had shared rooms in London before the war, and the Liberals appeared to differ between themselves on virtually every subject so that Party dogma and Party discipline did not threaten any great constraints on the Douglas Home conscience or tongue. Will's conversion to official Liberalism was accepted resignedly by the family, resignation severely tested only when he was asked to open the annual Douglas Flower Show, which had been opened by a member of the Home family for 120 years. Will took the opportunity to make a major political speech in the Liberal interest!

Will had fought a by-election in May 1957, and been beaten, without dishonour, by the Conservative candidate. Now, in October 1959, he found himself contesting the seat in a General Election, just as *Aunt Edwina*, too, arrived in Edinburgh. It was something of a distraction but on both fronts he did his best. There was nothing much he could do for *Aunt Edwina*, about whose fortunes he thought he could be reasonably optimistic. In the election he was beaten – by the same Conservative opponent, Michael Clark Hutchinson, and by a wider margin. But Jo Grimond's wife, Laura, later suggested to Will at a Liberal Ball, that any future candidature should not be attended by *Aunt Edwina*; something more edifying was her suggestion. Already in Edinburgh there was a whiff of disapproval of the *Aunt*.

It found full expression in most – not all – of the reviews. Will had thought the first night had gone tolerably but the critics differed and Will's confidence was slightly, if only slightly, jarred. The *Scotsman* was hostile and others questioned Will's subject and taste. The joke was not being taken. The accusations particularly irritated Will since he had just turned down an offer of £20,000 (a huge sum in today's money) to write the film script for Nabokov's *Lolita*, believing, as he said, that it might corrupt the young despite its brilliance. Will invited the veteran author Compton Mackenzie to the play and was relieved by his unequivocal approval, but there were inevitable shadows. In Dublin, however, reception was favourable and the *Irish Times* critic wrote a glowing review: 'A perfect lesson in how this kind of farce should be treated and a pure joy all the way.'

Then came London. And in the Fortune Theatre, London, the *Aunt* met the enemy deployed in full strength.

The audience received the play coolly. There seemed none of the spontaneous hilarity which at Eastbourne and Bristol and Dublin had approvingly greeted the unveiling of the central theme, the unapologetic joke, the appearance of the aggressively masculine and military, foxhunting Edward Ryan as a woman. If that first joke went flat so would the play. And next morning the critics were, on the whole, outraged at what they regarded as a wretched piece of atrocious taste. Humour tended to desert their pens, venom replaced it. Henry Kendall, who played Colonel Ryan, Aunt Edwina, wrote a commiserating letter to Will referring to the 'vicious press attacks' (the cast were loyal throughout). On the other hand not all criticism was rooted in malice or prejudice. One (friendly) letter from an admirer of

Will's work wrote: 'I'm sorry I didn't enjoy "Aunt Edwina". I found it too incredible to view as a comedy and not incredible enough to accept as a farce.' There was, perhaps, something in that. Nor was all press comment vitriolic, *The Times* temperately referring to 'a light-hearted, high-spirited, fox hunting, farcical comedy . . . bumping into more fences than it manages to clear'. This was not ill-natured; and not particularly hostile. But on the whole Edwina had few friends.

Was *Aunt Edwina* unfairly treated? Were the critics so obsessed with correctness and fashion as to ignore the straightforward technical merits of entertaining farce? Were those same critics unprepared to watch Will's plays objectively because of his past themes and light-hearted reputation? Or was the play itself an indifferent and tasteless work, justly condemned on its own merits or lack of them? *Aunt Edwina* may have been something of a one-joke play, but it was a good joke if allowed to be taken as such.

When the Court of Appeal in London hears a case it is often emphasised that the judges are not attempting to re-try a cause which has already been determined by a jury. The jury has had the benefit of seeing witnesses under examination and cross-examination, of forming a first-hand opinion of their credibility and drawing conclusions. The Appeal Court must simply rule on whether proceedings, including the trial judge's summary, were proper in law. In a rather similar way a play cannot convincingly be re-tried from the printed text. The jury, the audience, heard the case in the theatre and gave their view. Dramatic critics, influential though they might be, were essentially commentators on an issue whose jurors were in the body of the house.

By that test – a test Will always believed the only true test to which a playwright should submit – *Aunt Edwina* did, and continued to do, better than press comment implied; but not well enough. Audiences had received it, in Eastbourne, in Bristol, with gales of laughter. Perhaps those in the capital cities of Edinburgh and London (but not Dublin) were, or fancied they were, more sophisticated, more sensitive; more alive to the fashions of political correctness. Perhaps they were more inhibited, less ready to respond with the simple belly laugh with which earlier generations would have greeted a military master of foxhounds becoming a woman. Perhaps they simply had better taste. Whatever the cause, those latter audiences were insufficiently supportive of

Aunt Edwina to persuade managements to ride out the storm of hostile criticism.

At the end of the first week, with the box office at the Fortune Theatre doing badly, Paul Clift telephoned Will to say that he was taking the play off. After the Saturday matinée Will went on stage himself to speak to the audience, tell them that it was the end of the run, and invite their comments and a show of hands. As far as he could tell they approved of the *Aunt* and of him. Will then arranged to shoulder, personally, the expense of the production henceforth, apart from the expenses of the theatre. That night he again went on stage and announced that the run would continue; and got a good reception. At the same time Will sent telegrams to every London critic inviting them to join him on stage and debate the merits of the play. Unsurprisingly none accepted.

But henceforth, every night, Will went on stage after the final curtain and told the audience about the battle. For it was a battle. It was Will at his most combative, most obstinate – and most courageous. It was Will refusing to accept the conventional wisdom. It was 1944. It was Will *contra mundum*. In practical terms it was probably extremely foolish – Will had got a loser in *Aunt Edwina* and was refusing to accept the fact. There was, however, no mistaking the courage required. Will read to audiences extracts from reviews, ridiculed the reviewer, and derided his cowardice. He was extremely good at knockabout humour of this kind and he was enjoying himself. His nightly forays were also, of course, attracting a good deal of press attention. He had declared war on the big battalions. Every night Will appealed to audiences – what did *they* think of the criticism, of the play, of the accusations of bad taste and worse craftsmanship? And the box office was showing somewhat better. The cast of the play were entirely behind it and Will loved them for it. Nevertheless *Aunt Edwina* was obviously not giving the management an easy time, notwithstanding Will's major financial contribution.

Next, in the face of management's unhappiness at the controversial run of events, Will offered to shoulder *all* expenses. He was confident – or at least persuaded himself – that if the play could run on for a short time longer in the West End it would become established, critics confounded. Supported by Rachel's father he made a simple business plan and that night, on stage, told the audience that the *Aunt* would run indefinitely.

It was not to be. On Thursday of that week he was told that

management had finally decided to take the play off two nights later, on Saturday.

Will invoked the law. After discussion with his agent and lawyer he sought and obtained an injunction from a judge in chambers, preventing the management from taking the play off. In the following week a settlement was reached out of court. *Aunt Edwina* would continue, provided the box office reached an agreed figure; and Will had to provide significant financial guarantees.

The box office failed to attain the agreed figure. *Aunt Edwina* was to finish. She had given fifty-four performances. Then came a reprieve of a sort. The management of the Lyric Theatre in Hammersmith agreed to put the play on for a month, followed by a week at Brighton. It would cost the same as at the Fortune. Rehearsals at the Lyric started on the following Monday, despite the fact that the previous management forbade the use of the Fortune Theatre set, costumes and so forth. There were improvisations. Costumes were begged and borrowed. Rachel's fur coat was draped over the Aunt. When *Edwina* opened at the Lyric it was to a warm reception and Will went on stage with high hopes that the appalling past was behind him and his *Aunt*.

But the box office was still thin and Henry Kendall, playing the lead, had to leave the play because of another commitment. For the promised final week – at Brighton – Will himself agreed to take the part, and, nerves acute, he did. The takings at Brighton, furthermore, were more than the entire run at the Fortune. Audiences were enthusiastic. When *Aunt Edwina* finally came off Will felt justified. The play was afterwards frequently revived by repertory companies and amateurs. It was done by the girls of North Foreland School – Will was delighted to receive the headmistress's call asking permission. He had never surrendered, he had given a lot of people something to laugh about and enjoy, he had cocked a snook at humourless correctitude, he had been true to himself. Nevertheless, he was ultimately slightly more flexible in his position than he had allowed to appear during the battle. Years later he took friends to one amateur performance (well done) and afterwards they looked at each other as Will, with usual quizzical half-smile, observed quietly: 'I'm not sure that that's really a very good play!'

Will had stuck to his principles and suffered for them, expensively. He was now extremely short of money. He had only managed to finance the *Aunt* by asking and arranging an advance from Peter Saunders against future royalties – an advance of £1,500, specifically for support of *Aunt Edwina* and balanced by an option against any three of Will's future plays which Saunders should elect to produce. Managements were now receiving his plays with no enthusiasm whatsoever. He was by many regarded as a writer whose day had passed, one whose skills with dialogue and construction were overshadowed by his lack of feeling for contemporary life, or for the mood of contemporary audiences; one, furthermore, who had in desperation tried to turn a serious human predicament into a matter for laughter with a one-joke play in deplorable taste. The shadow of *Aunt Edwina* was long. But Will, as ever, would fight – in his own way.

CHAPTER VIII

Fight for Survival

There now began, for Will, a long campaign from difficult beginnings and in unfavourable circumstances. He had, in campaigning terms, suffered severe casualties. The imputations, hanging like poison gas in the theatrical air, were of frivolity, snobbery and bad taste. His technical skill and proven ability to make people laugh were forgotten or deemed irrelevant. The themes and settings of his plays were condemned as outdated, his attitudes of mind as insensitive and detached from the realities of life. His own origins were, naturally, dredged up on every occasion as being at the root of his psychological problems – problems which prevented him being taken seriously as a dramatist who had anything significant to say.

Will fought back, and the fight lasted some eight years, with frequent setbacks and a few transient victories. It was a war of attrition. His first move and instinct was to demonstrate seriousness – seriousness of matter even if lightness of manner; and his way was to draw on themes he, himself, felt most seriously about. In his next two plays he returned, as he often did, to the matter which never left a part of his mind – the issue of peace and war; and his own lonely protest. These plays, he seemed to be saying, might be rejected at the box office but nobody could say that their underlying sense was frivolous.

His first attempt – consistent with this feeling, albeit as scriptwriter for a film rather than as original author – was with a contract for a film about the Italian campaign in Abyssinia, being made by Dino de Laurentiis. This involved a spell in Italy (uncertain hours, stresses, confusions but sun); disagreements of concept since Will saw the story as necessarily having tragic undertones while his colleagues (and employers) wanted lightness and froth; and, ultimately, the sack.

Will's first play after the *Aunt Edwina* debacle, *Up a Gum Tree*, was produced in 1960 in Ipswich and never reached

141

London. An unashamed nonsense, set in some unspecified future, it shows a tropical island of imagined strategic significance. British and Russian paratroop forces are simultaneously tasked to capture it to prevent its exploitation by the other. The opposing commanders find themselves stranded, by the waywardness of parachutes, in conversational reach of each other. They discover an earlier acquaintance (in post-war Vienna) with the ladies each has thereafter married. The king of the island, a benevolent peace broker only wishing to save the place from the ravages of battle, suggests a deception of the higher authorities on both sides which will obviate the need for fighting and leave everybody hoodwinked and happy.

Conventional voices on both sides try to discourage the two commanders from the appalling prospect of avoiding a battle, while the ordinary soldiers cheer it. There are beautiful island girls distracting the warriors from ideas of war. There are familiar Will touches. The visiting general, who must be deceived about what has happened, turns out only to be interested in tropical butterflies.

BRITISH COMMANDER: Sir, would you like to hear about the battle?
GENERAL: Must I? Just like any other battle, wasn't it?

There is, of course, Will's characteristic parallelism – why should the British and Russians be contemplating fighting when each side's representatives are experiencing exactly the same human emotions? There are lines which would today be no doubt considered as in deplorable taste. The islanders are cannibals and ask their senior prisoner (the visiting British Prime Minister) his name: 'We want it for the menu!'

Up a Gum Tree is a deliberate absurdity throughout, a farce but a farce nevertheless wrapped round a serious point dear to Will, and resurrected on all conceivable (and many inconceivable) occasions by him since 1939. If, he is saying, we could only recognise ostensible enemies as human beings and subject to exactly the pressures – personal, political, psychological or whatever – that affect us all, we would surely be the more likely to conduct international relations in peace. The sentiment was one he had cherished all his life. He never accepted, as most people with whatever reluctance accepted, that such optimism about human nature is a simple blend of naivety and unrealism, and that it has little part to play in great affairs. Will held fast to his illusions. They derived from his ineradicable generosity of spirit. *Up a Gum*

Tree had little hope of commercial success, and despite some neat lines didn't deserve it. But it enabled Will to remind himself and theatrical managements that he had a message, and behind the laughter it was a serious one.

Also serious – and completely undisguised – was Will's next play *The Bad Soldier Smith*, produced at the Westminster Theatre in June 1961. The play was directed by Jack Minster, of *The Reluctant Debutante*. It is almost straight autobiography, based on Will's experiences at Le Havre. Characters are somewhat camouflaged, with attitudes (caricatured a little) ascribed to different figures from reality, but Smith/Will is set pretty accurately in the Douglas Home identity in Normandy. The salient features of Will's own story are there. The dialogue is true to life. Together the officers watch an air raid – it is even identified as that on Caen, which devastated much of the city:

SECOND-IN-COMMAND (looking at his watch):
> There. Finished. Dead on nine. By Jove the RAF are marvellous – two hundred planes – that's five a minute. On the bloody dot. It's bloody wonderful if you ask me. From all over the shop . . . I call it bloody marvellous . . . Don't know how they do it.

And later, raising his glass having stood drinks all round: 'To all the bloody Huns they blew to Hell in Caen, God rot them!' But Smith neglects to drink.

SECOND-IN-COMMAND: Smith, why aren't you drinking?
SMITH: Don't feel like it, sir.
SECOND-IN-COMMAND: Why not?
SMITH: I don't much like the toast.
SECOND-IN-COMMAND: Well, you suggest a better one.
SMITH: 'To all the bloody French they blew to hell as well', God rest their souls.

The Second-in-Command is a deliberately crude portrait, incorporating the insensitivity Will reckoned he had fought against. There are speeches by Smith/Will about the folly of the demand for 'unconditional surrender', about the humbug endemic in pretending that only the Germans had sometimes fired on the Red Cross, and so forth. Will's own rueful remorse is reflected – Smith says that there had been injustice in the treatment of Germany after 1918, 'and that's why Hitler came along'. A brother officer remarks of Smith's views, 'But you still became an officer.' 'Maybe that was a mistake,' replies Smith/Will.

Smith is tried by court martial, like Will. The play is soberly and straightforwardly written, dealing with war itself in a way which echoes, here and there, such works as *Journey's End*, much admired by Will. Le Havre is called Le Havre. Will's arguments for the possibilities of peace are as confused in the play as they were in life, but are consistent. And Smith, like Will, writes poetry when awaiting the court martial's outcome (and recites it). After sentence, the sympathetically drawn Medical Officer has a word:

MEDICAL OFFICER: Don't expect the world to treat you as a hero. Some of them'll say you're a coward and some of them'll say you're a bloody fool, but precious few'll say you're a hero.
SMITH: What'll *you* say?

And an ATS officer runs into Smith after the trial (this happened to Will in not dissimilar fashion) and accuses him of cowardice: 'I can't think why they didn't shoot you.' Smith denies cowardice. He says he *would* have fought at Le Havre:

SMITH: . . . I would have done because I would have lacked the courage not to. I'm not that brave. I would still have felt obliged to go round killing people just to prove that I'm a man to people like you – even though I think that human sacrifice is out of date. But when we wouldn't let the people out it gave me something to get hold of.

And later:

SMITH: Three thousand French civilians died – if that's of any interest to you.
ATS OFFICER: Ah, I see your line now – saviour of civilians! You're going to go on living on the very doubtful theory that lots of French civilians'll make a hero of you when they know you saved their lives!
SMITH: I didn't say that.
ATS OFFICER: But you meant it. And it won't hold water.

Will wrote a perceptive author's note to the printed edition of *The Bad Soldier Smith* and most of it gives a useful insight on Will himself. The play, he wrote, would be most effective when directed least effectively – with saluting, heel-clicking and such exaggerations absolutely eschewed.

Nor should the actors try to create drama, since to try to do so will, in fact, diminish it. Instead, they should be ready to leave all adornment and embroidery in the wings, where I have quite deliberately left that old ham actor, War. One only asks that they should be sincere.

The tragedy of modern war is that it is so all-embracing that humanity, perhaps in self-defence, has tried to treat it as an uninvited, unattractive but inevitable guest, like death, and bravely tried to carry on with well-bred dignity, like funeral guests at a wake. This play quite simply tells the story of a man who tried to break the party up.

The actor playing Smith should never become sanctimonious or sentimental. If he does so, he destroys the basis of the character, which is aggressive. In a world of paradoxes, Captain Smith is militant, much more so than his brother officers. As Dick remarks, 'I fight because it's much more peaceful doing that than what he's doing.' Let the actor playing Smith read, mark, learn and inwardly digest that line.

The Second-in-Command is crudely drawn, intentionally, because such men are crude. This does not mean, however, that he has no heart nor humour. Many men with rougher tongues than he have both. He need (and should) be no exception. Let the actor playing him remember, too, that, in the period in which the play is set, the lines he utters were a commonplace in any officers' mess. He should play them without passion, with sincerity and not for laughs (although it does not matter if he gets them).

The same applies to the ATS officer. She, too, is a recognisable type from any war. The actress playing her should not be tempted to assume that, just because she says unpleasant things to Smith, she is a bitch. She may well be a charming wife and mother who believes sincerely what she says and equally sincerely that it must be said. Her tragedy (if she is tragic) is her honesty.

The inevitable note of self-justification and grievance in *Smith* troubled some of Will's friends a little but this was good theatre. And good morals, too.

These plays, with their underlying gravity of purpose, helped Will in his defensive battle to remind others of his own inherent seriousness. They were unlikely to have public impact; they certainly did not obliterate his reputation as a writer of outmoded light comedy and little more. They gave both him and his supporters, however, something to stand on. They were the reverse of frivolous, despite the deliberate absurdities of the farce *Up a Gum Tree*, and the humour which frequently broke through.

Will, however, wanted not only to strengthen his defences but to counter-attack. His reaction to the previous nadir of his fortunes in 1945, a sentence of imprisonment and a certain degree of social ostracism, had been to write a play about it; to dramatise, mock and to some extent condemn the experience of prison itself. It had been a necessary catalyst and it had worked. *Now Barabbas* had marked the beginning of an ascent from misfortune to triumph, and the ascent, albeit uneven, had been steep and successful. Resolving in the same way to turn the world's derision into material for drama, Will now wrote *The Drawing Room Tragedy*. He was being jeered at for writing drawing-room comedies. He was mocked for producing light, flippant pieces, without serious social content. He seemed to know nothing of the seamier, sordid sides of life. Very well. He would take it from there. He would mock the mockers. *The Drawing Room Tragedy* – even the name, of course, was spoof – was produced in Salisbury in 1963. It had been preceded in 1962 by *The Cigarette Girl*, a pretty unconvincing attempt by Will at a little social realism, set in a nightclub/brothel and dealing – sentimentally and predictably – with a girl who works there and has a child by a youthful client. Not even Will's occasional felicities with the lines could save this from a critical hammering (the play reached the West End for an extremely short run), and in the view even of Will's most loyal friends the critics were right.

The Drawing Room Tragedy, therefore, was launched when the atmosphere for a play by Will was as unfavourable as it could have been; and it never reached London. Nevertheless the play shows the combative side of Will's nature and it did him good. It makes a counter-attack. It is an explicit, often exaggerated, often absurd, sometimes very funny, always unsparing attack on the 'New Wave' in the theatre. At the beginning, members of the cast of a new play by a Will figure, Tommy Brownlow, are assembled to start reading. Will lays his cards face upwards on the table at the very start when the homely stagehand, Bert, talks of a recent theatrical failure:

... the one that closed on Saturday was in a drawing room. The Manor 'ouse in Little Belping, Gloucestershire, it was. Now if it'd been the doss-'ouse in the County Penitentiary the critics would've eaten it.

The cast learn that a new director, Bill Rogers, has been enlisted, 'the chap who does all the kitchen-sink stuff'. The reading gets off to an uncomradely start with the veteran actor Hertford Bradshaw (something of a Hyde White) interrupting the stage manager's recital of the setting, to the Director's irritation:

SID [stage manager]: The scene is laid in the drawing room of the Earl and Countess of Crowborough's country mansion, somewhere south of Maidstone, with pleasant chintzes and a Gainsborough of an early Crowborough hanging on the wall.

HERTFORD: I like that.

BILL ROGERS: What's that, Hertford?

HERTFORD: Hanging on the wall, old boy.

BILL: What's wrong with it?

HERTFORD: Nothing, old boy. It tickled me, that's all. I mean to say, where else?

The absent-minded and geriatric Mr Heycroft, producer of the play, reminiscing about Barrie and asleep much of the time (only waking up sharply at the possibility of wasted money), is a useful foil, and the cast start reading, with Tommy, the author, present. Something like a parody of a comedy by Will then takes a few minutes, with Charles and Ruth, the Crowboroughs' children, balanced by Hawkins, the butler. But by then Bill has seen that everything about the play must be changed, starting with its title, 'The Staff of Life'.

HERTFORD [Lord Crowborough]:
Monday afternoon'll put that right.

BILL (stops them,
excited): Yes. Yes. Yes! That's our theme. I chased it all last night and couldn't find it ... then you read it. But so exquisitely. And I saw it instantly. We all did, didn't we? Even our author. I knew it was there of course – poor fool that I am ... thanks Bradshaw. Thank you Brownlow. 'Oh well, Monday afternoon will put that right.' Superb! This deadbeat, decadent aristocrat, relying on the future being like the past, and never realising that the tumbril has become the Welfare State and Madame Guillotine the Inland Revenue – still hoping against hope that Monday afternoon will save him, when, of course, it won't. 'Nor any other afternoon.' That's it! We've got our title, darling! Shove it down, Sid!

TOMMY: I prefer 'The Staff of Life'.

BILL: What's that?

TOMMY: The title of my play.

BILL:	Oh dear – I'm glad I missed it, darling. Might have put me right off.
TOMMY:	What's the matter with it?
BILL:	Queens Gate, darling. Bourgeois.

'Drawing rooms, peers, butlers – everything they're out to crucify!' Bill exclaims. 'To Hell with them,' Tommy answers. 'I daresay you're right as far as the next world's concerned,' rejoins Bill, 'but we're still in this one and we've got to eat.' Will was undoubtedly getting things off his chest! And the play is rewritten, extremely fast. Lady Crowborough becomes a drug addict, with Hawkins, the butler, as supplier – supplier and earlier seducer of both mother and daughter in the play within the play:

RUTH:	I'm carrying his child.
LADY CROWBOROUGH:	Say that again.
RUTH:	I'm carrying his child. I'm not ashamed of it. It's like a lantern in the midnight of my womb. He gave it to me in the Folly, by the croquet lawn.
LORD CROWBOROUGH:	He didn't touch my mallet, did he?

So there is drug abuse, seduction and incest (Ruth being also Hawkins's daughter). Criminality and imprisonment. Homosexuality. Further incest as Lord Crowborough, a drunkard, finds an unexpected daughter. Murder (by Crowborough of Hawkins).

HAWKINS:	You've done me in, my lord, and I thought you was joking.
CROWBOROUGH:	No, I'm sorry, Hawkins, but I wasn't.
HAWKINS:	And to think I could've gone to Mr Clore three years ago.

In the closing scene the play within a play is over and the cast are reunited on stage for a party given by the ancient producer, Heycroft, manager of the theatre. Morale is at the bottom:

CRYSTAL [Lady Crowborough]:	But darling, one boo doesn't make a flop.
TOMMY:	I never should have altered it ... the public would have eaten this if some slick operator hadn't come along and sabotaged it ... You're phoney, Bill ... You take my little play and trample on it with your big feet like an elephant in suede shoes. Every decent sentiment is squashed with your unerring instinct for destruction. And what do you substitute? Don't tell me, I'll tell you. Perversion, incest, crudity and human degradation.

And Tommy, by now thoroughly drunk and thoroughly enraged, continues attacking Bill: '... the trouble with you, and the likes of you – the reason why you phoneys serve up all this desiccated trash to those poor suckers out there – is because you've lost your sense of humour, if you ever had one.' But 'Nor Any Other Afternoon' is a smash hit. The reviews from the morning papers arrive while the cast are still on stage drowning their sorrows. 'Mocking message provides merriment,' runs one review, and another is read out exultantly by Bill as Tommy looks bemused: 'Brownlow, your name is genius. Shakespeare, look to your laurels. Shaw, to your royalties. Brecht take a back seat. Rattigan retire.' And much more to the same effect.

> '... and what a theme! For it is no less than the end of an epoch, the start of a new age! ... the eternal question, posed at Curtain-fall, "will youth be strong enough to fight against tradition?" ... Make your way to "Nor any other afternoon", dear reader, I beseech you. Double quick and join me there!'

Scattering fire over the whole 'New Wave', authors, themes, direction, reviewers and newspapers as well, it was unlikely that Will would make friends or score commercial success with *The Drawing Room Tragedy*. Even some friends thought and told him that they detected a note of bitterness and self-pity in the play, the pursuit of a private vendetta. But it undoubtedly gave him a lot of pleasure.

Will always enjoyed topicality. A morning telephone call to a friend would generally start in that designedly expressionless voice, with 'What do we think of ...?' and a reference to a morning newspaper headline, a current event, described in as contentious terms as possible. This was particularly so, inevitably, if the news touched his own family, his own plays or his own experiences. In the same way he could never leave alone any arresting political development without writing a letter to *The Times*, generally sardonic.

In the autumn of 1963 the Prime Minister, Harold Macmillan, had resigned on account of ill health. There was considerable excitement and uncertainty over who should succeed him. The Conservative Party – and since the Conservatives had a comfortable majority in the House of Commons it was assumed that whoever was invited by the Queen to form a Government would be, or become, leader of that Party – had never elected their leader.

There had, by custom, been a groundswell of opinion, tested by traditional methods, and somebody had emerged.

There were a number of strong starters among the senior members of the Cabinet, notably (in the Commons) Reginald Maudling and R. A. Butler, the latter a very senior and experienced figure. Two members of the field, however, were peers – Lords Hailsham and Home. A recent Act of Parliament had been passed allowing hereditary peers to disclaim their peerages for life and thus to be eligible for election to the House of Commons. It was generally accepted that in political (but not constitutional) terms a Prime Minister should in these days be a member of the Lower House. Hailsham and Home were, therefore, possible candidates; and Hailsham announced at the Conservative Party Conference in October that he was disclaiming his peerage. His hat was in the ring.

In the event Will's brother, Alec Home, was asked to form a Government and did so, disclaiming his earldom and becoming (as a Knight of the Thistle) Sir Alec Douglas-Home. There was an arranged resignation of the Conservative member for the Parliamentary constituency of Kinross and West Perth. Alec was selected and returned at a by-election, thus again taking his place in the House of Commons and now leading the Government of the country. Will's play *The Reluctant Peer* was produced at the beginning of 1964, by Peter Saunders; first in Brighton and then at the Duchess Theatre in London. From Alec's disclaimer of his peerage in October 1963 to Will's First Night was under three months – impressive productivity. Although Will, the nonconforming rebel, had had many differences about politics with Alec, senior and established Conservative figure, family feeling ran strong. In particular the sneers at Alec as 'the fourteenth Earl' who was unlikely to comprehend modern life, echoed, recognisably, the sneers by critics at 'The Honourable William' who failed to understand modern drama. This argument from origins rather than policies or achievements infuriated Will.

Although, as it were, triggered by Alec's experience, *The Reluctant Peer* was written by Will as a straight sequel, with the same principal characters, to *The Chiltern Hundreds* and *The Manor of Northstead*. Tony, the 'Reluctant Peer' himself – Lord Pym in the earlier plays – has inherited from the (A. E. Matthews) Earl of Lister and is now himself the Earl, with the delightful June his Countess, and with his eccentric old mother,

Molly, still surviving. The Cleghorns and Beecham are in place. A strong cast were led by the incomparable Sybil Thorndike as Molly, and Naunton Wayne as Tony. There is a Pym daughter, Rosalind, who has just emerged from prison for obstructing the law during anti-nuclear demonstrations and who is arriving to stay with Molly, her grandmother:

MOLLY: Thank you Beecham. And – treat her normally. Don't discuss the sentence with her, not unless she starts the subject herself. After all, it happens to the best of us these days. Always did, in fact.

Of course this was another 'drawing-room comedy' of the kind Will had been so excoriated for producing, but he reckoned that topicality, a certain chuckling irony in his relationship to Alec, and a star cast would turn the tide in his and the play's favour. Confidence was largely justified: *The Reluctant Peer* ran for over 500 performances. Will needed this badly; the years since *Aunt Edwina* had been, so far, lean and depressing. In fact Will in retrospect (and in autobiography) somewhat exaggerated the extent of his own eclipse. Critics and managements were supercilious or wary, but when given the chance audiences still remembered him and anticipated his work keenly and kindly, even in the darkest days.

In *The Reluctant Peer*, Will was again writing to his strengths, hoping that the prejudice against him could be offset by the wit of the play itself. There was also a political factor at work. The play was topical in more ways than one. Everybody expected the Conservatives to be beaten at the next General Election, after thirteen years in office and under a new leader – popularly caricatured as an aristocratic amateur, at sea in the complexities of modern political life and sophisticated economics.

The election was held in October 1964, and was won by Harold Wilson's Labour Party with a surprisingly small margin – Alec had done a great deal, against the odds, to reinvigorate his Party. He had been in office a year, and *The Reluctant Peer* had been running for nine months. Will had, whatever his deprecatory chuckles, been very proud of Alec's success and high office. At a Green Room Club lunch a few years later he thanked the Club for its hospitality: 'Of course you know me – I have a very famous brother who reached the highest office in the land – President of the MCC.' But his appreciation of his brother's

151

eminence, while always disguised, was entirely sincere.

Once again *The Reluctant Peer* conveyed Will's settled belief that politics should be good-tempered and that most of life can be improved with a joke. Molly is a lovable eccentric with near-total tolerance of human nature, the less conventional the better. She is also a secretive gambler on horses (and everything else). In the opening scene she hears from the Prime Minister's wife on the telephone that the Prime Minister is about to undergo an operation, and wants to see her son, Lord Lister. Urgently. Molly, of course, forgets to pass on the message.

Tony is shooting pigeons, and there are some enjoyable family jokes, in the Home manner, as the plot takes its fairly predictable course:

TONY: ... did quite well. Got fifty-seven. I got forty-five and Brown got ten.
MOLLY: How lucky you aren't Chancellor, dear!
TONY: Twelve, I mean.

Will was back on his own ground, and at ease. And Sybil Thorndike (Molly) got plenty out of the part, giving the 'mother's angle' to an intrusive reporter on the telephone, who is assessing the chances of the Prime Ministerial candidates before the choice is made.

MOLLY: ... I've backed him. Last night. Thirty-three to one. Because I always back outsiders, that's why. The more outside they are, the more I like them. Because when they win the lolly pours in – yes, of course they do. 'Sea Biscuit' did in the four-thirty yesterday. So I played up my winnings. Fifty pounds if you must know. I don't know, dear – I can't add ... Yes, of course I'm optimistic. But I think he's got too much weight. Well, the peerage. And of course he doesn't know the first thing about economics. He can't even work an each way treble out with any accuracy. Still, I doubt if any Prime Minister could have, except possibly Lord Rosebery. My dear young woman, that's a very silly question. Oh, I'm so sorry but you've got a very high voice, so I thought you must be. Oh dear, I'm so sorry. Still, if you will go tobogganing you've only got yourself to blame. But really – asking that! Have *you* got any children? No, of course – how silly of me. Well, I might as well ask you whether *your* mother ever thought *you'd* be a journalist! She did? Well then, all I can say is that she must have been a fortune-teller. She was! (to Rosalind – 'she was').

Sybil Thorndike had an enjoyable time with all this. Tony proposes to give up his peerage, as had Alec, and stand for the Commons. Nomination day for the by-election arrives and it takes a comparable course to the earlier plays, with June, outraged at Tony's intention to disclaim, finding herself standing against him as a Labour candidate and Molly, nominated by Beecham unbeknown to her, as a Liberal. Rosalind's bearded young Communist boyfriend, John, is also standing (and staying with the Listers). Molly wins, having not wished to stand in the first place, and then immediately resigns, in the manner of both *The Chiltern Hundreds* and *The Manor of Northstead*, so that Tony can be returned at yet another by-election and resume his place as Prime Minister. Beecham, as previously, has the last word; and, also as previously, has it on the telephone to a newspaper.

> ... the Dowager will be applying for the sequestration of Buckingham in the morning ... the Prime Minister will carry on until the by-election where it seems most likely he will be unopposed. Depressed? Why should he be? You are forgetting Bruce's spider, are you not? Or did your education not embrace the story of King Robert, either? It did. Then you will recall that that tenacious insect won through in the end – unhandicapped, I might add, by its family.

The Reluctant Peer did not signal the end of Will's period in the shadows – it would be a longer fight than that and the knives were still out for him. It was a characteristic Will piece, everyone in it tolerant and agreeable to everyone else in the end. The ideologues – both June and John at different parts of the spectrum – are disarmed by the courtesy of opponents. The fun was light-hearted, the relevance to actual events in the Home family smilingly agreeable. It did nothing – and was designed to do nothing – to upset the prejudices against Will's themes, assumptions and treatment. But it ran for well over a year and it did a good deal for his confidence and something for his finances. It would not be the last time he used a current political situation for a plot, but it was the most successful.

The premiership of the real reluctant Peer, his brother Alec, did not greatly impinge on Will's life. Only once was he summoned fraternally to Downing Street from Hampshire. One morning his telephone rang. It was the Prime Minister. 'Billy

Graham's coming for a drink at half past twelve. Elizabeth's going out so I'll be alone.' He asked – Will wrote 'with panic in his voice' – his brother to come up urgently. 'If we're alone he might ask me to get down on my knees and say a prayer or something.'

So Will drove to London and, having talked to Alec about racing before the evangelist's arrival, they all three continued talking about it – happily – until he left.

After a 'double bill' of two one-act plays (*Two Accounts Rendered*, 1964)[1] had been tried without much success at the Comedy Theatre in London, Will turned again to an historical theme. He had been feeling in some despair about his ability to produce another winner with a full-length play. *The Reluctant Peer* had had a respectable run but its topicality was finished – Harold Wilson's Labour administration was firmly in the seat of government and Alec Home had been replaced as leader of the Conservative Party in opposition by Edward Heath.

In this mood Will launched *Betzi*. *Betzi* appeared in four separate productions, at Salisbury, Birmingham, Cheltenham and Windsor. She was revived in another production, first at Guildford and then at the Haymarket, ten years later, in 1975, by which time Will's reputation stood at a very different level.

The play deals with a true episode in the life of Napoleon Bonaparte. It might be thought that Will, arch-apostle of peace between nations in every age, would not feel much affinity with probably the most famous of all practitioners of war, but it was a curious facet of Will's character that he had a great affection for the little Corsican Emperor. In *Betzi* he has him miserably languishing on St Helena, temporarily lodged in the house of the agreeable Balcombe family – Mr Balcombe is the representative of the East India Company. Napoleon appreciates the kindness and courtesy of the Balcombes and is enchanted by their delightful younger daughter, Betzi – and she by him.

There is – there can be – little plot and little action. The story turns on the exiled Emperor's reluctance to move to 'Longwood', the disagreeable, windswept house assigned to him by the British Government; and on the gentle, painful, mutual attraction of the

---

1. One of them, *The Home Secretary*, dealt with the issue of capital punishment – like *Now Barabbas*, but melodramatically and less effectively. Will was always in favour of its abolition.

forty-seven year-old Napoleon and the fourteen-year-old Betzi. The play is a skilful – and touching – little character study. There is virtually no dramatic tension, but the characters themselves are shrewdly drawn. They were also, as were the circumstances and background, scrupulously written from history by Will. He always enjoyed historical drama and historical research. The difficulty, as he knew as well as anybody, was to sustain enough interest in a story whose ultimate end was familiar to everybody, with few surprises possible.

Within these constraints Will, inevitably, managed to ride some hobbyhorses. Mr Balcombe, a familiar from many of Will's plays, is elderly, genial and tolerant. Betzi is pert, tolerated and adorable. And Napoleon – the 'Corsican Ogre', 'Old Boney' – is anticipated with terror by the Balcombe women when they learn, in the opening scene, that they are to share St Helena with him.

MRS BALCOMBE: There, there, he's going to be well guarded.
JANE BALCOMBE
(sobbing):   He's a monster, isn't he? I'm frightened, oh, Mama
– I'm frightened.

But Will, of course, quickly and sympathetically shows the suffering man behind the demonised enemy. The Irish Doctor Barry O'Meara, who has volunteered to accompany Napoleon, has known the Balcombes before:

WILLIAM BALCOMBE: But why the reputation, Barry?
O'MEARA: Propaganda, William, that's why. Every enemy of England needs must be a villain, as you know. Maybe they are – most of them. But not this one!

And Napoleon, determined at first encounter to stay at the Balcombes' house and not where the British Government have ordered, charms the family. When Mrs Balcombe, flustered, insists that there will be no problems, the house is small but the family can move out, Napoleon responds: 'If you, Madame, and your daughter, were to go to Jamestown then a far too large proportion of the charm that draws me to this place would disappear.' And Will, in a note to the script, reminds us that the real Betzi described Napoleon's smile as 'the sweetest in the world'. George Waring played the Emperor – the part taken by Herbert Lom at the 1975 Haymarket revival. His wistful affection for the little Betzi, and hers for him, are moving. The Balcombes are ultimately sent home and the last small ray lightening the Emperor's darkness disappears. After a farewell dinner, breaking every taboo, Betzi runs back to say goodbye; she weeps and Napoleon gives her his own handkerchief: 'Keep it, Betzi, it is all we share together – handkerchief and tears.' *Betzi* had, perhaps, too little substance to sustain a full-length play on stage but it showed the serious, emotionally vulnerable Will. The play deserved its shortlived revival ten years after debut, and although on no occasion did it break box-office records it was a satisfying, well-crafted and well-received work which Will had a right to feel reassuring.

Then Will produced a comedy wholly within his range, an excellent piece by general agreement of the theatrical world, well-constructed, entertaining and uncontentious. *A Friend Indeed* was conceived by Will during his visit to Rome for the Dino de Laurentiis film, and dealt with two senior British diplomats, one the British Minister to the Holy See and the other Permanent Under-Secretary at the Foreign Office. Will originally planned the play for Wilfrid Hyde White and Robert Morley but in the event David Tomlinson and David Hutcheson did admirably; many people reckoned better. Will was fond of large 'characters' of the stage, like Morley and Hyde White, but some of his friends thought that in some plays the size of those characters could leave too little room for his own dialogue to have optimum effect.

A Friend Indeed would probably have done better – it was produced at the Cambridge Theatre in April 1966 and directed by the redoubtable Jack Minster – had it not been tried during the period of Will's long, attritional campaign to restore confidence in his plays. All he asked, he repeatedly cried, was that his work should be judged on its merit alone, on its entertainment value, wit and skill. By every such criterion *A Friend Indeed* should have scored high. It didn't.

Sir Lionel Hibury (Hutcheson) is visiting Rome with Maud, his wife and their pretty daughter, Sheila, who has fallen in love after the briefest of acquaintances with an American Harvard undergraduate, Bobby Butterfield. Lionel Hibury, instinctively disapproving of so sudden a romance, is introduced to Bobby's mother, who turns out to be Rosie, an ex-chorus girl on Broadway with whom Lionel had a short fling during a wartime visit. Begetting Bobby. Incest looms – the situation is similar to that used by Will in the play-within-a-play in *The Drawing Room Tragedy*.

The appalled Lionel seeks the support of his oldest friend and host, Sir John Holt, in his efforts to pre-empt an engagement and to send his wife and daughter home:

SIR LIONEL: ... she's been properly brought up. She wouldn't dream of going against Maud and me. That's why I say you've got to back me up and make Maud see I'm right.

SIR JOHN: To tell the truth, I haven't seen it myself, yet.

SIR LIONEL: You mean you don't trust my judgement?

SIR JOHN: I'd like notice of that question.

But Sheila, of course, is really the outcome of an earlier fling between her mother, Maud, and John Holt himself, a bachelor who had long ago been in love with her. So, unbeknown to the principals, incest doesn't loom.

Will handled it neatly. John Holt (unaware of Bobby's paternity, until enlightened by Lionel) has been backing the young people's love against Lionel's horrified disapproval. Then Lionel has to explain:

SIR JOHN: Why couldn't it have been old Butterfield?

SIR LIONEL: Because she'd never met him.

SIR JOHN: Never met him? Do you mean she wasn't married?

SIR LIONEL: Married? No, of course not. I'm not that kind of a snake. She met him two months later. They got married, and the child was premature, that's all. Like Sheila was, if you remember?

SIR JOHN: Now you mention it, I do.

So Sir John, alone, sees that all is perfectly possible – especially since Bobby has inherited a great deal of money from the defunct show-business tycoon, Mr Butterfield. Sheila, innocent, loves John for his support:

SHEILA: Oh, darling Uncle John, you're so sweet and sentimental. ... If only you were Daddy, everything would be simple, wouldn't it?

SIR JOHN: Well, if you want a diplomatic answer – 'Yes' and 'No' – my dear.

Thus the curtain to the second scene of Act I. Will's curtain lines were always effective.

But Rosie enlightens Maud about Bobby, and Maud enlightens Rosie about Sheila. Only Lionel (of the older generation) is then in ignorance that there are no hereditary impediments to marriage. Thereafter there are ingenious complications, misunderstandings and impersonations on Will's inevitable telephone. There is farce, as the two senior diplomats try breaking in to the Americans' flat, and ultimately tell all to each other at the final curtain, confusing all, at last aware of all, and forgiving all:

SIR LIONEL:	You?
SIR JOHN:	That's what I said.
SIR LIONEL:	You mean that it was you who –
SIR JOHN:	Yes.
SIR LIONEL:	You're Sheila's . . .
SIR JOHN:	Yes.
SIR LIONEL:	Oh Johnny! John! (He comes forward and enfolds him) – my dear old friend!

A Friend Indeed ran for 125 performances. It was not enough. The play was adroit, and it was excellently cast and produced, but nobody could deny that it was a comedy in a drawing room (albeit one in Rome) and one dealing with socially eminent people in a wholly artificial situation. Thus it did nothing to break what managements saw as the Curse of Home, despite their professional appreciation of Will's talents and work. They knew him as a playwright in whose work it was never necessary to alter a line, whose plays were actable, ingenious and funny. But they were nervous.

A few critics were more perceptive. 'For some reason,' ran one piece about Will, 'William Douglas Home seems to be out of favour as a playwright – with the critics if not the audience . . . it is puzzling to know why.' And *A Friend Indeed* was described as a 'stylish, very elegant frolic', as 'superb'. Others, however, referred to the author's 'outdated attitudes'. This was to be humourless, as criticism of Will so often was.

Will was, therefore, short of remunerative work. He was contracted to write occasional film scripts but his talent for original creation was being frustrated and his income as well as his spirits suffered. He was an abstemious man and spent little on himself, but times were anxious. He needed a real and lasting success. He knew, without much surprise, that during 1967 his agent had sent another play to a number of managements and received discouraging responses. It had been written some time earlier. It was called *The Secretary Bird*.

PART III
1967–1992

CHAPTER IX

Winning Streak

The Secretary Bird first emerged from the egg, after a long time hatching, in 1967 before flying in the following year to London and proving to be Will's most successful play.

Will's plays can be placed in four categories, although a few of them belong to more than one. There are runaway winners and some undoubted losers in each category. The first category – *The Thistle and the Rose, Caro-William, Betzi*, and so forth – are the Historicals. Despite all their well-known difficulties of staging, their inevitable risk of loss of tension and surprise, Will enjoyed his Historicals. He remembered Gielgud in *Richard of Bordeaux* in the Thirties. Everybody knew, he would say, what was supposed to have happened to King Richard II but the predictability of plot did nothing to destroy the fascination of musical language, clever characterisation and dazzling acting. The past is a rich seam and Will mined it.

Second came what may be called the Topicals, plays in which Will exploited a particular near-contemporary event or mood, and dramatised it or satirised it or both: *The Reluctant Peer, The Grouse Moor Image, At the End of the Day*, arguably *The Drawing Room Tragedy*. These, by their nature, were unlikely to have great durability – they caught a tide and were designed to. The best of them, nevertheless, were undoubted successes for their fleeting while. Will was quick at touching a newsworthy nerve, and his ear and eye for public events and personages – and absurdities – was impeccable.

In the third category can be placed the Sermons. The Sermons held moral or political messages, conveyed by drama (*Great Possessions, The Bad Soldier Smith, The Bad Samaritan, Now Barabbas*) or by farce (*Ambassador Extraordinary, Up a Gum Tree, The Iron Duchess*), but the intention is always serious. Some of these later Sermons could, if not well-handled, lapse into a certain mawkishness but that, to Will, could and should be generally

161

cured by the robustness, as well as the intelligence, of direction and acting. Furthermore, any possible sickliness is almost always offset by high humour and by vigorous sentiments in the mouths of some of the characters as they confront moral dilemmas. The Sermons at their best (*Now Barabbas*) were brilliant theatre and intensely moving. At their worst their messages – for instance, and frequently, satires on the obtuseness shown by governments in the conduct of international relations – were simplistic, dramatically as well as intellectually unconvincing. And Will's own feelings sometimes got in the way.

The fourth category contains the straight plays, the dramatic works without explicit preachment or topicality or history. These range from the comedy, touched with a moving, elegiac note, of *The Kingfisher*, through the brilliant absurdities of *The Chiltern Hundreds*, to comedy shading here and there into farce such as *Lloyd George Knew My Father* or, notoriously, *Aunt Edwina*. The only category of play Will never attempted was the thriller or crime story, and the reason this genre never attracted him is clear. A thriller requires villainy and villains, and Will preferred not to contemplate – or stigmatise – villains; and thus did not like contemplation of evil or villainy. When he once appeared to break this self-imposed habit (with a play, *The Perch*, given at Pitlochry in 1977) it was a tease; benevolence to all broke through at the dénouement.

Of Will's comedies the most successful, without question, was *The Secretary Bird*. The play ran for 1,463 performances at the Savoy Theatre and marked a period of nearly eight years at that theatre during which a play by Will was continuously being presented. There were to be setbacks, but the war of attrition was over and Will had won it. Won it, furthermore, with honour and considerable profit. He was of that level of playwrights who received 10 per cent of gross box-office takings. The sun was out from behind the clouds. They had, at times, been depressingly black.

The triumph was slow to emerge. Eleven managements turned the play down flat. They reflected on the antipathy to Will of the dramatic critics and they had no desire to kick against the pricks. Will sent the play to Hyde White, hoping he might want to do it. He didn't; very fortunately, since Will's judgement was in this faulty. It is impossible to see Hyde White successfully doing the lead part which was brilliantly performed in London by Kenneth More – he would have been wrong. But Will was very anxious to get the play accepted and he knew that the climate of opinion in managements was such that only the promise of a star was likely to get *The Secretary Bird* flying. If then.

But Hyde White did the play a favour. He told Will that Anthony Roye, who was acting with him at the time, was keen to put on *The Secretary Bird*. Roye did a number of months in each year producing, directing – and often acting in – plays on provincial tours. He was enterprising, perceptive and ran his business on a shoestring. He had read and instantly liked Will's play – he did not personally know Will. He was enthusiastic.

Roye's insight was undoubtedly better, and braver, than that of the prestigious London managements which had so far looked without excitement at *The Secretary Bird*. He was, furthermore, an actor who instinctively understood Will's humour, whose mind – and speech – could move with the dexterity the lines demanded, exploiting Will's invariable economy with words. Will was instantly intrigued. Roye proposed that if Will gave him the play he should put it on at a new theatre in Swanage called the Mowlem, would direct it and play the lead himself. There would be a run at some five other provincial theatres. Will agreed; and shortly afterwards he met Roye's cast and heard their first interpretation of the play, which impressed him, as did Anthony Roye's professional and boldly practical approach to the whole business and the economics of it. The set for the play on tour would be the furniture, or most of it, from Roye's own flat. Thereafter Roye produced and directed seven of Will's plays, and acted the lead part, somewhere, in seventeen of them. He appreciated them at their true worth, relishing the way Will often gave excellent lines to even the smallest parts, savouring Will's curtain lines, and enjoying wholeheartedly the understanding Will, RADA graduate, showed for the actor's own craft. He knew Will's previous plays well and told him that *The Secretary Bird* was the best thing he had ever done.

He was right. In those early touring performances audiences were hugely enthusiastic. They were, furthermore, audiences of differing types, some smooth, some rough – and all lapped it up, appearing to give the lie to the idea that only one class of playgoer would appreciate Will. At Weston-Super-Mare, during Whitsun 1967, the queue for entry to the (very large) pavilion was so long that the curtain went up thirty minutes late. These were holiday-makers, the 'ordinary people' who critics so often suggested would be out of tune with Will. They weren't – and the auditorium had to be expanded by 400 extra chairs.

In London, John Gale – a distinguished manager who did not know Will, had never done one of his plays and had assumed, with the generality of opinion, that they were stereotyped, out-dated and likely to be unsuccessful – had been sent a copy of *The Secretary Bird* by Will's agent at the time, Aubrey Blackburn of the Christopher Mann Agency. Gale had read it and, to his own surprise, found it irresistible. Shortly afterwards he attended the annual Derby dinner, where Will was also a guest. Will sent over a note to a neighbouring table where Emile Littler and Peter Saunders were sitting with John Gale (who was unknown to Will). 'Which of you,' the note to Littler and Saunders ran, 'is the lucky man who's going to get hold of *The Secretary Bird*?' 'May I look at that?' Gale said to them. And he sent it back to Will with the answer: 'Neither, I am. John Gale.'

The *Bird* was about to fly at Swanage. Gale had no particular wish and felt no need to see the play on tour. He was completely confident. He was one who, like Will, could see a play's poten-tial effect from the not-very-explicit written pages. He was also confident – and right – about who should star in it: Kenneth More. It would mean waiting until the following year, and this was frustrating for Will, who was impatient. It was also uncer-tain – Kenneth More was as vulnerable as were others to false impressions about Will's work. When Gale gave him the play to read he first removed the page showing the author's name.

'It's wonderful,' More said, returning the typescript. He was now an enthusiast; and, when told of the authorship, a convert. There were still problems, however, before the *Bird* finally spread her wings. It was surprisingly difficult to find a director. Every director suggested – by management, by agent, by Kenneth More, by Will – turned the idea down. This was clearly becoming dan-gerous: Kenneth More's own confidence and enthusiasm might be dented if director after director showed such discouraging luke-warmness. Eventually a comparatively unknown director, Philip Dudley, was enlisted; and did superbly well. *The Secretary Bird* opened at the Savoy Theatre in October 1968.

The trial pre-London run had been at the Opera House in Manchester. Will felt confident. The audience had been enthusi-astic and he felt certain of success in a way he had not for many years. An inquest was customary the morning after the First Night and Will told John Gale that he regretted but he couldn't attend. He had an engagement at home in Hampshire.

This was remarkable. It was hardly professional. 'But haven't you any comments, criticisms?' Gale asked. Will reflected and said that the flowers in the set were wrong for a country drawing room – something more like delphiniums, herbaceous border flowers, would be more appropriate. That was all. With that Will returned to Hampshire. He knew he had, at last, written a winner. *The Secretary Bird* made £4,000 profit a week throughout its first year; and it ran in the West End over three years. £4,000 a week represented some £1,000 to Will, a figure which can be multiplied by at least twelve to reach the money of 1995. The sun was not only out from behind clouds but was shining with remarkable brilliance.

The Secretary Bird is high comedy, and contains, also, that vein of seriousness which gives savour to the best of comedies. It was this which made it outstanding among Will's plays (although not unique in this respect) and which the cast handled so admirably. Kenneth More – Hugh Walford, middle-aged author, a husband with an errant and younger wife, Liz, who is spreading her wings a little – had the sort of lines and personality Will did almost best of all, identifying painlessly with the character in his imagination despite his own happy marriage.

LIZ:	Do you mean to say you've noticed nothing, all this spring and summer?
HUGH:	I've been busy on my book.
LIZ:	Yes, that's the trouble.
HUGH:	One has got to live.
LIZ:	I'm sorry.
HUGH:	I did think to myself once – when I was playing golf in May, so far as I remember – that your hair was getting quite a beating up this year. But then I got a birdie and forgot about it.
LIZ:	What about the time you found me crying in the summer-house?
HUGH:	That didn't worry me unduly.
LIZ:	Well, it should have.
HUGH:	I don't see why. Women cry when they're happy – like men whistle.
LIZ:	In your books, I dare say.
HUGH:	And in real life.
LIZ:	I don't.
HUGH:	Yes, you do. You cried that time we saw the Northern Lights in Ullapool.

LIZ:	That was the whisky.

So far we are in Homeland – feelings leashed behind quickfire badinage, serious subjects well-camouflaged by talk of golf, travel, racing. But Liz plans to go to Milan with her young lover, John Brownlow, and Hugh takes deadly seriously her talk of not coming back, of wanting a divorce. Hugh, furthermore, has detected the affair since it started; and never said a word. He insists on asking Brownlow to stay – golf, the weekend, talk things over. Liz is appalled at the idea. Hugh has recovered a certain initiative.

LIZ:	Talking over?
HUGH:	The divorce, I mean . . .
LIZ:	You're going to cite John, naturally.
HUGH:	No, on the contrary. I'd like to give you a divorce.
LIZ:	That's too old-fashioned for words, darling.
HUGH:	Maybe so. But that's the way it's going to be.
LIZ:	You mean you'll go to Brighton with some blonde?
HUGH:	No darling – I won't go to Brighton – and the blonde'll come to me.
LIZ:	Here!
HUGH:	Yes – why not?
LIZ:	But what will Mrs Gray [cook-housekeeper] say?
HUGH:	Quite a lot, in Court – I hope!

Molly Forsyth, Hugh's attractive secretary, is summoned to stay. For Hugh, dégagé, easy-going, tolerant, entertaining, nevertheless cares about saving his marriage far more than he is prepared outwardly to demonstrate – cares, and plans intelligently to succeed in doing so. And the audience, while laughing delightedly at his wit and ingenuity, also cares. It is because so often there is constriction of the throat, a pricking behind the eyes as the laughs flood in, that *The Secretary Bird* shows Will at his best. And the contrivances – Hugh's pretend-affair with Molly, Liz's last-minute revulsion from what she intends, John's ineradicable promiscuity discovered at last curtain – all these work splendidly. *The Secretary Bird*, furthermore, shows Will as bold – and some critics were outraged and found the boldness of attitude deplorable – in the unfashionable lightness about sex he ascribes to Hugh. Hugh has summed up the situation. Brownlow is a good deal younger, has had several wives and much sexual success, is proficient with women.

HUGH:	I'm . . . a pleasure-lover, a narcissist. Someone who sees everything, including marriage, in relation to himself. And

	Brownlow's just the opposite, I should imagine – thinking only of you. I'll bet he concentrates like no one's business. You needn't tell me if you'd rather not . . .
LIZ:	That's most broadminded of you.
HUGH:	. . . Maybe men are like steaks – rare, medium or overdone. If so, I know which I am.
LIZ:	I'll second that.
HUGH:	I'm sorry – obviously I've been most inadequate. And you've been very noble, putting up with it for so long. . . . The break was bound to come one day.

And later, with John, the night before he and Liz set out for Italy:

JOHN:	It isn't only physical with her.
HUGH (putting his arm round John):	
	I doubt if she'd agree. You see, old fellow, let's face it I'm a pretty poor performer in that line. You don't mind me talking to you like this, do you?
JOHN:	I'm beginning to get used to it.
HUGH:	. . . Well, what I was going to say was that – in that particular sphere you make rings round me, I should imagine – like you do at golf . . . we're on two different wavelengths – yours is physical and mine is mental, broadly speaking. And the trouble from my point of view is that my batteries are running down.

This was the reverse of politically correct. This – for Hugh's *ruse de guerre* is successful, his marriage is saved, Liz perceives John Brownlow for the bore that he is and rejects the idea of running away (a decision about which some of the audience may have remained a little sceptical) – was to challenge a contemporary icon on the primacy of the sexual imperative. Hugh's wit, humanity, tolerance and intelligence win the day, and audiences loved it. 'The clouds dispersed,' wrote Will, '– so did the Inland Revenue officials. My bank manager actually smiled.' With reason.

The Secretary Bird flew happily in Germany ('Gute Nacht, Liebling!'); in France ('Canard à l'Orange) where the President's wife, Mme Pompidou, arranged a private performance at the Elysée Palace, since the President of France may not attend a public theatre; in America, where there was great enthusiasm. Reviews, even in London, and even among sharp critics of Will's style, were amiable, praising the neatness of the construction, the pace, the ingenuity. Will, once again, had scored a hit.

There now came an exceptionally productive period of Will's

life. Although *The Secretary Bird* was his outstanding play at the Savoy, in a sequence which continued until 1974, it followed another of Will's plays at that theatre – an 'Historical'. Although it had only a short run there, *The Queen's Highland Servant* had opened in May 1968 after a trial at Salisbury in 1967 and at Windsor. It was a play dear to Will's heart.

The play dealt with John Brown, the eponymous leading character whom the widowed Queen Victoria so treasured, and who caused a good deal of scandal as well as considerable resentment within the Royal family and the Royal Household. Will enjoyed the character of Brown. He enjoyed his uncompromising Scottishness of phrase and feeling; and he enjoyed Brown's robust, no-nonsense way with the Queen, wholly lacking in deference but rich in genuine, loyal, understated affection.

The Queen is lamenting to Brown about the Prince of Wales's behaviour, the blight he brought to his father's life by an affair with an actress in Ireland:

BROWN: That wee lass at the Curragh.
VICTORIA: So you know about it?
BROWN: Everybody knows about it, Ma'am. There's no a body in the country does'na – I'd be surprised if there's a beast up on the hill that does'na know about it.
VICTORIA: Why do people talk so?
BROWN: There's a lot of them have got nought else to do. But dinna let it worry you – it's not the first time a young man and young woman's got together and it willna be the last!

And when he tells the Queen that 'precious few young men don't' and she asks, 'Did *you*, Brown?' he responds: 'Well, that'd be telling, wouldn't it? But whether I did or didna, no one ever brought their father to the grave by tumbling a lassie. Yon's a crazy notion.'

In this play Will's warmth and common sense show strongly. And the relationship, always a shade ambiguous, between the Queen and Brown is convincingly drawn, with Victoria's ministers advising her frankly of the Highland Servant's unpopularity, and with her – a woman as well as a Queen, responding to a man as well as to a Highland Servant – defending him with loyal anger. Will introduced the political issues of that exact time – the resentment of the public at Victoria's long absence from London, the French adventure in Mexico, the change of Premier between Lords Russell and Derby – with considerable adroitness and without in the least overburdening the audience, or distracting from the central theme, which is personal and moving. Reviews were restrainedly favourable, with some in the popular press suggesting that the play might have enormous success. This was to be over-optimistic. Will's 'Historicals' were never likely to compare in box-office terms with the best of his comedies, but for sheer quality *The Queen's Highland Servant* (like *Caro-William*) has an honourable place.

During the years between 1968 and 1974 Will was prolific. For most of this time he had two, even three, plays running simultaneously in the West End. He was also writing, or trying to launch, one or two plays which had provincial runs while not reaching London, and he wrote pieces for television.

Also appearing in 1968, and thus overlapping the first year of *The Secretary Bird*, were *The Grouse Moor Image*, and a television play, *The Bishop and the Actress*. The first of these, which never reached the West End, is an unabashed reversion to a *The Chiltern Hundreds* type of comedy. It has Scottish country house life, financially hard-pressed land-owner devising new ways of attracting sightseers to the Castle park, American wife, arguments about inherited wealth, accurately observed quickfire repartee and, inevitably, a certain sense of *déjà vu*. The title came from the frequent sneers at Will's brother Alec, with accompanying comment that British political life had had too much of the outmoded 'grouse moor image'. The play is one of those which shades into farce and it was unsurprising that it did nothing significant. Reviews were poor.

Will's other 1968 production, *The Bishop and the Actress*, is a very different matter – one of his 'Sermons' and one of the best. It was written as a one-act stage play but was performed on television. A nineteen-year-old actress, abandoned by her boyfriend, the Bishop's son, is in her flat and about to take a drug overdose during what she knows is the wedding reception of the boyfriend to another girl. The Bishop, who has never met her, has temporarily left the wedding receptions, calls at the flat, instantly suspects what is going on, gets hold of the drug bottle, persuades her to get dressed and come back with him to the reception to wish her ex-lover happiness and purge her own heart. Will's Bishop finds exactly the right words to show the girl his own sympathy and humanity, to suggest that life is not really over, and to start the healing process. It is, quintessentially, Will at his most sensitive. The Bishop uses racy language and persuades her to let him open a bottle of champagne and have a glass:

ACTRESS:	Do you preach like this?
BISHOP:	Not with a glass of champagne in my hand, no.
ACTRESS:	I don't mean that. Talking like this, I mean.
BISHOP:	It depends on my Text. I've been known to tell a funny story with a moral. That's the built-in safety-belt – a moral. Not for a laugh, for the moral.

He tells one, crude in language but sincere in implication: 'To me it's an example ... of how a Christian ought to behave. That's to say, with dignity and understanding and forgiveness.'

Will certainly believed that. He also lived up to it.

In this period, of about seven years, Will produced some seven further plays. Although dramatic critics retained their capacity for periodic disdain managements had come round to the view that a play by Will was or could be an investment rather than a drain on the pocket. *The Secretary Bird* had converted them.

Will's comedies – indeed almost all his plays – were sprinkled with allusions to the pastimes he preferred, fishing, shooting, ornithology, bridge, golf. Above all, racing. 'You're letting down life, you're not giving it a chance,' says the Bishop to the Actress, 'You can't tip every winner. And there's always the four-thirty in the parlance of my racing friends – the Getting Out Stakes.' And when she replies, 'And if that one's beaten too?' he says, 'There's always Pontefract on Monday.' References to odds, tote doubles, handicaps and objections abound. It was always likely that at some time Will would build an entire play on a story set among the racing fraternity. In September 1970 *The Jockey Club Stakes* opened at the Vaudeville Theatre, produced by Peter Saunders.

Will's plays generally attracted stars. In *The Jockey Club Stakes* Alastair Sim led the cast of assorted Jockey Club stewards, trainers, jockeys and racing *prominenti*, with a genial, exuberant performance as Senior Steward, the Marquess of Candover. None of Will's plays was written with more relish. In some he had vicariously savoured politics, in others he had climbed on a soapbox and preached, in a few – always elegantly and agreeably – he had given a minor history lesson. In almost all he had communicated laughter. In *The Jockey Club Stakes*, writing of a background which delighted and intrigued him, he could simply relax and enjoy himself.

The play has an excellent plot and conveys that sense of inside expertise which generally flatters and attracts a readership or an audience. Will knew his stuff in the racing world and the script shows it. And because he loved, always, a touch of a world turned upside down, a Jack's-as-good-as-his-master atmosphere, poachers have become passable gamekeepers and vice versa. A Stewards' Enquiry is being held at Weatherby's in London into the remarkable running of a certain horse. The Jabberwock, heavily backed by Lady Candover without her husband's knowledge, has won, at long odds, having seemingly been pulled in an earlier race to distort his form. The Jabberwock's personable young trainer, Captain Trevor Jones, is in love with the Candover daughter, Ursula. Lord Green, Chairman of the Levy Board (former politician and something of a Lord Wigg lookalike), is a sworn enemy of the Jockey Club and suspects that the Stewards' Enquiry has been distorted by personal loyalties. From that foundation Will builds a most enjoyable romp, with a deliciously unsuspected dénouement and with every sort of betting skulduggery conducted for the best of motives by people of impeccable social position.

URSULA:	That's not what I'm talking about, Daddy.
MARQUIS:	Well, what is it then?
URSULA:	The Jabberwock! It wasn't Trevor's fault the Jabberwock got pulled at Catterick and Newbury. Or Brown's [the young jockey]. It's mine and Mummy's.
CAPTAIN JONES:	Ursula, he wasn't pulled.
URSULA:	He's only saying that to protect me, Daddy – but it's too late now. He's not to blame – it's me and Mummy.
MARQUIS:	There's no need to bring your mother into this.
URSULA:	It's all her fault. If she hadn't lost her shirt at Doncaster the first week of the season on the Lincoln, Trevor wouldn't be in trouble.
MARQUIS:	'Lost her shirt', Maud, lost her shirt! Your mother doesn't bet.
URSULA:	She bets like no-one's business. She's never off the telephone. (Imitating her mother, in a whisper) Hullo, Red Mullet speaking . . .
MARQUIS:	What did you say?
URSULA:	'Red Mullet'. That's her alias.

And a little later:

URSULA:	Sorry, Daddy, I can see that what I told you about Mummy's given you a shock.
MARQUIS:	I don't believe it.
URSULA:	That she bets, or that she lost a packet on the Lincoln?
MARQUIS:	Either.
URSULA:	Daddy, Mummy is a compulsive punter – she always has been.

MARQUIS:	How do you know?
URSULA:	Everybody knows but you. Even the Chairman of the Levy Board knows.
MARQUIS:	What, Lord Green?
URSULA:	Yes, he knows all right – he mentioned it last week when he came to dinner. He asked me if I knew how *much* Mummy had lost at Doncaster.
MARQUIS:	And did you?
URSULA:	No, but he did. Seven thousand.

It was inevitable that in a play built around the actions of Jockey Club stewards the laws of libel needed to be taken into account. Although the stage Marquess of Candover bore little resemblance to such senior Jockey Club men in real life as the then Duke of Norfolk, Will sailed, in his text, pretty near the wind. There were accusations in the play that wives and daughters of senior stewards had backed a horse knowing it had previously not run straight. There were exchanges between Will's lawyers and the lawyers advising the Jockey Club as to how stage characters might be further disguised. For a while it looked as if these difficulties might scupper production – no management wanted to invest under the shadow of a writ.

Will took on responsibility for tackling the matter and he did so. He talked to Sir Randle Feilden, influential steward. He made some amendments (a most rare occurrence!). Ultimately the Duke of Norfolk personally 'passed' the play, while recognising its innuendoes; and Will, in an 'author's note', thanked the Jockey Club for their cooperation and sportsmanship. The thanks were justified. Reviews were good. The run at the Vaudeville was succeeded by one at the Duke of York's, for, in total, nearly 300 performances.

Will's own racing career had started in the early 1960s and although he had enjoyed it and followed racing with the greatest assiduity, glued to the television during the flat racing season when not actually on the course, he had, at the time of writing *The Jockey Club Stakes*, never owned a winner. He had bought horses but their performance had disappointed. He had no real understanding of breeding or the Turf. But he loved the excitement of ownership. He loved being an owner, with an owner's privileges, in the paddock. The summit of all success in life, he said, would be to own a Derby winner. He backed his own horses, optimistically, defiantly, probably often imprudently. When he sold the film rights of *The Secretary Bird* he bought two new horses at Newmarket, with high hopes. Several times second, they never won. As with humans he disliked his horses being criticised, generally finding a word of exoneration to say after even the most disappointing running – and in defiance of objective fact.

In 1976 he bought the best horse of his career, the top-priced yearling at the Ascot sales costing 3,600 guineas, and named it Goblin. Trained by Bill Wightman it ran with some promise but without success four times at Newbury, once at Salisbury, and once at Goodwood – and at Goodwood, Goblin ran second, to Will's satisfaction despite the disappointment, for Goodwood was his favourite (and nearest) race meeting, a joyful event in his year.

But Goblin, still a two-year-old, needed to win and, entered for a maiden race at Newmarket in October 1977 with Lester Piggott up, win he did – easily. In the following year's Derby, Will persuaded Wightman that Goblin should try his luck. Finishing tenth (but going on to win twice at Brighton and Lingfield), Goblin at least gave Will a Derby runner and was accorded a complete chapter in his second volume of autobiography, *Mr Home Pronounced Hume*.[1] All this was long after the end of run for *The Jockey Club Stakes*. It was an expensive sport – to keep a horse in training in 1979 already cost £60 a week and it was soon to rise, sharply. Costs of purchase were also rising on average – Will, in October 1980, would buy a horse for over six-and-a-half thousand. But racing reflected one of Will's most persistent enthusiasms. As with many racing men, hope outpaced experience.

1969 and 1970 had, therefore, seen a strong recovery in Will's fortunes. 1969 had also brought sadness. Will's mother died. He was probably the only one of the family who could get away with a certain boisterous impudence towards her. Late in her life, when the family were largely assembled at the Hirsel and a big race was about to be listened to on the radio, Will said, 'Everyone must take a horse's name and part, move round the room, and when the commentator says, "So-and-so has now moved into the lead", accelerate past the others and get there.' Lady Home, surprisingly and obediently, took her place and – for her horse was well-fancied and soon took up the running – gamely accelerated

1. William Collins, 1979.

as the race went on. She had always been uncompromising in her frankness about all her children, including him – their views, their achievements, their shortcomings and flaws; and, like all the family, equally uncompromising in her loyalty. In his next play in the West End, Will returned to his roots.

The Douglas Cause was put on at the Duke of York's Theatre after *The Jockey Club Stakes*. It is not only one of Will's 'Historicals', but a family Historical. In it a fictional Scottish judge is dining with the Homes at Douglas in 1910, and the subject of the Douglas inheritance, the curious case of Lady Jane Stewart's family,[2] is given theatrical form. In the play the matter becomes a subject of dinner table conversation and the judge (convincingly played by Andrew Cruickshank) is intrigued. The young Duke and Duchess of Hamilton are staying at Douglas, for the first time since the inheritance dispute of 1760 had made a bitter rift between the families.

The judge, after the case has been outlined by his host, Lord Home, sits by himself in the dining room for a little, over his port, ruminating. What a fascinating challenge, he thinks, 'to try the Douglas Cause again!'

Then Will uses the device of bringing ghosts from the past. As in *Ruddigore*, from the portraits on the wall step principals in that historic case: the Duke and Duchess of Douglas; Archie Douglas, the alleged French impostor ultimately certified as heir; Stewart of Grandtully; and (slandered or innocent according to the verdict) Lady Jane. The play demonstrates Will's fascination – but never obsession – with family and family legend. The judge is given good lines. He keeps the advocates (one of whom is the young James Boswell) in order. He is sympathetic and fair. And he finally addresses a Lady Jane who has broken down in tears under the cross-examination and imputations of Counsel for the Hamiltons. Among other things she has been accused of a love affair with, and a child by, Lord Chief Justice Mansfield (when young Mr William Murray), a circumstance which allegedly biased Mansfield in her favour when the cause was heard in the Lords.

JUDGE: Lady Jane, please listen to me. As you know now, which you did not when you died, the Douglas heritage was not lost – since the House of Lords restored it to the Douglas family. And, furthermore, that it cannot be lost

2. See Chapter I.

now, thanks to a certain statute which limits the time in
which a verdict is reversible . . .

He puts to Lady Jane, for a last time, the vital question. Were
the twins hers? And she swears they were. She had fainted and
was unconscious immediately afterwards, after delivery.

Could they have died, and other children been substituted?
Lady Jane: '. . . It's possible my husband, out of feeling for me,
my Lord, substituted other children . . . but I do not believe it
happened.' And Stewart hotly denies it.

The judge sums up, fairly suggesting the possibilities, fairly
summarising what has or has not been proved. Then he wakes
up, having dozed over his port, disturbed by the butler. And gives
his own, private, surprising, non-legal opinion at the curtain line.
The Douglas Cause did not run long in London but it is, in
its own specialised way, highly effective theatre. It was coolly
received, although one critic's comment that 'The playwright is
struggling well beyond his capacity' was surely as far off target
as it was possible to be.

Soon after *The Secretary Bird* came off at the Savoy Theatre
after its superb flight Will had another play there: *Lloyd George
Knew My Father*. Under the title *Lady Boothroyd of the By-
Pass*, the play had had an earlier production at Boston in
Lincolnshire, yet another put on and directed by the faithful
and perceptive Anthony Roye. Roye used to ask audiences each
night after the performance whether they would like a share in
the London production and a mass of individuals came forward
with impressive amounts of money. The play's first performance
had, in fact, been at Eton in 1970 when a master who had taught
Will's son, Jamie, telephoned Will to ask whether he had a play
the boys could do. He was sent *Lady Boothroyd* and it was done,
Will acknowledged, most impressively; and John Gale had seen it
there.

In London it was jointly presented by John Gale and Ray
Cooney. They reckoned that a certain amount of work was
needed on the script, after watching the Boston production and,
rather unusually, Will did it. This was the play which brought
Will together with Ralph Richardson and Peggy Ashcroft (in a
part later taken by Celia Johnson).

Will, himself, could see Ralph Richardson in the lead part.
Cooney was dubious – Richardson was heavily involved with

prestigious productions, with the National Theatre. Later Will confessed that he had sent Sir Ralph the play, and later still, exultant, said that the star was keen to do it. He was seventy.

All lunched together. 'Who shall we have for Lady Boothroyd?'

'Peggy might do it,' said Richardson, to the astonishment of the others. Dame Peggy Ashcroft, at the head of her profession and a serious actress of enormous attainments, had not crossed their minds.

'I'll ask her,' said Richardson. And later he telephoned, 'Peggy will do it.' She did, but with a four-month limit; and was superb. The combination in the lead meant that the play could hardly fail.

Lloyd George was a successful example of the sort of comedy by Will which almost shades into farce. The underlying situation is normal and believable. Lady Boothroyd is determined to stop the building of a new bypass, her husband, General Sir William Boothroyd – old, dear and decrepit – is past minding, or minding so passionately. The incredible then intervenes. Sheila, Lady Boothroyd, has announced to an astounded family that she intends to kill herself in protest when the first work on the bypass begins.

Sally, daughter of the disagreeable Boothroyd son Hubert, an MP, is staying. She epitomises a favourite theme of Will's, a natural empathy between old and young, skipping a more conventional and less sympathetic middle-aged generation in between.

SHEILA: Your father said I mustn't tell you something – so I'm going to.

SALLY: Good for you.

SHEILA: ... I think you've every right to know about the family.

SALLY: Has Grandfather gone round the bend?

SHEILA: No dear – no farther than usual. No, it's me. I've told your father and your mother, and now I'm telling you. I'm doing myself in on Monday morning.

SALLY: ... But you've stood it so long, why give in now?

SHEILA: Stood what?

SALLY: Why, Grandfather.

SHEILA: Sally!

SALLY: I'm sorry, Sheila. Well, what is it then?

SHEILA: The bypass.

But Sir William/Richardson had the best lines, although it had been a near thing. Having been at moments uneasy about the play during rehearsal he was, Will remarked, totally in control from the First Night onward; a typically Richardson, apparently effortless, performance. The family discuss Sheila's suicide plans with the Vicar – and gloomily acknowledge her obstinacy.

SIR WILLIAM: She pestered Winston in the war about the toilet paper shortage in the village. Wrote him seven letters, till she got an answer.

VICAR: And I'm sure it was worth reading.

WILLIAM: Three-ton lorries, seven of them, packed up to the canvas. I doubt if they're through it yet. You weren't here then, were you Padre?

VICAR: No, no – I was serving in a frigate.

WILLIAM: What's that?

VICAR: (louder) Frigate!

WILLIAM: What did he say, Hubert?

HUBERT: He was serving in a frigate, Father.

WILLIAM: My mistake.

And farce comes as Sir William orders the butler, an old soldier, to sound 'Last Post' for Sheila's suicide in the garden, and himself dons uniform and sword and salutes her through the French windows at the appropriate moment. During which scene, of course, Sheila slips back into the room and talks to William without his at first noticing. It is a beautiful morning, and the best 'Sheilas' were able to suggest a lyrical note, an inability to leave even this flawed world on such a day. This goes beyond the script but Will left it as an opening to a perceptive player. He often did.

Ralph Richardson did not take kindly to changes in the actresses playing opposite him and grumbled when Peggy Ashcroft left the play after her contract, to be replaced by Celia Johnson. John Gale, the producer, expressed the hope that he was still happy. He was scoring a huge success in the play. 'Oh, yes. But I don't think she's *quite* as good as Peggy!'

But the truth was that she was getting longer and louder laughs!

Lloyd George, like *The Secretary Bird*, also touches genuine emotion. The two gloriously eccentric characters who dominate are moving as well as hilariously funny. They are absurd but they care – not least about each other. There is a catch in the throat beside the laughter. Some critics thought the play 'flimsy', but it ran for over 600 performances in the West End, it is often revived and it is loved in France ('Ne coupez pas mes arbres') where, for example, it grossed £40,000 in 1992–93, to *The Secretary Bird*'s £80,000; an illustrious double for two plays which have become classics of the French stage.

Will enjoyed hugely his holidays, generally taken abroad in a borrowed or rented house with friends and families. He was always delightful with children of any age, talking to them in exactly the same tone and with the same turn of speech as to their elders. He enjoyed playing games with them – bridge if their age made it possible, charades, chess at any time of day; he had always been a good chess player since Eton days. He could be bored or secretly irritated by adults, often slipping away under some excuse, particularly from a crush, a party, which could give him a certain claustrophobia. With children he felt unpressed and happy. Particularly on a holiday.

He loved beaches, the sea – brilliant or cold weather, it didn't matter. He enjoyed exploration of new places. In 1971 and 1972 he took the family with friends to Elba – the Napoleonic association pleased him, they took a house near Capoliveri on the south-east coast, and the bathing was superb. *The Secretary Bird* was nearing the end of its triumphant run at the Savoy, *The Jockey Club Stakes* had been filling the Vaudeville, *The Douglas Cause* was about to open at the Duke of York's. *Lloyd George* was being prepared for the following year. The sun was shining, and not only in Elba. Will enjoyed the drives across France and Italy with the children and both families. After a long day's driving through the Alps the companion car stopped and turned. Will's friends had left a piece of baggage at the customs by mistake and would now be an hour behind the Homes. When they arrived at Aosta, the agreed night-stop, it was to find Will with his usual suppressed grin at the hotel's front door – despite prior booking there was always some uncertainty and competition between families. Will opened their car door with a salesmanlike flourish: 'You want the best rooms. We have them!'

Will explored Elba, even (without enthusiasm) driving on the hair-raising ascent to Procchio and other mountain villages in the centre of the island. Driving through or over the Alpine passes always posed a particular problem for the Homes since Will hated heights and Rachel had a phobia of tunnels. Once, long before, he had driven with her from Marbella in Spain up the dramatic road to Ronda, a bend with an unfenced outer edge and a thousand-foot drop every fifty yards. The children had, on that occasion, been young and left with the Home nanny at Drayton. 'I've sent Nanny a telegram,' said Will in sepulchral tones to Rachel, having ultimately reached the top and found the Ronda telegraph office. 'I've just said, "Bring the children out here. I'm never coming down!" ' He had always loathed the idea of travel in an aeroplane. Even when he and Rachel went to South Africa (Rachel's sister, Tessa, had married Julian Ogilvie-Thompson, of the Anglo-American Corporation) they went by boat.

Almost above all, Will enjoyed places where there was varied bird life. A year or two after Elba he went with the same friends and the same children to the Ile de Ré, opposite La Rochelle on the French Atlantic coast. It is a superb spot for any ornithologist, and to be with Will on the '*Marais*' with the great variety of seabirds and waders provided fascination for all. He was observant, knowledgeable and funny. The house taken by Will and Rachel was on the far north-western corner of the island, a house on a small hill (almost the only hill on the Ile de Ré) with an enormous picture window looking towards the Atlantic and the sunset; and beyond it numbers of different birds and small animals would silently appear in the early morning. Other friends came to stay. Celia Johnson came – and, although the house party didn't know it, was at that time about to have yet another triumph in a 'double' of Will's with Ralph Richardson. Bathing, bird-watching, games and laughter filled the days, just as laughter and singing – especially Scots ballads, with Will leading – filled the evenings. And Will was as happy as he was, again, successful.

After *Lloyd George*'s run at the Savoy Theatre Will's next play, also at that theatre, was one of his 'Topicals', although slightly after the event rather than catching a tide. It was, nevertheless, a comedy drawing on a real situation and on real people, without apology. *At the End of the Day* continued a run of Will's plays at the Savoy which lasted seven years and ten months, a playwright record. It was splendidly cast with John Mills, Michael Denison and Dulcie Gray.

The play saw Will back on the familiar ground of a General Election. The Conservatives under Edward Heath had been in office since 1970 and it is their victory in 1970 which forms the basis of the play. *At the End of the Day* was an often used cliché of Harold Wilson, now leader of the opposition but the Prime Minister defeated in 1970, the play's notional date. The play was produced in October 1973 and as a 'Topical' was therefore already behind the game, recent history rather than current affairs.

It didn't matter. General Elections, in the autumn and winter of 1973, were again news. The Government were in trouble and the electorate restive. The National Union of Mineworkers had directly challenged Heath's Administration over pay – there was a statutory incomes policy and a miners' pay claim was in breach of it. An Arab-Israel war had just broken out with consequential effect on supplies of oil to Britain, and increased dependence on the coal which only the miners could deliver. A General Election looked likely earlier rather than later, and there was little expectation that the Conservatives would win it (although in the event it was held in February and they nearly did).

In the play the incumbent Labour Prime Minister, Henry Jackson, a Harold Wilson 'lookalike', faces challenges from an Edward Heath 'lookalike', Lew Trent. The play opens with a live TV interview by 'Martin Knight', a Robin Day 'lookalike', bow tie prominent. Knight is examining a supremely confident Jackson. Mrs Jackson is in the room and Jackson/Wilson's assured mateyness, his equivocation behind a mask of no-nonsense Northern frankness, are beautifully done. Jackson/Wilson takes a cigar from his mouth and sticks in the familiar pipe just before the cameras roll.

HENRY JACKSON: ... there were times when we were most unpopular. But, Martin, popularity was not what we were looking for. It was prosperity, security, and all the rest of it. And that's what we're offering again. Not just a free for all, a scrimmage, like Lew Trent wants, but a balanced, sensible and fair – above all fair – economy, which we can all share. Martin, I'll tell you something – have we got a moment or two? –

KNIGHT: Yes, yes, carry on, Prime Minister.

HENRY JACKSON: Well, I believe in Britain. It's my country. I was born and bred here. Brought up in it, Martin, through the slump and the depression and the unemployment – I went through it all, and so did Mabel.

It was all deliciously well observed, Will at his most authentic. And the Prime Minister uses the interview to tell the public that there is to be a June General Election – it is already the Easter recess of Parliament.

The election – a happy stamping ground for Will – takes

place in Act Two. Jackson is confident with the way things are going – 'The dear old British Public's got its head screwed on the right way, I always say. And that's what counts at the end of the day . . .' – and he takes from his Private Secretary a draft of his planned first speech on TV after victory and tries it on the Private Secretary and Mrs Jackson. He recites the promises made during the election campaign – the consolidation, the reductions in taxation, the 'full and frank discussions' about the Common Market, and to act according to 'the interests of ourselves, of Europe and the world'. 'It's non-committal, that's the great thing,' he says, 'leaves our options open.' He throws away the Private Secretary's proffered alternative draft – in case of defeat. Then they start, at Downing Street, to listen to results.

And the opinion polls have got it all wrong. Jackson is defeated – and Will handles his defeat with humorous sympathy. Trent/Heath moves into No. 10 and after Will has given the two opponents (meeting, rather implausibly) an exchange in which some of Will's own scepticism about the political battle (but fundamental belief in democracy) finds expression, there is a highly ingenious final curtain. Reviews were good. 'Go and see for yourself,' *The Times* bade its readers. Will was in favour for a while. 'In his quizzical glance,' Harold Hobson wrote accurately, 'there is neither envy nor hatred nor venom.'

The play, light-hearted and entertaining though it is, shows yet again Will's innate generosity of spirit, his entire absence of prejudiced partisanship; some would say his lack of political passion; certainly his dislike of doctrinaire ideology. The two principals – Jackson/Wilson and Trent/Heath – feel the bitterness of rivals but share an understanding of the difficulties which any Prime Minister faces, an understanding based on experience in the case of the defeated Jackson, and a perception dawning in the case of the newly victorious Trent. The lead players – John Mills, Michael Denison, Dulcie Gray – were exactly right for the mixture of scepticism and rueful generosity which the parts demanded. The play, like almost all Will's work, breathes charity through the laughter and leaves an agreeable taste in the mouth. The humour of some dramatists grows darker with their output. Will's never.

CHAPTER X

An Extraordinary Record

Within the theatrical profession Will was often criticised on a number of counts. The first of these, experienced by almost everyone who had dealings with him, was obstinacy. He wrote his plays as he and nobody else envisaged them; and often very quickly – he talked fast, thought fast and wrote fast. He needed directors whose minds worked at equivalent speeds. He scribbled countless amendments in the large, hard-backed exercise books in which most of the work was done; he changed tack as he spoke to people and collected opinions during the writing; but he completed a play, more often than not, with remarkable rapidity.

When he had got it to his satisfaction, that was that. Only with the greatest difficulty could he be persuaded to think again about essential parts of it. The play was his child, he felt protective, paternal, defensive. He disliked the interference of others – managements, directors, cast. It had been so from the beginning, from *Great Possessions*. Will never changed. He was obstinate. He would say – did say, in his autobiographical writings – that an author must, in conscience, stick to his own view, back his own judgement. Except on rare occasions he wouldn't budge, although later in life he showed more readiness to entertain the suggestions of others.

This obstinacy was probably often justified. Everyone recognised Will's flair, the excellence of his touch when the dialogue was actually running; he was always the author of whom experienced directors said, 'You never had to alter a line.' But sometimes it probably wasn't. There were plays of Will's which had short provincial runs and never reached the West End, plays which, in the view of friendly commentators and managements, would have been more successful had he agreed to a somewhat different ending, to the excision of a scene, to a shift of emphasis. Who was right on such occasions will never be known because the issue has remained untried. Argument about it

182

is as speculative as debate on whether a battle would have ended differently had some commander taken an alternative course. We shall never know, although we may opine. What is certain is that pride of authorship, his naturally combative character and – as the years passed – considerable experience made him an obstinate (albeit utterly charming) man to deal with in professional matters. Yet those who dealt with him always acknowledged, gratefully, his ability to make audiences laugh – and, often, to make them think; his timing, his verbal felicity, his audacity. It was acknowledged that his dramatic ideas were as original as they were ingenious.

Another dart sometimes thrown at Will was the obverse side of one of his most agreeable aspects – his light-heartedness. Sometimes this, wrongly, was characterised as irresponsibility. It showed, some thought, in his attitude to the whole business of theatrical production. He enjoyed what might be called – although again, perhaps, wrongly called – the amateur approach to serious or professional matters. In fact, when engrossed in a play, Will gave it his whole attention; knowledgeable and expert, he was a professional to his fingertips, described by some at the summit of the theatre as probably the most talented and underestimated playwright in England. But like many Englishmen (although fewer Scotsmen) he preferred expertise and seriousness of approach to be concealed by a curtain of flippancy, to be leavened with reference to lighter concerns, in the theatre and in life. Thus he relished, for instance, Wilfrid Hyde White's taste for the Turf, which Will so greatly shared; it made him more than an actor, it made him a racing man. He relished Celia Johnson's suggestion of Jack Merivale to play the young man in *The Reluctant Debutante*.

'Is he good?' they asked her.

'I don't know, but he can drop me off on Henley Bridge to pick up my car every evening, on his way home.' More than an actress, therefore, a wife and mother. Such reactions always tickled Will's fancy. He would relate with enjoyment (nobody knew with what accuracy) how his brother Alec opened a Cabinet meeting with a congratulatory word to a colleague on a sporting success scored by the colleague's wife, thus showing that he was more than a Prime Minister; he was a sportsman.

To some, this sort of thing appeared deplorably frivolous. To Will it demonstrated a sense of proportion. It is echoed again and again in his plays. In the *Debutante*:

SHEILA: Why did he get a peerage?
JIMMY: ... the river Itchen ran through his garden and the
            Prime Minister was fond of fishing.

This *dégagé* approach made, of course, a considerable contribution to the dislike Will and his work aroused in some
critical breasts, as surely implying a lack of dedication as well
as more than a small touch of aristocratic complacency. But to
Will – and the matter went far deeper than literary or artistic
style – it was essentially a moral question, although he would
have thought it pretentious to say so. To him, civilised human
beings *ought* to temper their professional talents and pursuits
and preoccupations with sufficient touches of the frivolous, the
sporting, the light-hearted.

But those who supposed this attitude of mind might nullify
Will's own skill of dramatic appraisal did not know their man,
although it perhaps here and there blunted the sharpness of his
judgement. He disliked unprofessional conduct very much indeed,
but he found a touch of amateur ambivalence so endearing that he
may have occasionally smiled with too forgiving a smile. It was a
similar, but lighter, aspect of the Will who could only contemplate
misery or wickedness by invoking some saving humour; who, like
Brian in *The Bad Samaritan*, saw 'how much there was in life
that's sad' and – as Jane said to him – had to joke about it for
that reason. So with Will, whose 'Sermons' were never bare of
laughter.

A third criticism sometimes made of Will was that he was
too prolific, that he wrote too much and that some of it was
of poor quality compared to his best work. This is probably
fair – few creative artists in any discipline are consistently at
their peak. Will, as even his most loyal admirers conceded, wrote
some awful plays; not many, but some. He was, however, tireless.
His span of active work probably exceeded that of any other
dramatist, certainly in our time; his first play was produced in
March 1937, his last in November 1989 – over fifty-two years.
Like most people he was not always the best judge of his own
work. 'Can't you bring yourself, when the general consensus is
that the play you've written is not a good one, to *tear it up*?'
ran a letter from an influential old friend. Will seldom saw it like
that. His plays were his children, not to be disowned. He could
sometimes, but rarely, bring himself to speak critically of a play

but it was almost with the difficulty he found in speaking critically of a person. One shrewd, and not unfriendly, observer said that Will wrote some of the best light comedies in the language; and some of the worst. The trouble, he added, was that the author failed to distinguish between the two. This was harsh, but there was a grain of truth in it.

Two things drove Will. The first was money. He was always very conscious that to live as he wished to live, and where, to keep his family and help their launch in life (about which he was extremely generous), he had to work, to succeed. Lack of success at the bad times disturbed him – perhaps less than it would have disturbed one more financially aware, but sufficiently. He was not extravagant but was temperamentally improvident. He was open-handed and would have preferred hunger to disappointing a needy friend. He was not self-indulgent – was, indeed, rather abstemious in most things, caring little for instance for fine food and wine – but he spent what seemed to be there (and in good times a great deal seemed to be there) without the sort of attention to financial planning which penal tax rates and periodic backlog of debt made necessary, whatever the gross take from the dramatic successes when they came. He lived comfortably, he travelled a good deal, not least to look at provincial showings of his plays. He was immensely hospitable. He loved golf, and played it as often as he could – not well but enthusiastically, flippantly and in a most companionable way. He went to the races; and there was, it must be said, his racing account which, whether as owner or punter, did little to make his finances more secure.

But the second thing which drove Will's output was, quite simply, his creative urge. It seldom weakened. He was unhappy unless writing a play, or meditating a play, or negotiating the production of a play; and very often during his life it was all three simultaneously. He was restlessly inventive. His mind was searching and formulating drama all the time. The people he knew or met, the settings in which he encountered them, their voices, their attitudes, their expressions, all produced scenes in his mind for future use. It had always been so.

During the next four years – from 1974 until 1978 – Will brought out a further eight plays, six of them produced in the West End. It is an extraordinary record. Two were flops. One, an 'Historical', returned movingly and successfully to Will's well-honed theme of mutual understanding between enemies in time of war, while another, also an 'Historical', had had an earlier, provincial run ten years earlier. One was a 'Topical', a parody on the power of the media. Another was one of Will's 'Sermons'. And two were comedies, named from a fishing beat and a bird respectively; of which the latter was a work of genius, a triumph.

First the flops. *In the Red* was first tried out by Anthony Roye at Boston in Lincolnshire and was later put on by John Gale at Windsor (where Will had had frequent successes) to a good reception. But Will knew that in spite of a strong cast all was not well. 'It's a bugger!' he said tersely to John Gale, and he was right. In spite of an encouraging run at Richmond, Gale, agreeing with what Will had undoubtedly felt at Windsor, decided not to try to take the play to London. Nobody else wanted to.

Will then embarked on one of his major imprudences, with echoes of *Aunt Edwina*. Together with the gifted director, Allan Davis, he decided to underwrite a London production himself. He managed to get the Whitehall Theatre (largely associated with Paul Raymond's revues or Brian Rix's farces), and *In the Red* opened there in March 1977; and closed in April. It was losing £2,000 per week (in 1977 terms) and was near universally damned.

In the Red has, as central character, David Clifton, an author (addicted to racing) with a very large overdraft and a very large unpaid tax bill. He has written successes in the past (hence the tax bill) but none for a long time (hence the overdraft). Except for financial anxiety he lives comfortably in the country, and the family are served by an Italian couple. A new bank manager, Bentworth, calls – an amateur enthusiast of the theatre. His news for David Clifton is very bad indeed and he listens to David's (wildly improvised) ideas for new plays, plays whose success will solve his problems. Bentworth is unimpressed. Head office are being adamant. No more credit.

DAVID: No more cheques! Do you know what you're saying?
BENTWORTH: I'm afraid I do.
DAVID: Then you're a heartless bugger!
BENTWORTH: Mr Clifton, I am acting on instructions.
DAVID: That's what the Gestapo used to say.

The bank manager, however, is seduced into a change of heart. David backs more losers but his scheming succeeds. The first part of *In the Red* is as painfully autobiographical as *The Bad Soldier Smith*, and this was probably one of its troubles. The play seemed too close to the most unappealing aspects of many people's lives

– indebtedness, anxiety, a disappointing professional future. The dénouement was inventive but improbable. Some professionals thought that *In the Red* might have benefited, even turned into a triumph, had Will been prepared to see its imperfections, reach for scissors and pen, work at some changes. He wouldn't. As it was, *In the Red*, although Will was courteously described in the *Daily Telegraph* as writing with all his 'loose-wristed fluency' (a pleasing image), lost him a considerable amount of money.

A few weeks later Will's other flop at this time was produced at the Shaftesbury Theatre in May 1977, and taken off after three weeks.

Rolls-hyphen-Royce had a huge cast. The play, an 'Historical', was based on the partnership and stormy relationship between the peer's son, the visionary Charles Rolls, and the gifted, gritty, self-made engineer, Henry Royce. It received thoroughly bad notices and brought Will few new admirers.

Will was particularly exasperated by two aspects of this failure. First, Wilfrid Hyde White (playing a comparatively small but pivotal part, Claude Johnson, the entrepreneur and narrator) chose to ignore the script of the opening speech Will had written for him, and to ad-lib, irritatingly and less than amusingly. Second, critics (as so often) used the play's historical subject to play tunes on the theme of class distinctions (Rolls and Royce), a trivialisation of a great story about the origins of an historic British marque. Will was fond of the play and saddened by its failure. It is written episodically, with a large number of small sequential scenes and a narrator (Johnson/Hyde White). As a stage play it is hard to imagine it working well, but, as always with Will, there are shrewd and entertaining passages. Will, after careful research, had injected human interest into the story of mechanical invention, experimental aviation, the taking of business risks, the tragic death of Charles Rolls, and some past associates were appalled by the critics' reception. 'I don't know what's the matter with these beasts!' wrote one leading actor, but general press comment was 'a poor play'. The world stayed away. Those who wrote that the theme probably had more of a future on film may have been right.

These were the flops. Before this, however, Will had produced another, and better, 'historical'; a delightful play.

The Dame of Sark was produced by Ray Cooney at Wyndham's Theatre in October 1974. The play was based, pretty accurately, on the German occupation of the Channel Islands during the Second World War. The Dame of Sark, Sybil Hathaway (played by Celia Johnson), is determined never to yield an inch in dignity or practical concession to the invaders, except by force. Her American husband (in origins and on stage; in reality he had been naturalised British after the First World War) is, in mid-play, deported to Germany. Her 'people' on Sark are terrified and confused, and look to her for leadership. An SS officer, Dr Braun, acts as interpreter to Sark's German commandant, Major Lanz: the former is disagreeable, the latter courteous and correct. In overall command, based on Guernsey, is Colonel von Schmettau, played most convincingly in London by Tony Britton.

Von Schmettau calls at the Seigneurie on Sark to offer his condolences on the death in action of the Dame's stepson, an officer in the Royal Air Force. A sympathetic relationship is depicted between the German colonel, an old-type officer manifestly out of sympathy with the Nazi regime, and the Dame and her husband. News of the war's progress broadcast by the BBC (forbidden listening) periodically cuts into the play. Von Schmettau has occasions to visit Sark, and on one such, when fresh restrictive measures have been ordered by the Germans after a British raid from the sea and the killing by British commandos of two Germans, he meets fierce frankness. The Dame is quick-tempered.

SYBIL: We didn't start this war, Colonel, you did – or, rather, your Führer . . . you've no right to be in Sark or Guernsey or any of the Channel Islands – or in Poland, come to that . . . No one invited you . . . Now you must take what's coming to you and, make no mistake about it, it *is* coming – slowly but inevitably, and your despicable little Führer will be defeated and your precious German Army beaten . . .

Von Schmettau demands an apology. Sybil: 'I'll speak exactly as I like!' But, urged by her husband, she grudgingly says she's sorry. And when Major Lanz has left the room:

VON SCHMETTAU: Now it is my turn to apologise.
SYBIL: And so you should.
VON SCHMETTAU: Major Lanz heard you insult the Führer and – I had no alternative but to demand an apology. I have every reason to believe that Major Lanz admires the Führer greatly – as we all do.

SYBIL: We're alone now, Colonel.
VON SCHMETTAU: As we all do, Mrs Hathaway.

So Will propounds, entirely fairly, a favourite proposition
– that the enemy individual may be deeply unhappy about
the duty he has to perform but must still act correctly and
cannot appear to condone disloyalty. This was the Will who
had, rightly or wrongly, protested that the Allied policy of
demanding 'unconditional surrender' from Germany had helped
deprive the anti-Hitler elements in the German army of hope.
The connection was never wholly convincing and Will never
faced fully the fact, which his own text in this play indicated,
that a man like von Schmettau, however unhappily, believed in
obedience.

Von Schmettau does (and in fact did) all he can to protect
the islanders from the more oppressive directives of Berlin, but
is recalled in the summer of 1944. He knows that he is in bad
odour with the Reich authorities, and probably in trouble. He
comes to say goodbye – the Allied invasion of Normandy is about
to begin.

SYBIL: Goodbye – and good luck, Count von Schmettau.
VON SCHMETTAU: Thank you. I shall need it. (He salutes) Did you
      hear the aeroplanes last night?
SYBIL: Yes, they woke me up.
VON SCHMETTAU: There were very many of them – British and American.
SYBIL: Oh, really?
VON SCHMETTAU (as he smiles and turns to go):
      What a pity that you have not got a wireless set!

The play ends with the liberation of Sark. Like most 'Historicals' it suffers from a certain lack of dramatic tension since the
ending – liberation – is sure. But *The Dame of Sark* handles deli-
cately and convincingly a theme near Will's heart: the possibility,
indeed the normality, of enemies in war sharing the same human
qualities and recognising them in each other as transcending the
external circumstances which have set them in opposition. Von
Schmettau's son (killed in Russia) was an ornithologist. The Dame
and the Colonel speak of birds, photography. His conscience and
unease about the war are never exaggerated or implausible, while
the claustrophobic atmosphere of a community under enemy
occupation is persuasively conveyed. Will is fair to all parties.
He generally was.

The play ran at Wyndham's for over six months and was

made into a TV film (with Johnson and Britten) by Anglia. Critics were appreciative, although one, Irving Wardle, wrote of von Schmettau's loyalty to a government whose policies he is shown deploring, 'Mr Home is not one to open that can of beans'; or so Will quoted,[1] adding indignantly that it was exactly that can of beans he had opened and explored for a year at Wakefield and Wormwood Scrubs. But J. C. Trewin wrote of a 'heartening night in the theatre', remarking that he was bored by the condescension and inverted snobbery shown by too many of his colleagues to Will's plays. Will had written the *Dame* in five days and greatly liked it. The theme absorbed him. Characteristically he arranged at his own expense for Sybil Hathaway's maid, Cecile, who had never before left Sark, to fly to London for the First Night. The play pleased the von Schmettau family.

The Dame of Sark was followed in London by another of Will's 'Historicals'; one already described, which had run in the provinces ten years earlier when the atmosphere for Will had been particularly inauspicious. In 1975 *Betzi* was produced by John Gale at the Haymarket.

The critics were not hostile, although some fastened, with a certain justice, on a central weakness. The placing of the exiled Napoleon in a story told 'in terms of domestic light comedy', as one (friendly) observer noted, had inherent difficulties – 'a very difficult combination of mediums'. Perhaps; yet Will could have responded that to show a gentle, ambiguous side to the great conqueror's nature did not necessarily lack drama.

There was, however, another recurrent criticism. The actual relationship between the Emperor and Betzi was thought by some 'too slight to involve us'. Will wrote the story romantically, touchingly. The language aimed, wittily, at the heart. Yet it is clear (and historically accurate) that this was no 'grand passion' or adult love affair. 'It seems a bit excessive,' wrote Irving Wardle, not perhaps unfairly, 'to pull out all the romantic stops at the end to express regret for something that never happened.'

Will's 'Sermon' in this period of his writing was *The Lord's Lieutenant*, performed at Farnham, and in several places (including in several Hampshire churches) in 1977. In fact there are two explicit sermons in the play – one of them an actual sermon, preached in the closing scene by the (sympathetically

1. *Old Men Remember*, Collins & Brown, 1991.

drawn) vicar, the other an indignant diatribe by a county Lord Lieutenant at the nervous concessions to intellectual fashion made by too many cowed 'ordinary people'.

Both are effective. The play is concerned with an agreeable and fundamentally conventional girl, Rosemary, who is in love with a pop star, a flamboyant, rebellious, agnostic figure who seems to love her in return. The girl is the beloved daughter of the county's Lord Lieutenant, Lord Froxfield, who thoroughly disapproves of her pop star and all he epitomises.

Rosemary dies in a car crash (Johnny, the pop star, driving). To general consternation Johnny attends the funeral. It is followed by a Communion service, at which Johnny may or may not go to the altar rails to take the sacrament. We are given the general impression of a conversion (or reawakening: Johnny has, in fact, been confirmed). The Vicar's sermon (before Communion) is significant in indicating a view often propounded by Will about survival and life after death. Whatever its theological standing, it is how he felt.

VICAR: ... there's no rebirth, the cynics say. The whole conception of the Resurrection's phoney ... It doesn't work, that trick, they tell us. He existed, yes, we all accept that, but He couldn't have been resurrected, that's a load of rubbish, no one ever has been, no one ever will be. So the unbelievers argue, and they could be right, let's face it. After all the Church has no monopoly of truth. Although I might get into trouble with my Bishop if he heard me saying that ... Was Christ resurrected? What's the answer, yes or no? It may surprise you when I say this ... does whatever answer each of us may feel bound to make really matter? Is not Christ ... alive still through His teaching? And is not God the Father ... alive too? If not, who is? ... the trees, the birds, the sea, the hills, the butterflies, the apple blossom and the daffodils. Don't tell me no one made them.

This, of course, was to argue for Christ the teacher as preeminent, rather than Christ the Crucified, the Redeemer. And the Vicar's sermon continues with the argument of the Creator amply demonstrated by the example of Creation, and with the question of survival (and, by implication, the historical Resurrection) left as a matter of hope; and faith; and doubt. Will felt so strongly the presence – and, when they died, the memory – of people he loved that he found that fact itself a sort of indicator of immortality, without commitment to any specific formulation of dogma on the subject. The Vicar's sermon was not far from his own feelings, carefully speculative as it was. 'Lord, I believe – help thou mine unbelief.' There was much of Will in it.

Lord Froxfield, austere, conventional but also sympathetically drawn, harangues the village audience who have earlier attended a debate in the church between the Vicar and Johnny, a debate in which Johnny has derided the idea of the sacrament of Communion, and most of the Christian story; and pronounced a hedonistic philosophy of free love and personal liberty in all things.

FROXFIELD: His [Johnny's] approach is symptomatic of the malaise I've been trying to describe. A deep-seated desire to bully.
JOHNNY: No!
FROXFIELD: Yes. A desire to bully all of us, especially the Vicar. A desire to shock us – make the things on which we've built our lives, the basic tenets that we learnt respect for at our mothers' knees, seem silly, trivial and childish and, above all, untrue . . . Well, don't you stand for it. Ignore the fellow . . . Hang on to your faith. It's the only thing in life that matters . . . Hold on to the fact that faith is not – and is not meant to be – founded on intellect, only on instinct. You know in your heart of hearts that Christ was born and died and resurrected, and that God the Father so arranged it . . . So hold firm, and *don't be bullied*. That's all, thank you.

If there was a good deal of Will in the Vicar's sermon, there was not a little, too, in Lord Froxfield's words. Will, too, had fought many a battle against the bullying propensities of modish fashion. The play was well received ecclesiastically, the Bishop of London being keen to get it put on in a church in London but finding opposition from the Greater London Council; and the reactions of young members of audiences were generally reported as favourable. Some, indeed, found it intensely moving – especially the Vicar's sermon. Harold Hobson called it 'glittering', in what Will termed the best review he'd ever received.

Of Will's straight plays during this period, the first, produced at the Pitlochry Festival in 1977, was called *The Perch*. It appears to breach Will's unfailing aversion to plays about crime, criminal passion or violent wrongdoing. A 'closed' situation with a number of people (and suspects) isolated in a Highland fishing hotel, it has excellent pace and suspense. 'Douglas Home in Christie-land' was the *Financial Times* headline, and the play was described as one of Will's 'more disciplined efforts' as well as 'impressing with its wit and charm'. *The Perch* may have owed something to Will's performance in 1948 in a showing of *Shall We Join the Ladies?*, Barrie's classic, with every member of the cast (a dinner party) gradually disclosing an unsuspected past, an unavowed relationship, a motive for murder – if there has been murder.[2] *The Perch* is a shrewdly concocted little piece, full of surprises, adorned by plenty of fishing expertise. It shows Will's ingenuity at plotting. In the dénouement Will springs the ultimate surprise – and is true to himself.

The Perch also provided an example of Will's obstinacy. A theatrical trick – a skilful pistol shot which cuts in half a cigar – was used by Will. Not essential to the plot, it was impossible to demonstrate on stage (as opposed to film) and merely left the audience bemused. Will, who had driven to Pitlochry to see the play, refused to accept this in the slightest – 'They seemed perfectly happy!' he said as the audience filed out after the curtain. *The Perch*, a child, was beyond criticism.

In March the following year, 1978, *The Editor Regrets* opened at Henley, ran at Bournemouth, at Brighton (where Will stepped into the breach when Anthony Roye became ill, and played the lead for several performances) and at the Greenwich theatre. Before its opening at Henley, Anthony Roye had put on there his solo miscellany *Just Home*, giving excerpts (taking several parts) from a number of Will's plays, from *The Chiltern Hundreds* through *The Reluctant Debutante*, *The Queen's Highland Servant*, *The Secretary Bird* and *Lloyd George* to *The End of the Day* – a bravura performance, first presented at the Mayfair Theatre in London in 1974, and perfectly designed to remind audiences of what Will had done and could do.

The Editor Regrets is in a sense a 'Topical' (although timeless) since it deals with the themes of media intrusion and blackmail, as fiercely debated in 1978 as 1995. The setting is political – Will enjoyed putting his characters not too far from Westminster. The daughter of a distinguished politician has been indiscreet, and photographed in mid-indiscretion. The story, with pictures, is about to break and with it is likely to break the political career of the daughter's fiancé (deceived by her) as well, of course, as her engagement. Father – a Will-figure, tolerant, principled but uncondemnatory – approaches the newspaper proprietor about

2. See Chapter V.

the treacherous gossip columnist concerned:

SIR ERIC: If you recognise he's a bastard, why do you employ him?
THORNTON: For precisely the same reasons that your gardener puts manure on your roses, Eric, to encourage growth. I reckon he's worth a quarter of a million copies to me every Sunday.

But Thornton, although an old acquaintance, has always been covertly attacking Sir Eric and there is war between them now. Will has a good time firing salvoes at the hypocrisy of newspapermen – and proprietors – and Sir Eric, with smart footwork and a private detective, turns the tables. It is fast moving, entertaining, unmemorable stuff, and made no great impact. It did, however, enable Will, once again, to show his detestation of double standards, and the humbug with which those in positions of power condemn their opponents – or victims – for actions indulged with impunity by themselves. Whether in war or peace this was a fundamental concern of Will's and he attacked it ceaselessly.

Some people – they included Kenneth More, to whom Will sent the play – thought it too hostile to the press as well as being incredible. Some, and this was a rare accusation to be levelled at Will, thought it surprisingly bitter. Although there was some critical approval of 'Mr Home's impish humour' there was a general reluctance – perhaps predictable – to see much good in the play, or anyway to write it. During the run at Brighton and Will's emergency playing of the lead he was alleged sometimes to forget his lines, and the fact did not pass without comment. Much of the published criticism was sadly humourless. *The Editor Regrets* lost money. But before this, in 1977, a kingfisher had flown up the river.

When Will had been conducting his solitary, valiant, doomed battle to keep *Aunt Edwina* running at the end of 1959, he had signed his agreement with Peter Saunders. In return for an advance of royalties he would give Saunders an option on a number of future plays, yet to be written. The advance had enabled the *Aunt* to continue briefly. The option remained, and Saunders proposed to take it up for the third time in respect of *The Kingfisher*. It was clear to him that Will had written – after a sadly extended interval – another first-class play. Saunders had put on *The Reluctant Peer* and *The Jockey Club Stakes*, but these had been some years ago. Will's winners were too long-spaced. It looked as if one was again within sight.

Others were also enthusiastic about *The Kingfisher*. At the National Theatre, Sir Peter Hall was particularly anxious that Ralph Richardson should play the lead part – Cecil Warburton, the ageing reminiscent writer in the evening of his life, reminded suddenly of long past loves. He asked Saunders to give up his option so that Richardson, generally agreed to be perfect for the part, should play in *The Kingfisher* at the National. Richardson was keen – he had been working for some time at the National. For Will to have a play put on at the National Theatre would clearly be a significant feather in his cap and one not yet worn; indeed – together with possession of a Derby winner – it was one of his two greatest ambitions. Will, having met and liked Peter Hall, was also keen, although he was worried by Hall's wish for a different ending to the play. Saunders agreed to give up his option on the play in return for an additional option on a play of Will's in the future.

Soon thereafter, however, Hall proposed to put *The Kingfisher* on as a National Theatre production but in a West End theatre, at least initially. Will understood that building problems and scheduling had led to this. There would be a preliminary out-of-London tour and Lindsay Anderson would direct. Now, however, Will was informed by his agent, Laurence Evans, that the Society of West End Theatre Managers were taking strong exception to a National Theatre production of Will's play coming on in the West End and, in effect, competing with the commercial theatre by using public money. There was, Evans told Will, likely to be a press campaign – or leading article – against the National Theatre and its director, Peter Hall, on grounds of the iniquity of subsidised theatre distorting the theatrical market in the West End in this way. This was comprehensible to Will. He had once tried *The Queen's Highland Servant* on the National Theatre, to be told in a letter that 'We make it a matter of policy as far as possible not to trespass on the commercial theatre's traditional ground.' To West End managements the trying out of a play by William Douglas Home was trespass on 'the commercial theatre's traditional ground' if anything was.

It looked as if *The Kingfisher* might first fly during a nasty public storm. After a meeting of interested parties Will – who, it was agreed, should have the deciding vote – asked for the play back from Peter Hall. He had concluded that the atmosphere would make a National launch unpropitious. He was probably right. Hall made no difficulties, and wrote thanking Will for his 'tolerance and fairmindedness'.

Will, however, then turned the situation into a question of principle. He decided that the Society of West End Theatre Managers were seeking to use their dominant commercial position to 'dictate' to a playwright where and under whose management he should launch a play. He wrote to *The Times* (as always in any controversial situation) attacking such attempted dictation, and saying that his play would not be performed until he had been assured in writing that the playwright's 'freedom of choice' was and would always be inviolate. Peter Saunders did not wish to reclaim the option he had generously surrendered to Hall and a few days later John Gale proposed to do the play. In response to Will's arguments it was arranged for him to receive a letter which appeared to satisfy him. Thenceforth *The Kingfisher* flew triumphantly.

In all this it is difficult to argue that Will did not get the wrong end of the stick. The entirely fair letter he received, signed by Michael Codron, made it clear that the Society of West End Theatre Managers were not seeking to dictate to a playwright. It seems, rather, that they were making a perfectly legitimate point about the operation of the market in the commercial theatre, and were questioning (or were reported as being prepared to question; it never came to it) the propriety of subsidised productions competing on the same ground with productions riskily backed by private money. There may, obviously, be a response to this, a counter-argument; the Society may have been unreasonably provoked. But Will's reaction was not in the least concerned with the rights and wrongs of subsidised theatre or its relationship with commercial theatre. Instead, he struck an attitude for the liberty of the creative artist, surely with very little rational justification.

The Kingfisher, therefore, flew into the Lyric Theatre in May 1977 (a normal commercial production), some pretty disagreeable communications having passed between the main parties concerned. It is a delightful play and it shows, tenderly, the way Will was able to blend witty dialogue, perfect rallies back and forth across the net between two artists at the game (initially Ralph Richardson and Celia Johnson), with a gentle, moving depiction of the process of ageing, of earlier emotion recollected in tranquillity – but tranquillity still liable to upheaval despite the advance of the years. It shows, too – most of Will's serious plays show — the way he preserved a play's integrity. There is a theme and a story and the playwright holds the audience to it. There are seldom distractions or diversions simply to introduce an irrelevantly amusing line or incident. 'I don't want any jokes!' Will used to say to a director, and he meant it. There were, of course, jokes galore but they were in the script and the script stuck firmly to the evolution of the plot, economically constructed, economically written, whether high comedy, near-tragedy or near-farce.

But there is in *The Kingfisher* an elegiac, reminiscent note, naturally sounded by the story itself, which is of three elderly people — witty, attractive, in two cases distinguished, but unquestionably elderly people. And the note reflected Will's own age. He was sixty-five. He was still entirely prepared to invent, to fight, to argue, to oppose, to protest — there were plays yet to come which would show it. In *The Kingfisher*, however, more than in any play before it, Will is relishing a certain rest from conflict; a rest, too, from the implacable energies of the young, however sympathetic the young.

In the play the distinguished author, Sir Cecil Warburton (Richardson), is expecting a visit from Evelyn, Lady Townsend, whose husband Reggie has just died, on a golf course. She is returning from the funeral. Cecil, we are asked to believe — and she, only half-credulous, is asked to believe — was passionately in love with Evelyn fifty years ago. They have not met since. Now he wants to renew acquaintance, perhaps with a view to marriage. He is confident that her husband had bored her for fifty years. Hawkins, faithful servant of Cecil for all that time, is inevitably jealous, but Evelyn charms him. And Cecil makes her laugh, in a way (we guess) that she hasn't since marriage.

CECIL: ... he liked the good things of life, obviously. What hole did it happen on?

EVELYN: The seventeenth.

CECIL: Oh, nearly made it. Was he doing a good round?

EVELYN: Twelve over. Not bad, for him. And his tee shot was pin high. It's quite a short hole.

CECIL: Were you playing with him?

EVELYN: No, no. I was playing bridge back in the Clubhouse ... I'd just gone Six No Trumps when the Pro rushed in.

CECIL: Did you make it?

Facetious. Implausible. But behind the deliberately heartless *farceur* image Cecil makes Evelyn, and us, realise he really cares about her love. He knows that laughter is the way to her heart, if there is a way, and Will knew the same.

EVELYN: You sit there asking me to marry you and then, without a blush, you tell me that you've done the same thing to two other women when their husbands died.
CECIL: What's that but honesty?
EVELYN: For one thing it's bad manners.
CECIL: Not at all. You must remember that I'm getting on. I have to take my chances when they come. For all I know, old Reggie might have gone on playing golf till kingdom come. Well, he did, didn't he? So you can't blame me.

They both feel the sense of limited time:

CECIL: They issued us with return tickets when we came into this world, remember? Now we're on the way back. And soon we'll hit the buffers, crash-bang –
EVELYN: Don't.
CECIL: Why not? One may as well face facts. The only truth in life is death.
EVELYN: You might as well say that the only truth in death is life.
HAWKINS: You'll pardon me for saying so, it could be wiser to avoid the subject altogether.
CECIL: You keep out of it!

Hawkins gives in his notice later, is charmed by Evelyn into withdrawing it. Both she and Hawkins have never stopped loving the outrageous, selfish, irresistible creature, young or old, that is Cecil. At the end, their future not quite certain, Cecil and Evelyn hope they may spy the kingfisher along the river as they did on an enchanted evening fifty years ago. The 'beat' of Will's dialogue, the harmonious economy, the transitions of sound were never better, and the play was a superb vehicle for the stars who adorned it.

There was a near-disaster on the First Night – an electricity failure led to a long delay in starting, and to intense cold. Ralph Richardson did not respond at first to a call – he was suffering from hypothermia. He recovered, and triumphed. Rex Harrison and Claudette Colbert played it in New York; Harrison and Wendy Hiller, with Cyril Cusack, in a television film. Some critics thought *The Kingfisher* too light, flimsy; but a sufficient number used words like 'gentle', 'skilfully crafted' and 'tender'. They were right.

The flurry about the National Theatre and the legal advice

which Will took about his 'option' agreement with Peter Saunders[3] were not the only troubles to beset *The Kingfisher*.

A Mr Basil Ashmore brought an action against Will in 1978, an action which dragged on through more than five years. It concerned *The Kingfisher*, and ultimately judgement with costs was given in Will's favour in February 1982. Ashmore appealed. The appeal was dismissed and full costs (some £28,000) were recovered, but the whole business was not cleared up until January 1984. The action had been for infringement of copyright and breach of confidence.

Briefly, what had happened was this. Ashmore, interested in collecting old plays, had in mind to adapt a short one-act play written in 1908 into a longer play, with four parts. The theme was that of a selfish old man, refused in old age by a woman he had declined to marry in youth (having, daringly for the period, proposed love without marriage). Ashmore hoped for a second act drawn from a play by Max Beerbohm and a third act based on a work by Wedekind. He approached Will to write a fourth act.

This had happened some time before *The Kingfisher* flew. Will had replied in friendly terms. Meanwhile the executors of both the Beerbohm and the Wedekind literary heritages had refused authority for the proposals. Ashmore produced no original work but – because of the theme envisaged – argued that *The Kingfisher* owed everything to his ideas. In effect, he accused Will of plagiarism; and he launched his attacks having read about (but neither read nor seen) Will's play. He demanded financial recompense and, failing this, sought redress in law.

Will found this intolerable. He had at no time made an agreement with Ashmore; nor had he received any money in advance for the work the latter proposed he do. And Ashmore held no copyright.

There was also the matter of breach of confidence, the suggestion that *The Kingfisher* would not have been hatched had Ashmore's idea of joining up three existing plays (and getting Will to add a fourth) not been discussed. Will disputed this strongly and Judge Mervyn Davies, in an extended and entirely

3. It ended with Will, who had disputed, writing in generous terms to Saunders to say he was legally and morally in the wrong, and that no further action was contemplated.

lucid judgement, found for him. Will had, throughout, maintained that *The Kingfisher* owed nothing to any man but himself. It had, however, been a long and at times a worrying episode.

The Kingfisher, as a final disappointment, was taken off while still playing to excellent houses and making money. Celia Johnson's contract was up for renewal and she did not wish to continue; while Ralph Richardson (personally keen) would not agree to any of the substitute actresses proposed. It is an exquisite play.

CHAPTER XI

Portraiture and Pain

Will was incomparable company with his friends and with children. He had an ageless, Peter Pan-like quality, never changing, always delighting. With strangers, however, he could – but generally only at first – appear oddly uncommunicative, often to their disappointment. Hoping to meet a man of the theatre whose wit they admired and of whose charm they had heard, they found instead an enigmatic person who tended to speak in short, jerky sentences, sentences not apparently aimed with any particular interest at the person addressed; the Ludgrove shyness never altogether vanished and newly introduced acquaintances could find it unnerving. He could seem, in a curious way, unsociable; even offhand.

This was a mask. In reality Will was always observing. He had, as became clear after a little to most people meeting him, a most engaging gift of making another feel both important and unique, but he was also recording in his mind nuances in a voice, in turns of phrase, in conversation. He was reading characters, composing lines for bit parts, sitting in the stalls. For him people had to find their places in the cast of his unceasing drama. At first a stranger might be hard to place, part unlearned. Will would – an introductory gambit – lightly touch the arm, with an irrelevant one-sentence anecdote out of the blue. 'My friend, Mr Washbrook, says that he saw eleven of his cows standing in a circle in the moonlight, all rearing up on their hindlegs. Is that true, do you think?'

Or something equally preposterous. A nervous chuckle of acknowledgement, a perplexed expression and Will would pass on to another. 'Perfectly charming fellow!' he would mutter, apropos the stranger just addressed; or, 'She's a lovely girl!' had it been a perhaps seventy-five year-old lady. Yet whenever he came into a room those in it looked up with anticipatory smiles of enjoyment; and any sense of offhandedness in treatment would be replaced by a feeling in everyone contacted that he or she had found a friend. He made people feel valued. Shyness and initial inscrutability spoiled nothing.

Will wrote many plays, or fragments of plays, which were never produced, or which were performed once or twice in such places as village halls, or in churches. He might try these, without success, on commercial managements, but the exercise had given him satisfaction whatever the outcome. He sometimes wrote at the behest of a friend or a cause. *Uncle Dick's Surprise*, a children's play, a Christmas mystery story written in 1970, was one such – kindly reviewed, too, by a few critics who came to see it in a village hall and who recognised behind the charming fantasy a note of seriousness familiar to all who knew him well. His pen was always active. He had an idea – more often than not an excellent idea – and he started to write. He needed to write. He wrote as other men sing in the bath. Lines, with natural rhythm, came to him with remorseless felicity.

Plays, if not immediately tried on agents or managements – or if tried and rejected – would be stuffed into drawers and perhaps pulled out long afterwards. He also had a considerable following in France and Germany. The French warmed to his sensibility, his generosity of spirit, his manifest family feeling and his wit. His brand of humour, rooted in his own background and origins, might have been supposed too alien to evoke sympathy; the contrary was the case. In France his humour was '*toujours aimable*'. '*Il ne blesse jamais*' – he is never wounding – ran one biographical note, and it was true and congenial. His stance in the matter of the bombing of Le Havre was remembered, and by no means to his discredit. He was, they reckoned, '*le gentleman britannique par excellence*', and his plays were translated and performed with understanding and enjoyment. A particular wing of the modern language faculty of the Ecole Centrale at Lille University, the Centre de langues vivantes, is named after him.

Will's wit, in France, was likened to that of Wilde, and his delicacy with the emotions found not wholly unlike Marivaux, even Alfred de Musset. His battle with critics who condemned for reasons of class prejudice rather than artistic judgement was quoted with approval. In a French 'portrait' of Will his own words were greeted with understanding.

'You are a reactionary and an aristocrat and a relation of the Leader of the Tory Party.' 'Ah,' said I, 'There speak the politicians.' And that, of course, is what they were. They weren't critics in the true sense . . . artistic critics, taking every offering at its artistic value, quite regardless of its subject or its setting. Had they knocked me for my lack of skill in writing and construction, for ineptitude, for being boring and long-winded, that would have been legitimate. But they did not do that or – if they did – it was because, in their view, all those faults were automatically the lot of such an author as myself, writing on subjects that they disapproved of . . .

The French like good robust blows given and taken in the world of letters and drama. Will's vigorous defence of his philosophy was enjoyed by his admirers in France as much as his wit was relished.[1] He had, they said, taken on the 'dragon' of contemporary criticism *'pour faire partager au public, ravi, son univers secret, magique, légèrement fou, où le rire optimiste et l'amour raisonnable triomphent . . .'* Such tributes were as elegant as they were perceptive.

His plays were presented and ran at intervals all over the world. He himself had said at the height of the 'New Wave', when his own writings were ignored, jeered at and unremunerated, that a well-made play would always one day find its audience; and his own work demonstrated it. Inevitably the better plays are those which revive; but Will would not have resented that, and he realised (although seldom with public acknowledgement) that however loyal he was to all his plays, his 'children', some were better favoured than others.

In the next decade of life, from 1978 to 1988, Will was as busy as ever, writing a large number of plays both performed and unperformed, both for stage and television. His next published work, however, was a second volume of autobiography, published by Collins in 1979. He called it *Mr Home Pronounced Hume*, drawing on a line of witty abuse by Kenneth Tynan, who once wrote, 'Mr Home, pronounced Hume, makes me foam, pronounced fume.' Will's book was a general survey of life to date – primarily professional, playwriting life, although the events at Le Havre and the subsequent experience of prison were given another short chapter. The book reflected, on the whole, Will's contentment. He wrote charmingly of Rachel and his good fortune; she it was who had once restored him to confident health and bolstered his creative power, and he knew it. He worried

1. 'William Douglas Home', Hélène Catsiapis, Paris, 1992.

about Trades Union power as a threat to democracy (a worry to find expression in a play, *The Eleventh Hour*). He relived the struggle over *Aunt Edwina*. He had a brief tilt at drama critics – some people found a touch of unwonted bitterness here, but considering what Will had suffered it was extremely restrained. He wrote a little – hopefully – about his racing. He summed up.

Of Will's plays which have not so far reached a stage several were written during this period. *The Eleventh Hour* was a 'Topical', anticipated by the *Evening News* in January 1979 as 'a new comedy . . . about Trades Unions and a female Prime Minister'. The actual female Prime Minister was, in reality, some months away and the run of circumstances which attended Margaret Thatcher's first year of power were essentially different from those sketched by Will, but he aimed to catch a tide and it might have been effective. In the play there is a looming general strike, a political crisis, a coalition government (this from Will, enemy of coalitions!) and threatened unrest. The Prime Minister, 'Mary Teacher', makes a resounding (but excessively long) speech at the Guildhall calling on the 'militants' supporting the strike to go home, since otherwise the whole system of democracy will have broken down and Britain will be ungovernable. The curtain falls on a question mark as the clock strikes. Will they? Will was unhappy at what seemed to many an arrogant misuse of economic power by some union leaders, followed by supporters bullied into acquiescence.

By making the play's *pièce de résistance* the eloquence of the Prime Minister, Will was, in effect, preaching the possibility of reason, conveyed by well-conceived and well-spoken words, triumphing over brute force – and without need to resort to countervailing brute force. The hope and the possibility were congenial to him. Theatrical managements were sceptical as to whether audiences, as Peter Saunders put it, would want to come and see 'a series of political viewpoints'. This was surely right; *The Eleventh Hour* is polemic, without much other interest. It is, however, strong polemic. It showed Will, unusually, somewhat depressed about human nature. The forces of reason, compromise and moderation, as expressed by the Prime Minister and her coalition, may triumph; but probably won't. 1979 was an uneasy year for Britain. Soon the play would be overtaken by events. It was not, fortunately, very accurate in prophecy.

Another unperformed play (also written up in the press) came later. *Retirement Age* was an enjoyable skit on Denis and Margaret Thatcher, with Margaret planning retirement and having taken up golf. It was entertaining, perceptive as to character, light-hearted and not unkind. There were others during this period – plays about the judiciary (*Contempt of Court*), with extended treatment by Will of his *Honest Burglar* theme; about the Royal Family – particularly sensitive for Will, since he was well-acquainted with several members of it; yet another about the double standards applied to each other by British and Germans (*The Ski Instructor*); about the medical profession. There was a one-act curtain-raiser, *Dramatic Licence*, imagining a scene from the lives of Gilbert and Sullivan and D'Oyly Carte, written to precede a production at the Savoy of *Trial by Jury* in the centenary year. There were TV plays – *On Such a Night*, a partner-exchanging frolic; *You're Alright, How am I?*, a send-up of psychiatry which drew a good many snorts from TV critics. None of this made many ripples – or significant money.

There were also, however, six straight plays, and although four were exercises on familiar themes and made little mark, two were near Will's heart.

Of the first four, one, *Her Mother Came Too*, at least showed Will's ever-present generosity. Hermione Baddeley played the lead. It was a well-crafted 'mother-in-law' play, produced at Leatherhead in 1982. Unfortunately the star forgot a good many of her lines on the First Night, when, as hoped, West End managements were represented at Leatherhead on reconnaissance. There was embarrassed disappointment; but when Hermione Baddeley took her curtain call to applause (she was perennially popular) she raised her hand and said, 'Don't clap me. I was terrible. I owe you all – and the rest of the cast – an apology. But come back in a few days and it will be terrific!' This, of course, went straight to the audience's hearts and she received an ovation. Will was completely relaxed about it. A bad First Night on a provincial 'try-out', with visiting London managements represented, was inevitably disappointing but his magnanimity never wavered. He was as incapable of recrimination as he was of condemnation, and he told everyone that the play would be fine and that the leading actress was superb. It never reached London.

Four Hearts Doubled, produced in 1982 at Windsor was – in the words of Peter Hall, who turned it down for the National – 'full of your usual grace and wit'. It is an elegantly constructed

little charade of matrimonial switching, unfaithfulness and suspected unfaithfulness; of much-married Americans, dinner and
bridge. Reviewers wrote of 'genuinely funny scenes . . . as always
with Mr Douglas Home', but it was found somewhat too predictable. This was Will in Coward-land, where he was perfectly at
home in terms of pace and wit; but his talents were best used in
a less brittle mode.

The Golf Umbrella had been tried at Birmingham in 1981.
Another verbally sharpshooting quartet (one of whom is an ageing
playwright who fears he has written himself out) play the ball to
and fro over the conversational net with Will's usual skill; and
with (as often) a strong autobiographical touch, as the playwright
wrestles to evolve new dramatic themes and more believable
characters. It probably reflected Will's own sense that ideas were
not coming to him with their previous ease – understandably.
Reviews were friendly and some managements were tempted but
didn't fall. 'A hilarious comedy, bearing all the hallmarks of the
playwright's skill and panache,' ran one paper; and another – a
very fair comment on even the least distinguished of Will's work
– 'We laugh some of the time, chuckle most of the time and feel
all the time that we are being entertained.'

The fourth play in this quartet, *After the Ball is Over* was
produced by Anthony Quayle's 'Compass' productions at the
Old Vic in London in March 1985. It was a curious essay for
Will and many thought it an aberration. In the play there is
to be a Hunt Ball at Drayton Castle, where the Duke of Drayton,
Master of Foxhounds, is getting ready amiably to preside – many
of Will's stage characters and settings were named from his own
families, friends, home. We appear to be comfortably in Douglas
Home country, and many critics – absurdly – concentrated on
this fact and expressed their distastes for Dukes and Hunt Balls.
There is, in the play, an anti-hunting lobby active, and a vote
against hunting has just been passed by Parliament. Battlelines
have been drawn and, as so often with Will, there are sympathetic characters both sides of the lines. Another posse of critics
supposed the play to be primarily concerned with the argument
about blood sports and reproved (or, in one case, approved) Will
for appearing ambiguous on the issue.

Sadly, the critics should (and a good many did) have fastened
on a wholly implausible element in the play, which most people
thought wrecked it, whatever its other skills or demerits. At the
end of the first act the Duchess of Drayton and the Hunt Secretary

(they were lovers long ago) fall to their deaths from a balcony – the crash is heard on stage. Sudden death must be inappropriate to the comedy-shading-into-farce which *After the Ball is Over* constitutes. The fact that, at the moment the deaths are discovered, a hunting horn blows 'The Kill' in the ballroom (presumably instructed by the Duke/Master) appears extraordinary and tasteless (and no doubt to many incomprehensible). The atmosphere was entirely wrong and audiences could not easily understand what sort of a play they were supposed to be watching.

Reviews were harsh, surely with justice – 'A sad business indeed'; 'This Ball couldn't end soon enough.' The Duke – designed by Will as a bluff, sympathetic, tolerant character of the kind he so often drew well – is made by the turn of incredible circumstances to appear callous and unattractive. It was most unusual for Will to mistake mood in this way, or to appear insensitive to it. The points made (on both sides of the argument about hunting) were fair and often funny; and, as ever, there were entertaining exchanges. It was not enough.

Very different were the two plays in this period which came from Will's heart: *David and Jonathan* and *Portraits*.

Throughout 1981 Will was frequently warned, and was gloomily convinced, of the seriousness of his financial situation. There had been no real commercial success since *The Kingfisher* (1977), which had narrowly made a profit but had not been the sort of earner represented by *The Secretary Bird* (1968) or even *Lloyd George Knew My Father* (1972). The only play pending in autumn 1982 was *Four Hearts Doubled*, and in the event it did little. Will was told that his debt to the bank was increasing at a rate astronomically higher than his actual income; and astronomically higher even than his anticipated income (and his anticipations were implausibly optimistic) unless some remarkable success appeared. In his play *In the Red*, Will had depicted only too faithfully the plight of an author whose takings are episodic, unpredictable, and which – in his case – carry regrettably long gaps from one financial success to another.

This was at the heart of the problem. Will was still drawing, at uneven intervals, very respectable sums in royalties from his plays. He was by no means extravagant (except perhaps in one respect). He was exceptionally benevolent, but he lived moderately. His expenses, however, were financed too often and for too long by the bank, when plays failed to come up to expectations; and borrowing was, inevitably, financed by further borrowing. He thought the bank (National Westminster) unreasonable in their (as he saw it) stringency, and exchanged letters with the Chairman. Courteously but unproductively. On top of this was Will's determined refusal to understand much about taxation; and his diminishing reserves of capital. He had illusions about what could be achieved by promotion, actually, for example, subsidising his publishers (to a significant sum) in order to advertise *Mr Home Pronounced Hume* – with little result. Letters from his conscientious accountants became gloomier and gloomier through 1981 and the three years following, and there was no theatrical winner on the horizon. His foreign rights, often so profitable, were in a serious mess. His racing account was unfortunately getting more and more heavily into debt. His accountant asked him at least to examine the possibility of some savings. Somehow. Somewhere.

'I've had an idea,' said Will.

'Yes?'

'What about my not paying your last bill?'

He never allowed these concerns to cloud life or reduce the fun and enjoyment his company gave to others. They never reduced his quiet generosity, which was exercised as much in this difficult period as ever. He was greatly in demand as an after-dinner or guest speaker and his quizzical, detached humour always delighted. He found the right anecdote or throwaway line appropriate to the particular company. He spoke on P. G. Wodehouse at the National Theatre. At an anniversary dinner of the Garrick Club he quoted a Scottish peer asked to toast 'Absent friends' at an Archers' Dinner in Edinburgh: 'My Lords and Gentlemen, I give you "Absent Friends", and in that category I include the wine waiter, who I haven't seen since the beginning of the evening!' He was also brilliantly accomplished at any sort of Memorial Address, speaking with great beauty – and with as much wit as on any other sort of occasion – at Celia Johnson's Memorial Service at St Martin-in-the-Fields. Will's financial problems were vivid but they never subtracted anything from his style or his charm. Furthermore – and here pride played its proper part – he never allowed them to bother others. Deep down, perhaps, a certain aristocratic disdain for money matters influenced him; his mind, had he bent it to them, was well up to it but he left such things to others (although he enjoyed, periodically, the detail of contracts and he positively loved the detail of betting transactions). Friends had often sought help from Will, and generally got it. He never reciprocated. The difficulties were his own, and he, not others, would bear them; and solve them. He simply reached for his pen.

In 1984 *David and Jonathan* was produced at the Redgrave Theatre, Farnham. In reviewing it Harold Hobson, an admirer of most although not all of Will's plays and a reviewer of immense experience, wrote, 'More critical injustice [has been] done to him than to any other British dramatist of our time.' 'The strength of his convictions,' Hobson added, 'tends to be hidden from a superficial glance by the urbanity of his style.' It was a fair comment on one of the most unusual of Will's 'Sermons'.

David and Jonathan is a play about homosexuality. Will depicts two young men who have been in the Navy together (one still is, the other has been dismissed); and in love with each other since schooldays. The elder, David, is now engaged to marry a girl, Mary. The younger, Jonathan, is heartbroken. He and David have gone through a form of homosexual 'marriage', conducted, illegally, by a 'nutcase' parson in London; and Jonathan persuades himself that this, with his (genuinely felt) love for David, constitutes an 'impediment' to the latter's marriage to Mary. He interrupts the reading of banns in Mary's parish church, and the whole action takes place in the vestry (although the audience on occasion hears what is going on in the church itself) with, in succession, the Vicar, the Rural Dean and the Bishop interviewing the various parties, in the hope of persuading Jonathan to give up his damaging objections. Mary's father, a bookie, is furious at the disclosures about David, and in an attempt to pressurise Mary into calling the wedding off has talked to the press.

There is plenty of tension. Will Jonathan interrupt the banns a second and a third time? What will be his reaction to senior clerical exhortation? How will it all turn out? The underlying situation is a strong one and Will was commended in reviews for giving it 'thoughtful treatment'. 'Douglas Home triumphs again,' was a headline after the First Night. The dialogue between all parties is sensitive and believable; there is sufficient – but not too much – humour to lighten things. The ending is happy, in that the marriage of David and Mary proceeds (the Bishop officiating) without mishap – the Bishop, indeed, frankly referring to David's earlier homosexuality and admitting the same himself, as a schoolboy; dismissively and convincingly before the congregation. The ending is also possibly happy for Jonathan, who in Will's ultimate version seems likely to have 'emerged' from homosexuality, becoming (in an epilogue) a godfather to David and Mary's baby, and on the way to heterosexual love with Jennie, Mary's sister. In an earlier version (which Will called 'Marriage Rites') this latter development is left uncertain, even improbable (although Will had written it in his original text), with Jonathan still in an emotionally broken state.

Will expounds the background situation without equivocation.

VICAR: You're going to tell me David's married, are you?
JONATHAN: That's right.
VICAR: And you know who to?
JONATHAN: Yes.
VICAR: Who then?
JONATHAN: Me.
VICAR: I beg your pardon?
JONATHAN: I said 'Me'. Me and Dave's married.

Nor is Will equivocal about the ecclesiastical reaction to this (a 'certificate' has been produced).

JONATHAN: It's signed, too. By the bloke who did it.
VICAR: Yes, I've heard of him. He's done this sort of thing before, you know. And maybe since, assuming he's not been defrocked. It isn't binding, you know.
JONATHAN: Isn't it?
VICAR: No, not in anybody's eyes but his.
JONATHAN: And mine. And Dave's until he ran out on me.

Will's own attitude was tolerant – he was tolerant of all minorities and most points of view. He resented bullying attitudes, whether in majorities or minorities, but his stance throughout *David and Jonathan* was one of sympathy – from a distance. Homosexuality was something to shrug, perhaps smile, about, something certainly to tolerate: something inevitable in some conditions of society, some organisations, some phases of life, often something from which to emerge.

VICAR: The world's not like it was when we were their age, Mr Graham – it's more tolerant and understanding.
MR GRAHAM [Mary's father]: More's the pity.

VICAR: I'm afraid I have to disagree with you – broadmindedness is not a fault. Indeed, in my book its a virtue.

Mr Graham reckons that homosexuals like David 'don't reform'. The Vicar suggests they grow out of it – and that, anyway, Jonathan's love, errant or not, is sincere. The Dean (the next cleric to get to work on the situation) tells Jonathan that David 'has now moved on'. The homosexual marriage ceremony was 'illegal, a mockery, a fraud, a gimmick'. He asks Jonathan 'to give up this silly nonsense'. 'He's grown out of you. He's passed that stage of adolescence.'

But Jonathan does not see it like that. Obstinate, he reckons that the love David and he have shared has validity. Only when the Bishop talks to him, drawing on his own experience, does he, miserably, yield.

BISHOP: Schoolboys tend to fall in love with one another, when they're good-looking; I know I did.
JONATHAN: You did!
BISHOP: Yes – why not? ... When youth and beauty meet I find it very hard to think of sin ... You see, adolescence automatically develops into manhood, if you are prepared to let it.

Will, therefore, resolves the play's situation by depicting the love of David and Jonathan in terms of a 'phase' – as most have at some time experienced – rather than an expression of congenital homosexuality, unlikely to change or incapable of doing so. This, although the earlier sequences, and Jonathan's fumbling, miserable declaration of his feelings, suggest the latter.

Some people felt that Will was dodging an issue here, sliding away from the real emotions he had realistically described in the earlier scenes, sliding away with a tolerant, no-nonsense, understanding pat on the head. They felt that in suggesting that a 'cured' Jonathan may end up satisfactorily partnering Jennie, Will was being altogether too tidy; was ducking out. The whole situation would, of course, have been subjected to different conventions and correctitudes a few years later; but even at that time Will was thought by some evasive. Others thought the play suffered from lack of a strong, high-tension confrontation at some point between the two young men. When reviewing *Now Barabbas* long years ago, James Agate wrote:

> 'Now Barabbas' swims in homosexuality [this was overstatement, but certainly Will wrote two of the characters as explicitly

211

so] – homosexuality treated in comic and sentimental but never in a realistic vein . . . what the governor in this play does is to shelve his problem by sending the young man to another gaol in the hope that the change of air will turn his tresses into a crop of manly stubble . . . I do not believe in placating the censor by throwing a sop.[2]

Had Agate lived to see *David and Jonathan* he would have fulminated in the same way. Will was placating no censor but he was – as often in very different works – easing an emotional dilemma by pushing it into a context of everyday development and experience; of 'normality'. The genuinely 'abnormal' was, perhaps, too tough to contemplate. He had no wish to condemn it: he did not desire to explore it. In some eyes, therefore, *David and Jonathan* represents trivialisation of a serious theme and it is certainly true that when faced with a really big emotional fence to jump Will, in his writing, could often be accused of avoiding it. Nevertheless it is a moving play, and although it had no commercial triumph it showed Will's skill and seriousness again.

In 1985 Will's life was dominated by two happenings, both of them traumatic, and both surmounted with grace and courage.

In August, Will and Rachel moved from Drayton. House and garden had been bigger than they needed, and were expensive to maintain. It was essential to cut costs and raise some capital. Recent years had not been financially successful. They sold Drayton, lodged for a little with Rachel's widowed mother at Mill Court, where they had first become engaged, and then moved to Derry House in Kilmeston, Hampshire, a village near Alresford. The house was smaller, the garden more manageable. They did not have the superb view enjoyed from Drayton, but the position of Derry was excellent, the village charming and the country around was Hampshire at its best.

The decision to sell was inevitably and deeply disturbing. Drayton had been their home from almost the beginning of their marriage. They had brought up their family there, seen success and failure, disappointment and triumph. It was a byword for fun and laughter to a very large circle of their friends, who felt as wretched as did Will and Rachel at the move. But the resilience

2. 'Ego 9'.

and courage of both soon carried them forward. Rachel, especially, was very skilful at decoration, at exploiting the possibilities of a house; and, above all, of a garden. Surprisingly soon 'Derry' was as synonymous with enjoyment and hospitality as Drayton had been; but the sale had felt like an amputation.

The second dominant event of 1985 was the condition of Will's heart. He felt rather unwell for about five days (attributed to hay fever!) and Rachel became anxious and sought a second medical opinion. This directed him instantly to the King Edward VII Hospital at Midhurst, where it was discovered that his heart was in a bad state and had almost stopped (he insisted that it had altogether stopped and that he had represented a revolution in medical knowledge!). A pacemaker was fitted at Midhurst which left him in considerable discomfort. A second, more permanent, article, was inserted on 24 October at the Middlesex Hospital in London, to which Will was moved; and where he was almost immediately entertaining friends and keeping them in such irrepressible bouts of laughter that the Ward Sister's authority was endangered and she complained that the number of visitors exceeded all previous limits and experience. On the day of the operation, furthermore, a horse of Will's, a hurdler, won its race; and was sold thereafter. Back at Derry life soon resumed almost as if heart attacks and domestic moves had never been.

Will's next play was *Portraits*. With *Portraits* Will went back to war. War on war. The central character (*Portraits* is, in effect, an 'Historical') is Augustus John, played initially by Keith Michell – 'infinitely better company,' wrote Irving Wardle in *The Times*, 'than the ingratiating landed gentry of his light comedies'; a comment of the sort Will by now took with resignation. The play was put on at the Malvern Festival in May 1987 and tried at Winchester. It was produced in London at the Savoy Theatre in August 1987.

Portraits has a number of interweaving themes and they are all in different ways and degrees absorbing. 'A long, taxing but always enthralling text,' ran the *Evening News* review, and it was fair. The play also reads beautifully, perhaps better than any other by Will. He put a great deal of his heart into *Portraits*. It was not particularly successful commercially but it was well received, acknowledged as honourable, technically skilful and theatrically compelling – 'a play for acting', as the *Financial Times* had it and as could far more often than not be said of Will's work although not always recognised.

The themes Will wove were, firstly, the character and, as the play runs (it opens in 1944, closes with John's death in 1960), the decline, of Augustus John. The great painter, still capable of sporadic brilliance to the last, feels himself abandoned by his muse. Will gave Augustus John excellent lines, salty and convincing. He is painting his friend and fellow artist, Matthew Smith, who has abandoned his own painting in misery at the loss of his two sons early in the war.

AUGUSTUS: I've not done much of this, have you?
MATTHEW: No.
AUGUSTUS: I've painted myself, often. But then I'm a damned good model. Fiery and flamboyant. And more often pissed than not. All the correct things. Whereas you're like old Dodgson's dormouse looking longingly towards the teapot with a view to tucking up inside it. Still, I'm quite enjoying myself.

And he and his beloved Dorelia manage to persuade Smith into returning to his easel. But at the play's end Augustus is wretched about his own decline:

AUGUSTUS: When I've emptied this damned bottle – I won't keep it, will I? ... I'll get another one, that's full ... and that's the way it used to be with women in the old days – but it isn't any longer. All that I can manage now is uncork the occasional half-bottle when I get a model who's sufficiently besotted to survive the operation ... so I can't paint and I can't screw –

Will's second theme is unhappiness at the threat of war, particularly the nuclear war which occupied most attention (improbable though it was) in the Fifties and Sixties. Augustus joins Bertrand Russell on an anti-nuclear platform in Trafalgar Square. Back in his Dorset studio he is painting Cecil Beaton.

AUGUSTUS: ... I was in the Gallery. And so I tottered down the steps and went across the road and sat beside him on the platform. Did they have a photograph?
CECIL: They did.
AUGUSTUS: What did I look like?
CECIL: An old tramp on methylated spirits.

There are three portraits painted in the play – of Cecil Beaton (the only personality in the play actually known by Will), Matthew Smith and General Montgomery, and each was played in turn by the same actor, Simon Ward. Each is entertainingly and persuasively drawn by Will, and each reacts to Augustus in his own way – Beaton and Smith are old friends of his, to Montgomery he is a (most extraordinary) stranger. The Montgomery portrait is the first to be introduced. It is 1944, before D-Day, and Will has Monty accompanied to the London studio by a young and very handsome Aide, who knows something of pictures, admires Augustus's work and in turn immediately impresses Augustus, not only by his looks and charm but because (Augustus feels, as does Dorelia) he has a look of death upon him, will not survive the campaign. This happens – the character as drawn is fictional. Augustus periodically harks back to this incident, reinforcing, as it does, his antipathy to all war.

The exchanges with Monty are believable. Augustus cannot capture – or evoke – animation and feels gloomy.

AUGUSTUS: She [Dorelia] finds the shadows overwhelming and depressing and the whole thing ugly – not excluding me – and so she shuts her eyes and chatters like a magpie instead. When's the Second Front?
MONTY: I don't know. And I wouldn't tell you if I did.
AUGUSTUS: You do know, General, but you're not saying.
MONTY: Then why ask me?
AUGUSTUS: Just to see if your eyes lit up.
MONTY: Did they?
AUGUSTUS: No – they flickered, that's all. And you can't catch flickers with a bloody paintbrush.

He persuades Bernard Shaw to come and talk to Monty,[3] to 'lighten him up' – with a degree of success (although perhaps fewer degrees of authenticity). Will had a sympathetic feeling for Shaw since his loyal friend Nancy, Lady Astor, soon after his discharge from prison, had once driven him to Ayot St Lawrence to call on the aged seer, had found GBS incommunicado, working in the garden shed in which he wrote, and had banged on it shouting, 'Come out of there, you old fool, you've written enough nonsense in your life!' Will (and probably Shaw) had enjoyed this. He and Lady Astor were devoted to each other.

The Montgomery portrait (by Augustus) is not a success.

3. This happened, as described in Montgomery's *Memoirs* (Collins, 1958).

AUGUSTUS: You're not the kind of subject that appeals to me. I'd rather paint a gypsy or a tart, and, through no fault of your own, you're neither.

And Will (somewhat incredibly) introduces and ascribes to Shaw a sentiment of his own in respect of Monty:

SHAW [to
Augustus]:   I wouldn't be at all surprised if the Field Marshal wouldn't like to see old Winston playing politics again, by offering the boys in Germany who don't like Hitler peace-terms.

This was Will astride a hobbyhorse and however retrospectively laudable it was historically implausible and dramatically ineffective. But Will needed to make *Portraits* (and the Montgomery portrait inevitably bore the brunt of this) a vehicle for reiteration of the sentiments he had so long held, wishful though some of the thinking may have been. There is some straight 'nuclear disarmament' talk near the end – Will managed to elide this campaign with his own loathing of war in almost all its forms, and the play was written and produced before the (peaceful) success of a completely opposite policy had been strikingly demonstrated to the world.

Near the end, however, Will returns to the dying Augustus in a lyrical passage. Augustus is with Cecil Beaton.

AUGUSTUS: Do you know what I'd do if I was young enough to do it, Cecil?
CECIL: I could make a guess, Gus.
AUGUSTUS: . . . I'd go off to the gypsies . . . and I'd sing the songs we used to sing together round the fire. And I'd sleep beneath the moon with some young creature who'd never bruised the soles of her feet on a city pavement. And I'd wake to the dawn chorus and the rising sun to meet a fresh day, and we'd look at one another and see beauty, newly woken in each other's eyes and in each other's bodies. And we'd know what freedom was and what God made the world for.

When dealing with the human heart rather than strategy or politics Will was unquestionably more perceptive and *Portraits* shows it. Augustus John's family did not like the play, considering among other things that it misrepresented the artist's essential good manners. Nevertheless there is beauty and insight in it; and the politics cloud but do not spoil that beauty and that insight.

In 1985 Will had published a selection of the letters he had written home from his time of wartime service in the Army and from prison,[4] thus reminding himself and others of an ancient wound. In February 1988 a number of newspapers reported that he was hoping to obtain a pardon[5] in respect of his conviction by court martial long ago. The wound still itched.

4. *Sins of Commission*, Michael Russell, 1985.
5. In fact, a review of sentence; but 'pardon' was often, albeit inaccurately, reported.

CHAPTER XII

The Unhealed Scar

The wound still itched.

The immediate cause, the catalyst, was the affair of Dr Kurt Waldheim, President of Austria and a previous Secretary General of the United Nations. Waldheim had been an officer in the Wehrmacht during the war and certain hostile newspapers reported that he was known to have signed, or at least connived at, orders for the deportations of some categories of prisoner and some Jews from occupied Yugoslavia and Greece; deportations which may have led to their deaths in concentration camps. For Waldheim it was pointed out that he had been an extremely junior officer at the time, simply performing a routine and bureaucratic task, obeying orders whose significance was probably unclear and with whose origins he had little or nothing to do. A later report by independent historians could find nothing to support criminal charges. The public dispute (with difficult and provocative diplomatic overtones, since the head of a friendly state was being criticised) occupied a good deal of media attention. One of its consequences was, of course, to raise again the matter of culpability if legal orders are obeyed in war whose consequences are – or later prove to have been – deplorable.

Will joined battle. He consulted his lawyers and applied for a review of his own case, a review at which he should be legally represented. His arguments (if they were permitted to be put) would be chiefly addressed to the circumstances at Le Havre at the beginning of September 1944; and in particular to the alleged refusal of the British authorities to allow the German commander to evacuate civilians. Some 3,000 French civilians had been killed by the subsequent British bombardment and it was (Will might contend) for debate whether this bombardment, following that refusal, did not constitute a circumstance which made orders to take part in the subsequent assault illegal – as being an exploitation of a 'war crime'; or at least possibly so in the eyes of a troubled and conscientious participant. If, Will argued, Dr Waldheim was to be categorised as a potential war criminal because he had played a tiny part in a chain of events which had led to the death of Jews or Greek and Yugoslav partisans, the implication must be that his moral duty had lain in disobedience. What, therefore, of Lieutenant Douglas Home? Where had his moral duty lain, when ordered to play an equally tiny part in the battle of Le Havre, where measures (resumed aerial bombardment of a civilian population, in effect) were planned which would also, in all probability, lead to the deaths of numerous French people? People whom a different policy and agreement to a truce might have allowed to reach safety? Had his duty, like Waldheim's, been disobedience? And if so, why cashiering and a year's imprisonment with hard labour?

There was a further point. Will reckoned to have discovered that at Calais and Dunkirk, whose investment by the advancing Allies had followed that of Le Havre during the 1944 campaign, an agreement had been reached between besiegers and besieged that civilians might be evacuated. He contended that this policy, different from that adopted at Le Havre, implied a tacit acceptance of the underlying reason for his actions; as, possibly, did a subsequent change of policy towards the Allied bombing of French towns in the course of the campaign. There was a quasi-technical point also averred. Will had pleaded Not Guilty at his trial, enabling him to enter a written statement in defence. To the extent that these latter points − inconsistency of British policy − could be regarded as relevant to his defence it might be suggested that a court martial should have investigated their substance; and did not do so.

Will petitioned in the first instance, in March 1988, against the court martial's sentence; and when that petition was denied success by the Army Board he applied himself, through his legal advisers, to seeking a new hearing, with legal representation present. He was not, in fact, accorded a hearing − his petition was read but no arguments were entertained beyond those recorded in it. He was informed that it was not possible to have a sentence reviewed without review of findings, so this he now sought.

Before Will's campaign − in the first instance, for a review of the court martial's sentence − had got far the BBC proposed to make a programme, a film centred on the affair at Le Havre. The programme, made by the Documentary Features Department, would be shown in the following year, 1989. It was intended as a long (three-part) programme, of which the third part would be a debate about a soldier's duty in circumstances which place moral strain on conscience, and about Will's case in particular. Will provisionally agreed to take part, anyway in the debate at the conclusion. Wisely, he consulted lawyers – clearly the publicity aroused by a programme of that sort could affect the minds of those who would presumably one day consider his application for another hearing. The effect might be beneficial; or neutral; or injurious.

The programme makers then began to seek contact with large numbers of former members of 141 Regiment, Royal Armoured Corps, an assiduous effort which lasted most of 1988. A good many soldiers who had served with Will, long retired, had of course read of his efforts in the newspapers and some had already written to him. Now, in many cases, they had to make up their minds about whether themselves to take part in a programme: if so, what to say; and thus what, after forty-four years, they thought.

Opinions differed. Some, of all ranks, wrote to Will wishing him good luck in his endeavours and were strongly sympathetic. Some spoke in the same sense to the BBC programme makers, sending messages of encouragement. One ex-officer, who had acted as escort to Will when he was in arrest, wrote of how impressed he had been with Will's arguments at that time and with the moral basis for the stand he had taken. 'I hope they listen!' wrote an ex-trooper of the Buffs. 'I would like to wish you success in your appeal to clear your name.'

Some felt otherwise. They remembered Will's often expressed determination to make some sort of demonstration against Allied policies with which he disagreed, particularly the demand for 'unconditional surrender'. They believed that with those views he had been irresponsible to accept a commission (Will, of course, argued that he had attempted to resign it, but that was of dubious possibility in wartime). They resented the fact that Colonel Waddell (who had died quite recently) had been a victim of Will's actions – attempting to be forbearing he had, in effect, been dismissed for condonation. Waddell had received scant recognition for a wartime record which had been zealous and honourable; and the hurdle which had brought him down was Will. He was a man whose achievements both in business and athletically were outstanding – at Fettes, captain of cricket, hockey, rugby football, capped fifteen times for Scotland, one known not only for his prowess but for his kindly encouragement of others. Although he had been promoted afterwards his loss of regimental command did not dispose people in Will's favour. And some suspected (wrongly) that Will had himself supplied lists of names to the BBC and was a prime agent of the programme as something which might help his case for a pardon. They felt that a programme which might leave a general impression of Will as martyr would probably blur the essential fact that he had deliberately refused to take part in a battle; a battle in which a good many British soldiers had died. Had self-preservation played no part in his calculations at the time?

Some wrote to Will expressing doubts about the proposed programme. Such letters were friendly, but critical. Will, in replying to them, reiterated his well-known views: that his treatment reflected double standards and that the public reaction to the Waldheim case showed it. Why punish Home for following his conscience in refusing an order while simultaneously arguing that Waldheim and others should have done exactly that? In Will's replies a long-held misconception again appeared. He supposed that the cashiering (as opposed to the imprisonment) was a particular disgrace and could be annulled. Not so: an officer had to be stripped of rank – cashiered or dismissed the service, whose effect was the same – if he was sentenced to serve time in prison. It had been a necessary legality. In Will's letters, however, it was once again plain how deeply the whole incident had marked him and marked him still. He was accused of bringing up again after over forty years a 'very small incident' in the story of the Second World War. 'But not small to me,' Will replied, 'it was very, very BIG and still is.' He knew, too, that the cashiering had particularly wounded Lord Home, and that probably continued to give remembered pain.

But the programme was never made. Will disliked the suggested format. He disliked the element of 'faction' which he thought was now intended, the emphasis on his own background, upbringing and education. This smacked a good deal of the sort of stereotyping he so loathed in criticism of his work as a dramatist. Will's contentions and arguments deserved, he thought, to be examined on their own merits and not to be coloured by a tendentious and probably class-conscious personal treatment. Few people will dismiss his concerns as baseless, and most will understand his withdrawal from the programme, which was discontinued.

There were, however, two other television programmes which dealt with the matter, either centrally or peripherally. In March 1988, Central TV broadcast a programme on the general question of obedience to orders in war. Will appeared, and spoke well in a restrained way along familiar lines before a studio audience. And in June 1991, BBC2 broadcast a programme, 'Hero of Le Havre?', which had Will and his actions at its centre. In this programme – one much more acceptable to Will than the earlier confusion of issues with 'background' to which he had objected – Will discussed the matter with an interviewer, George Hume. The programme dwelt on the appalling suffering the British bombardment, particularly the first raid which took place on 5 September 1944, had inflicted. Citizens of Le Havre questioned – not unfairly – the British targetting policy which had claimed thousands of French lives and hardly killed a German on that occasion. And some British officers also spoke of their horror at the destruction and their reservations about its necessity. Will was not alone now – unlike in 1944, as it had then appeared to him, although even then some old friends had found his actions extremely brave.

Some press comment – as well as a very large number of personal letters – was favourable to Will, many seeing in his stand a lone and conscientious opponent of the policy of aerial bombardment which had claimed so many civilian lives. Some was hostile. Newspaper commentators varied between the *Observer*'s 'Anyone who sees this programme will almost certainly wish him the best of luck', and the *Daily Express*'s 'This unbalanced documentary was special pleading of a high order.' Will was described as using a 30-minute soapbox 'to whinge about how jolly unfair it all was'! The silliest journalistic comment was that if Will had been of humbler origins he would have fared worse – a private soldier would have been shot. No such sentence had been contemplated for an act of indiscipline since the time of the First World War. But among private correspondents – inevitably those wrote who agreed with him – there were many who felt that his act of conscience had made them feel very much better. Nor was it the case that the writers of these letters were ignorant of war. Many had been in Normandy at the time, as soldiers, and wrote with sympathy and encouragement.

So much for the media. The 1991 programme was broadcast a few days after Will's lawyers received a letter saying that the Army Board of the Defence Council had denied his petition against the finding and sentence of the Field General Court Martial held on 4 October 1944. That was the end of that.

People again began discussing the legal and moral issues involved.

It can never have been very likely that Will would make much headway in legal terms. He had initially hoped to challenge only the sentence of his court martial, and in particular the sentence of cashiering which he felt dishonourable. Only when told that to attempt this it was necessary to challenge the verdict itself, the verdict of guilty, did he deploy arguments for acquittal. These were slender. He argued that he had felt 'mentally unable' to obey the order he was charged with refusing: the Judge Advocate at the trial had addressed the Court on that point – surely pretty convincingly.[1] He had pointed to the non-examination by the Prosecution of inconsistency of Allied policy in respect of bombing, as it bore on his case: it didn't much, would be the ordinary lay reaction. He had, yet again, pleaded the inhumanity of indiscriminate bombardment of civilians, a proposition easy to endorse but harder to connect directly with his own offence.

For the fact, which few of even his most sympathetic friends felt disposed to forget, was that Will, knowingly and deliberately, had refused to obey an order in battle. Obedience is at the very heart of military duty. Every civilised man can accept that an order, even a nominally legitimate order, may be morally odious and that conscience may struggle with legality; but in Will's case the order, by his legal superior, was simply to take a subordinate and routine part in the battle to assault Le Havre. The preliminary bombardments – their necessity, targets, timing and effects – were not for him, and he had in any case known little or nothing in detail about them. The legality of the order given to him was virtually impossible to challenge except by contending that the whole conduct of the battle (because of the bombardments and the possible effect on civilians) was by definition illegal, and thus excused all participants from their obedience. This can never have been easy. In the light of the circumstances of 1944 most people would have supposed it near-impossible and most people would have been right.

Will, however, was fighting on moral rather than on legal grounds. He wanted to establish in the world's eyes that he had not behaved dishonourably – unwisely perhaps, illegally perhaps,

1. See Chapter V.

but not dishonourably. There was plenty of understanding of his views on 'unconditional surrender', the wisdom of which had often been widely questioned in the post-war years; but Will's contention that the war itself had become no longer 'a just war' aroused few echoes. His friends knew he had long argued that the whole struggle had been avoidable and could have been stopped earlier – knew and were unconvinced. He had, some thought, developed a monomania on the subject. Furthermore Will was thought by many to be confusing the policy of demanding only unconditional surrender from the German Reich (whether wise or unwise) with the treatment of German commanders in the field. He seemed to be thinking – indeed at times he wrote – as if the latter might more easily surrender were Allied governmental policy different. This was most improbable.

Will's most deeply felt point, raised by him at every stage and raised both at his trial in his Plea in Mitigation as well as in his Statement of Defence – and at the root of his attempt to obtain a review – was the issue of double standards. In support of the general thesis that war crimes were, arguably, committed by both sides he pointed to the partiality of Allied propaganda, which (for instance) depicted only the enemy as capable of firing on the Red Cross whereas his own experience showed differently. If the Allies were preaching to the enemy's armed forces that individuals should follow conscience and refuse to obey orders which involved participation in war crimes (and would one day be prosecuted by the victorious Allies if they chose otherwise), then where was consistency unless one applied the same criteria to the behaviour of our own people?

There are two separate aspects of 'double standards' here. First is the simple matter of how such a disobedient British soldier – disobedient on grounds of conscience – would be treated. Will had proposed to test that matter by offering himself as living example, and thereafter insisted that British failure to respect his conscience and acquit him of an offence proved inconsistency and hypocrisy. But the second aspect, *on which his argument of course largely depended,* was whether the action on which he based his disobedience – the bombing of Le Havre with considerable civilian casualties, after a refusal to agree a truce for the evacuation of civilians – constituted a 'war crime' in moral if not legal terms, and could justify his calculated act of insubordination.

The legitimacy or otherwise of the bombing of targets which will cause widescale civilian casualties has been debated at length.

In the Second World War, certainly by the time Will made his gesture, such bombings had been extensively practised by both sides and horrific casualties inflicted. Because Allied air power far exceeded that of the enemy, by mid-war Allied bombardment caused far greater casualties than German. By the middle of 1944 the air raids on Germany were claiming a huge weekly toll of dead and injured, and this would continue to the end. Most of these were civilians and many were women and children. Moral repugnance at this had not wholly disappeared but it had been largely overtaken by an understandable popular sense that the Germans were reaping many times a crop they had sown; and that victory, the ultimate benefit, demanded these actions.

To distinguish between the air offensive against Germany and the bombings of targets (in pursuance of the same object: victory) where the casualties might be 'friendly' was and is defensible in political terms and understandable in psychological terms. It was not particularly sound in moral terms. The target areas (and it is unlikely that Will knew anything about them) at a place like Le Havre were, arguably, military; but were so delineated (and based on less than perfect Intelligence) that a large number of civilians might also be brutally affected. Similarly the raids on German cities were targeted as 'industrial areas' or 'centres of communication' – legitimate targets; although, increasingly as the war went on and Allied bombing power increased, the object was to demoralise (in other words 'terrorise') the German civilian population to the point that they either fled, were useless for work or were dead. Civilians who suffered were, simply, unlucky to be there. This was somewhat different from the 'incidental' losses caused by air raids such as that at Le Havre but it cannot, surely, be argued that the latter were only more morally culpable because the victims were French. At issue were the morals of aerial bombardment. On the scale of such bombardment undertaken in the Second World War there was virtually bound to be civilian suffering on a horrendous scale.

'Indiscriminate' aerial bombardment of military and civilian targets was forbidden in a draft international convention in 1923 which was never ratified. Such raids as most of those on Germany between 1942 and 1945 (and on England in 1940, 1941 and 1942 as well as by the V-weapons in 1944) would inevitably have been debarred. It was generally claimed that such raids (when conducted by the enemy) were barbarous and contrary to all civilised conventions, but it was – perhaps sadly

– inconceivable that by 1944 such actions, however regrettable in political or human terms, could be regarded as actually constituting a crime. Too much had been done, by both sides, to have made such a proposition credible. Anyway, nobody could contend that the raids at Le Havre were truly indiscriminate, although their targets may have been selected with inadequate knowledge or scrupulosity. Le Havre was a defended place, a fortress.

Will, however – and he was explicit about this, both in his statement at his trial, and in his writings afterwards – *was not making a protest against, or primarily against, the bombing in which civilians died*, much though he deplored it for humane reasons. He was protesting at the bombing after civilians had not been allowed, by the Allies, to be evacuated under a truce; at the infliction, in other words, of *unnecessary* casualties. It was this, he was implicitly arguing, which had produced in his own mind an inability to take part with good conscience; and which might indeed (had the enemy's conduct rather than our own been at issue) have been denounced as a war crime.

There is no convention in international law or the usages of war which *binds* a commander to accept such a proposal for a truce. It may be humane; it may be practicable; it may, on the other hand, disadvantage the pursuit of the objects of battle; it must be discretionary. Will, on hearing of it after the event, formed the instant view that discretion had been exercised inhumanely and that this at once justified his own subsequent actions.

In legal terms this must be difficult to prove and in moral terms highly debatable. When Will's attempts to obtain a review were publicised, however, and when his original actions received widespread notice again between 1988 and 1991 it was, inevitably, on this aspect that opinion focused, as well as on the actual tragedy, the civilian losses themselves. He became the man who had protested against the unnecessary killing of large numbers of French people. His moral courage in so doing was lauded by correspondents in both France and Britain. Letters – including very moving letters from Le Havre, from people who had lost whole families and homes – flooded in. Some letters told Will how much the writer had always agreed with him, how brave was his stand, and how inexplicably inhumane and obtuse was now the attitude of the authorities, just as it had been at the time. The complexity of the case he had attempted to make was largely blurred and instead he was depicted simply as one epitomising humanity amidst the carnage of war. But the difference in the climate of public opinion between 1944, when people in Britain were losing friends and relatives daily and wanted to defeat and punish the enemy *coûte que coûte*, and 1991 when they weren't, and felt otherwise, showed very plain. In the earlier year Will was near universally excoriated. In the latter, near universally praised. The BBC programme title, 'Hero of Le Havre?', summed it up.

Nor, despite the complexities, was this wholly unfair. But, lastly, it will be best to see what had actually happened at Le Havre, in the late summer of 1944.

The Canadian First Army, the British I Corps and two British divisions, 49th and 51st, took part in the battle as well as numerous formations of the Royal Air Force and several warships of the Royal Navy. The German commander, Colonel Wildermuth, commanded some 11,000 men.

A defensive line with an anti-tank ditch and extensive minefields had been constructed by the Germans to the north of the town, with further minefields and a canal line warding the east. The south and west flanks were protected by the sea. Part of the town was designated a 'fortified camp' by Wildermuth, including two massive forts and the enormous dock area with its facilities.

Wildermuth, not a regular soldier but an officer of the Reserve who had fought in the First World War and was not a Nazi, had received explicit orders. Le Havre was to be held 'to the last man'. He believed, and told his officers at a late stage in the battle, that it was an important object to tie up maximum enemy troops for as long as possible in a battle for Le Havre; and to deny to the enemy its use as a port, also for as long as possible. With these objects in mind he organised the defences and, later, conducted the battle as effectively as he could; did his best to stop demoralisation and defeatism within the garrison despite the obvious grimness of the situation – for instance confirming the death sentence on a soldier found guilty of spreading such demoralisation on 4 September when the decisive battle was imminent – and with defeat ultimately inevitable: did his duty.

Wildermuth had few illusions. On 25 August he had told his superiors that Le Havre could only be held for some twenty-four hours against determined attack. The 25-kilometre perimeter was too long, the resources too few. He had some thirty 88 and 75 millimetre anti-tank pieces – powerful guns but insufficient in number, and his infantrymen were very thin on the ground. He

227

suggested destroying the port facilities and evacuating the garrison (Le Havre was then about to be isolated by the forward movement of the Allied armies). Instead he was ordered to hold. He began destruction of the port facilities – and prepared to hold.

It was clear that an enemy assault would lead to street fighting and considerable destruction; and might well be preceded by aerial bombardment. Wildermuth decided to try to evacuate the civilian population – a huge and probably impossible operation. Some German transport would, he said, be made available. He made this an order to the civilian population on 31 August (his relations with the French civil authorities were correct and cordial). A good many people had already left and the streets were comparatively deserted.

This did not, however, work. The French Resistance cells issued instructions to the population to stay in their homes, and fear of looting deterred many from leaving. By 2 September, with little German military activity within Le Havre but destruction already in progress at the port, the French population had largely returned to their homes. Wildermuth, who had supposed his earlier exhortations had had effect, was disturbed. He saw the Mayor and issued 'orders' – which he can hardly have supposed could be enforced without measures he had no means to undertake – that the whole French civilian population living east of a particular line (and thus in what he presumed would be the combat zone in a land assault) was to be evacuated from Le Havre the following day, Sunday 3 September, by midday. The Mayor protested at the impossibility of this. There were no means by which instructions could be given or arrangements made. 'Do your best!' Wildermuth said. Some people left but in most quarters the evacuation order was treated with derision; and, as wholly impracticable, it was revoked at four o'clock in the afternoon of 3 September. Although of only theoretical relevance, it may also be noted that the civilians to be evacuated under Wildermuth's order were not those living in the area of heaviest bombardment when that bombardment came.

On this Sunday, 3 September, General Crocker, the Commander of I British Corps, gave out his orders. All measures were to be taken to prepare for a land assault. For logistic reasons such an attack could not be mounted before 8 September, and the attack would only be made 'if necessary'.

Crocker very much hoped that it wouldn't be. His divisions

– 51st from the north in due course, 49th already from the east – were taking position round Le Havre, and the latter division was already 'tapping in' to the German defences. He proposed to invite the surrender of the German garrison, whose position was clearly hopeless. Crocker knew well that the port facilities were being destroyed, and the earlier he could take the place the more likely it was that it could play a useful, perhaps vital, part in the advance of Eisenhower's armies; but he had no desire for an expensive street-fighting battle if it could be avoided.

Crocker had one powerful card of inducement – the threat of massive bombardment. A German plenipotentiary was received late on that Sunday afternoon and a British message was delivered under a local armistice, an armistice which lasted until the following morning, 4 September. By this message Wildermuth was told that a refusal to surrender would be followed by extensive bombardment preparatory to an assault. During the same armistice, however, Wildermuth asked that a subsequent 48-hour truce should be agreed, during which the French civilian population should be evacuated on 5 and 6 September (he had already revoked the order to them, or to some of them in the east of the city, to leave their homes). Both requests – Crocker's to the Germans to surrender, Wildermuth's to be allowed to evacuate civilians under a truce – were refused by Wildermuth and Crocker respectively. Wildermuth had no authority to negotiate such a surrender; and Crocker reckoned that a truce such as that proposed would take the heat off the German commander – and probably allow further port facility destruction. He needed to make progress as quickly as possible although he still hoped to avoid a land assault. Meanwhile Le Havre was isolated from the outside world.

When it was known that the summons to surrender had been refused, the British decided not to attack immediately but to allow the initial bombardments to go ahead and to take effect. As well as a huge allocation of bomber aircraft artillery regiments now ringed Le Havre. Two cruisers of the Royal Navy, with 15-inch guns, were tasked to support the assault and silence the coastal battery in the north-western outskirts. The air raid programme was to start next day, 5 September.

The air bombardment was scheduled on four days. Every possible check was built into the programme so that it could be stopped at any moment – but only if the garrison surrendered.

Crocker hoped that, despite Wildermuth's refusal, a surrender might yet come. He hoped that if it did not come before the first raid, on 5 September, it would come thereafter, when Allied air power had shown itself. And he hoped very much that he would not be forced to a ground assault. If, however, that was to happen it should happen, if possible, on the following Saturday, 9 September.

Three hundred and forty-eight aircraft took part in the first raid, beginning at six o'clock in the evening, dropping 1,812 high explosive bombs and a huge number of incendiaries. Some 650 acres of Le Havre were set on fire. The raid lasted two hours and was expected to have a devastating moral effect. It also killed some 2,000 French civilians – the most terrible, in that respect, of the four raids, for three others followed. During this first raid, which involved six successive waves of bombers, the most historic part of Le Havre was pounded into dust. Large numbers of people were burned to death. When the raid was over a desperate delegation of priests called on Wildermuth, beseeching him to surrender – surely his military honour was now safe? Failing that, would he authorise a deputation of the clergy to go to the Allied lines and plead for the population?

Requests refused.

Next day, 6 September, the second raid took place in the morning. Preceded by target markers, four waves of Lancaster bombers, about forty aircraft in each wave, came over Le Havre. Fewer civilians were killed. The third raid, scheduled for 7 September, was postponed by bad weather until 8 September. When it came it was chiefly directed, with considerable accuracy and effect, on the outer, northern and north-western, defences, accompanied by naval gunfire. All raids were overlaid by British artillery fire. There was very little German anti-aircraft action at any stage. From time to time leaflets encouraging desertion were dropped on the garrison, and amplified loudspeaker calls in the same sense were directed at them.

When Will was first told by a brother-officer of what had happened 'up your street' (Wildermuth's refused request for a truce to evacuate civilians), the first two raids had already taken place. Although Will couldn't know it, of the total number of French civilians killed in the raids the majority had already died. Wildermuth had categorically refused a summons to surrender. Crocker had refused Wildermuth's application for a truce two

days earlier. Another air raid (the third) was soon to take place
and an evening bombardment by heavy artillery (claiming more
civilian but very few German casualties) on 9 September. Will's
regiment was to move on that same day into position for the final
assault, which took place on 10 September after yet another air
raid, the fourth, by sixty-five aircraft.

The assault itself, accompanied by extensive direct air attack
on the defences, was wholly successful. At dawn on 11 September
Wildermuth realised that no sort of counter-action was possible.
His troops were still fighting, doing their duty. Next morning he
moved from his command post in one of the forts into some public
gardens and was badly wounded in stomach and thigh, his legs
ultimately both being amputated. Soon afterwards the battle was
over. The surrender was recorded in the War Diary of I British
Corps as taking place 'at 11.30 hours. Commander of garrison
(wounded in leg) extremely uncooperative'. Unsurprisingly so.
The assault had cost some 200 British lives, out of a total of
some 5,000 dead in all.

It is very unlikely that Wildermuth's attitude and actions
would have been different had Allied policy not been predi-
cated on 'unconditional surrender'. What would have changed
them would have been different orders to him. Wildermuth was
ordered to hold as long as possible. He told his men that this
might be near-hopeless but it was comprehensible, strategically,
in order to deny the facilities of Le Havre for as long as possible
to Germany's opponents and to tie up maximum enemy troops.
With those orders he felt he had no alternative but to do his best,
and he did it. Had he been given discretion to surrender he would
probably have used it – he was no Nazi, no fanatic. But he was a
dutiful, principled man and there seems little reason to suppose
he would have acted differently if offered some inducement of
terms by the enemy, against the orders of his own authorities.
Will may have supposed so, but in this as on other occasions
he was probably applying to the particular case the general (and
justified) political objection he had to the policy of 'unconditional
surrender'. He failed to appreciate the simple, not unheroic, sense
of duty of a man like Wildermuth, not actuated by political considerations but acting within a stolid tradition of discipline and
obedience.

Did the British air raids constitute a breach of the usages of
war such as to justify Will's contention that to take part in such
a battle implied condonation of an outrage? An outrage against

the general sentiment of humanity; one which might well be held a crime – at least in others?

These raids, and the losses they produced, were regrettable. They were politically harmful, and remain so – the British Cabinet were already considering with disquiet evidence of French bitterness at the casualties inflicted by Allied bombing policy. They were inhumane, in the sense that all war, and particularly that involving the massacre of non-combatants, is detestable. The selection of target areas on the first raid, 5 September, which caused most of the civilian casualties (and very few German), was, arguably, imprecise and generalised to a fatal degree – German headquarters were 'thought to be' in that quarter of the town and awful damage was done. But as means of persuading the German commander to consider surrender, and as means to reduce the will and capacity of the defenders to defend, these attacks were surely not different from the many bombardments, throughout history, of defended places under siege. It was entirely understandable that grief – and indignation – at the suffering should have inspired the main reaction to Will's case long after the event, among the French, the people of Le Havre, and many who could afford to react with simple humanity to past suffering. But the real culprit was war itself. Under its grim compulsions – vividly felt in 1944, virtually forgotten in 1995 – the actions of the British authorities at Le Havre appear wholly comprehensible.

The critical point was the non-evacuation of civilians. Will's contention was that to refuse Wildermuth's request was inhumane and that this, and perhaps only this, created the 'outrage' which led to his own insubordination. The case is hard to maintain although it may evoke our sympathy. The dilemma of Crocker, faced with an enemy proposal which might significantly delay the taking of the port; the additional time which a 'truce' – *for it was a truce Wildermuth requested, not simply the opening of British lines to French civilians, an easy matter* – would give the German defence for preparation and for port facility destruction; these factors, as well as the saving of French lives, must be taken into account. And if Wildermuth was in the least minded to surrender under the shadow of impending bombardment (and that was the hope) would he not be the less minded if he had lifted from his conscience the 'guilt' of provoking so many French deaths? Would agreement to his 'truce' not ease his decision and fortify his determination to resist? Such considerations were complex but real.

Will over-simplified. It is improbable – those who knew him well would say impossible – that fear of personal risk played any part in the way he decided and acted. His whole conduct from the beginning had been consistent and there is no reason to doubt the sincerity of his attitude, while its courage is beyond question. He was sick at heart about the war and the way it was going. He hated what he thought of as smug self-congratulation about the virtues of our own side, engaged in a 'crusade' (alongside the Soviet Union, improbable crusaders) and the evils of the enemy. He loathed double standards as he saw them. He abominated cruelty. Suffering and humbug turned knives in his heart. He needed to shout a protest and it was unlikely to be impeccable in logic, or particularly just, or even reasonable. At each twist of the argument there is a rational point to counter his. But, in the ultimate, we are left with 5,000 dead, a devastated French city, and a slender, lonely, defiant figure in British uniform proclaiming that there had surely been another way, and prepared to face prison for it.

The battle for a review of his court martial took a long time – a battle which Will sometimes referred to as one to clear his good name. That was wrong; to people who knew him and understood the issues his good name had never been in question. Honour does not necessitate impeccable judgement or consistency of argument. It necessitates sound ulterior motive and honest behaviour in conformity with conscience. It has nothing to do with the judgements of society, themselves vulnerable to fashion and external events. It certainly has nothing to do with the punishments society exacts. Will's honour was and always had been secure.

The battle, however, had lasted over three years from 1988 until the summer of 1991. During it, in winter 1989, there had been a Christmas Truce.

Will's play *A Christmas Truce* was produced at the Haymarket Theatre in Basingstoke in November 1989. The play memorialised the remarkable events in December 1914 when, from the trenches in one sector of the Ypres salient, first German and then British soldiers climbed, walked towards each other across No Man's Land unarmed, exchanged tobacco, food, greetings, showed photographs to each other of family and sweethearts, played football, fraternised. A united church service was held between the two lines of trenches to celebrate Christmas, with ranks of British and German soldiers standing facing each other, their officers in front of them. It was a spontaneous, extraordinary event – angrily deplored by the High Command on both sides. It lasted until 3 January 1915.

Will had always found the story intensely moving. It corresponded and gave tangible form to his own feelings – about the reality of shared humanity by ostensible enemies, about the unreality of the reasons advanced by governments for hatred between nations; about, in the end, the triumph of goodness, however fleeting this particular demonstration. It was not difficult for Will to find the words to enrich this historical incident and give it dramatic impact. The play, with his pen active, could write itself.

The play's action, inevitably, was predictable (and in outline faithful to fact). A German and a British soldier start shouting Christmas wishes to each other and gradually the soldiers on each side begin climbing from their trenches and meet, at first with suspicion and then with increasing, surprised friendliness. Two sergeants (drawn on each side as the least sympathetic, but who succumb ultimately to the Christmas spirit – and the drink); two young officers; two company commanders; two Protestant chaplains. In the second Act the two Colonels join the rest. The exchanges become rather less credible as ranks become higher – Will did the cockney badinage and its German equivalent very plausibly, but the 'parallelism' he needed becomes a little artificial as the play goes on.

It doesn't matter. The production was admirable and the spirit of the thing is moving. As Ian Mullins, the producer, wrote in a production note, the music was important, with some good singing, both of carols and traditional songs. He also insisted, wisely, that the German-language lines (some of the Germans, reasonably, are depicted as English speakers) should be spoken in German – they are short, the drift is clear, and it is conducive to atmosphere; indeed essential.

In the exchanges Will introduced almost a parody of pacifist idealism – war is made by high-ups, 'ordinary people' are the unenthusiastic victims. It has echoes of Remarque's *All Quiet on the Western Front*.

PRESTON
[British padre]:What would Jesus say to that? . . . If he was sitting here between us on His birthday, what would He be saying? . . . Would He say 'what in hell are you two doing, sitting out here playing soldiers when you ought

to be at home telling the big boys in your country where
they get off. What do you think?

To which Brandt, the German pastor, after reflection (and,
it may be thought, with some sense) replies: 'I think we are not
strong enough to interfere in politics, so it is better we do what
we can to help our comrades in the trenches.' And Will speaks,
once again, through the young British officer, Wilson, to his
counterpart, Brunkner:

WILSON: . . . the trouble is we all get taken in by bloody politicians
telling us that this war is the one to end all bloody wars and
that we've got to win it, whereas it's quite obvious that if
we win the bloody thing – or if *you* win it – never mind
which – all it will achieve . . . will be to sow the seeds of
the next bloody war.

Will accepted – unusually for him – some suggestions on
some of this, but it was reminiscent of a good deal of earlier
Will argumentation. And speeches are made about 'international
organisations' (and forces and commanders) who must in future
make conflict between nations impossible.

This was Will politicking and – perfectly legitimately – extrapo-
lating his own lifelong yearnings on to a genuine incident in 1914.
Reviews were good, and although some critics thought the characters stereotyped most found the play moving – 'powerful'; 'a
cry for peace among all nations'. Some felt (perhaps inevitably)
that the most effective element lay in the true facts – the
instinctive friendliness which found human expression despite
the killing (and this was surely Will's intention); and that less
convincing was Will's imposed philosophising, his pointing of
pacific morals which somewhat diminished the credibility of the
characters. It was possible to find the philosophising facile and
yet to be powerfully affected by the story itself. But Will had to
beat his drum and he beat it. His last performed play, as this was,
took its place, therefore, as both an 'Historical' and a 'Sermon';
a sermon whose text he had been preaching for most of his life.

CHAPTER XIII

Curtain

In 1989 Will completed an amended version of a play, *Pocket Money*,[1] which was based on an idea and synopsis provided by his friend, Otto Herschan (he who had once driven to Spain with Will in pursuit of Rachel Brand). The Herschans, Will and Rachel had dined together and Herschan had told Will his thoughts about a play. Will listened, fascinated.

'Go straight home and write it.'

'I can't.'

'Then give me a synopsis, and I will.'

He did and he did. Thereafter they cooperated in detail. The flow of dialogue, the treatment, is Will's. The ground was to some extent unfamiliar to him but he showed insight and understanding. The joint work took only three months.

It is a remarkable and moving little play. A sympathetically drawn and elderly Irish priest, a Canon with a liking for whiskey and golf, finds himself unexpectedly well-off. He has never been other than poor, and anything he has possessed he has generally given away with incurable and improvident generosity to the undeserving, but now a distant Irish-American cousin has left him a legacy – $20,000. His friendly bank manager and golfing partner, sworn to secrecy (since otherwise everyone will arrive to prey on the Canon) opens a bank account for him, arranges to control it and agrees to dole out a ration of 50p pieces with which the Canon can be generous to those in need. The ration soon has to be increased.

But since the Canon's poverty is well known his sudden bountifulness gives rise to belief in a miracle – for his goodness is also well known. A cult begins. Busloads arrive. Visitors travel from America. The village prospers. The Canon, suspected of deception of the faithful by one or two people (including his own

1. Not yet (1995) produced.

curate) replies that he has never deceived. He has said and done nothing. The self-deception and wishful thinking of some may have brought them a little joy, and the village some increased prosperity. That is all.

Eventually the money runs out. The bank manager tells him there is and can be no more. The last 50p piece has been shaken from his trousers, the account is empty. Thousands have been given away to thousands. And now the Bishop has heard of the whole business and is uneasy. The Canon is confronted and confesses all. He has, if not practised, condoned deceit. Exposure is inevitable – the 'miracle', a fraud, must anyway cease. And there is worse: the Canon confesses to the Bishop that throughout his priesthood he has sailed under false colours.

CANON: I don't believe in God.
BISHOP: Since when?
CANON: Since I first heard of Him.

He became a priest, he says, only because his family expected it. He has faith in goodness, in humanity, but as to God: 'I have always held the strong conviction that the Doubting Thomases in life are there for a purpose – which is to encourage others who feel the same.' The Bishop is shattered. The Canon – an old friend and once his supervising tutor – is guilty of blasphemy. He must, the Bishop decides, leave his parish as soon as possible, must be found some help to live in agnostic retirement somewhere, while memory of the 'miracles' – wrought in the eyes of the self-deceiving faithful by a God in whom the Canon cannot believe – must be allowed simply to die away. 'The divine gift' can forsake a worker of miracles and so it will be supposed.

The Canon is mortified, wretched. He never intended dishonesty. He hates the idea of leaving his people, deceived (harmlessly) though they may have been. He says frankly that he contemplates the sin of suicide. Horrified, the Bishop prays: 'Lord God, I beseech you grant to that unhappy man for whom I'm praying – grant that he may turn away from all the wicked thoughts that now beset him, and that he may start a new life in your faith and fear.' But there is a knock at the door. The Canon's housekeeper says that a familiar local ne'er-do-well has turned up asking for a handout and that she's explained there's no money. But the ne'er-do-well says that 'surely there's one coin somewhere in the bottom of his pocket!' The Canon, from force of habit, feels in his pocket. And to his astonishment huge handfuls of coins cascade onto the floor as he falls to his knees. The Angelus begins to ring.

A number of themes coalesce in *Pocket Money*. There is Will's reiterated sense of religious doubt – 'Help thou my unbelief' – already strongly deployed in *The Bad Samaritan, The Lord's Lieutenant, The Queen's Highland Servant* and to be uttered again in his last and valedictory piece of writing, *The Club Bore*. There is his corresponding belief, voiced by the Canon, that an undogmatic, a generalised sort of faith in humanity and in goodness may be as near to God as man can get, if God exists and whatever He means. There is Will's sympathetic understanding for the elderly Canon – generous, tolerant, enjoying his golf and his whiskey – who finds himself at the centre of a deception he has not willed but which has not, he decides, done anybody any harm. There is the rational (and also sympathetically drawn) attitude of the Bishop: disciplined, deeply upset by faithlessness, full of affection, notwithstanding, for the faithless. The Canon, saintly sceptic, is drawn in sharp distinction from his puritanical curate, Father Daniel, whose well-reasoned rigidities and assertive confidence Will gently mocks. Finally there is the superb, unnerving *coup de théâtre*, a wholly unexpected miracle which leaves all things uncertain but which, perhaps, demonstrates Will's ultimate sense of the triumph of good, the vindication of the humble doubtful; mysteriously demonstrated.

It is a Christian play, with admirable understanding of a Catholic society. There is, at the end, that sense which Will always enjoyed, of a world turned upside down, reasonable certainties confounded, as, to our astonishment, the Canon's doubts (and perhaps the playwright's) are overshadowed by the miraculous hand of God – full of 50p pieces. God, the all-comprehending, *may* exist, after all. Golf, whiskey, laughter, and human frailty all have their parts to play. Little is beyond sanctification. There are few corners, however improbable-seeming, where grace in some guise may not penetrate; even, perhaps especially, when they are dark with doubt.

In 1991 Will published the last volume of his autobiographical writings. *Old Men Remember*[2] covered some of the same ground as the earlier books – childhood, boyhood, parents, family, school, the world of the stage. The style is different; easier, conversational, gently reminiscent. Even more than in previous volumes the pages

2. Collins and Brown, 1991.

are filled with friends, friends in the theatre, friends in Hampshire, friends from youth. And friends were dying. Will was seventy-nine and the valedictory note is unmistakable.

In dealing with his experiences as a playwright there is less of the tinge of bitterness, mild though it was, which some had detected in *Mr Home Pronounced Hume*. Instead Will's natural benignity, his incapacity for dislike or grudge-harbouring, illumines the book. He describes in it his routine at home now, his household chores, his happiness. The book refers to the writing of a new play. He asks himself whether he is finished as a playwright, and answers – 'Not finished, no, but out of fashion yes, a hundred times yes.'

But he also, accurately, observes that his plays are still being extensively performed by amateurs, by repertory companies, and in France and other countries. Fashion may have deserted him in terms of West End managements and new plays, but 'William Douglas Home' is still a name and a reputation. Indeed, for the discriminating, it remains a name near-guaranteeing a well-made play, a talented vehicle for a talented cast, an hour or two of happy unmalicious laughter – or a few unembittered tears.

The new play to which Will referred in this last book was *The Club Bore*.[3] In it the valedictory tone is clear. The construction is simple – a number of elderly and distinguished members of a club, a Bishop, a general, a senior diplomat – have known each other throughout their lives. They reminisce, boring but only half-boring a young member. Each in turn dies and the remainder gather, remember, joke. Finally only one, the oldest, is left.

Themes worked often by Will appear and reappear. The humbug many an illustrious life conceals; schoolboy absurdities and adolescent homosexuality; peace and war; religious doubts – on Christ's divinity, on the Virgin Birth, on the possibility of Resurrection. And each member is wondering who is next to go. There is the ever-present question, occasionally put: 'Are you frightened of death?' The play, in Will's unchanging manner, cloaks the fundamental issues of life and death with the jokes, badinage and allusions of a self-confident, half-troubled, elderly élite. They tease their eldest, The Club Bore, incessantly: 'I'm only joking, old chap.' – 'Thanks for telling me.' Or: 'That goes without saying.' – 'It's a pity more things don't, if you ask me.'

---

3. Not yet (1995) performed.

There is pathos here, but no self-pity. The bell, however, is beginning to toll and Will's dexterous one-liners and repartee are certainly not designed to drown it. One but last of the group to go is the Bishop.

'Well, he should find out soon.'

'Who find out what?'

'If everything he's been on about for the last ninety years is based on fact or fiction.'

Will's own life contained still much – perhaps all – which had enriched it now for forty years. Derry, his home in Kilmeston, had replaced Drayton to a wonderful degree, largely through Rachel's skill and because their friends loved them and sought them wherever they were. Will saw all his children frequently: three were married and he got enormous fun from his several grandchildren, relishing their charm, good looks and impertinence, so reminiscent (as it was) of his own.

Afternoons at Derry, if not spent on the golf course, were generally dedicated to the racing programmes on television. He did the *Times* crossword daily. He still exchanged a near-daily telephone call about racing form and the tips of the day with his brother Alec at the Hirsel – Will had undertaken to share his winnings (but not his losses) in return for advice, which was often shrewd. He still conducted weekly (at least) conversations with Brian Johnston, giggling happily at the latter's most recent outrageous anecdote and quickly relaying it to others. He still flourished his large handkerchief as a sort of prop, placing it on his head to amuse children, which it generally and inexplicably did. He still spread marmalade stickily everywhere when he ate breakfast, as messily as in the Hirsel nursery. He still loved writing doggerel with all his old facility on every sort of occasion – the birthdays of friends and relations, unexpected happenings in the family circle, current events which caught his eye or his disapprobation.

He still covered an enormous mileage in his car – to friends' houses, to race meetings, to London, to Scotland at least once a year and often more. He still went to the theatre as often as he could. And new ideas for plays still bubbled in his mind and in his conversation.

On 22 July 1991 Will and Rachel marked their Ruby Wedding, with a large lunch party at Derry; and on Wednesday 3 June 1992 (Derby Day, as it happened) Will's eightieth birthday was celebrated with an evening party for an equally huge number of friends. It was probably impossible for anyone present to believe in the reason for the occasion. Will, Peter Pan, was exactly as he had been for those who remembered him in boyhood, at Oxford, at RADA, in the earliest days of his successes on the London stage. His half-suppressed chuckle, his teasing voice, his quick movements and gestures, his repartee, his zest for life and the things he loved in it – all were unchanged. Two days earlier, on 1 June 1992, a 'Festschrift' in honour of Will had been produced by Ian Mullins before a large audience at the Redgrave Theatre in Farnham. The Redgrave had replaced the small (and charming) Castle Theatre, and from the beginning Will had been involved in the project – the building, the launch, the continuing prosperity of this admirably conceived open stage house. A celebration of his birthday, the evening was also a celebration of his life, his time at Oxford, his wartime pain and struggle, his plays – with excerpts from a number of the better-known (not excluding *Aunt Edwina*!) interspersed with extracts from his writings. Both light and moving (and produced with remarkable speed and little time for preparation or rehearsal), this occasion touched Will deeply. He found it impossible to make a speech – a huge number of his friends had assembled and he was overcome. He finished the evening with one joke from the stage and left, near to tears.

On Monday 28 September 1992 Will was in the garden at Derry after lunch. He and Rachel had been at the wedding of a friend's daughter on the Saturday, where he had been as cheerful and light-hearted as ever. Now he felt tired and unwell. He came into the house from the garden and sat down, at first rejecting Rachel's suggestion that a doctor come to see him. A little later, anxious, she telephoned to ask for one. Soon after he arrived Will, very quietly and peacefully, died.

He was buried on 2 October in the churchyard at East Meon, his parish church for all the years at Drayton, years which had seen the upbringing of all his children; had witnessed every play's birth from *The Manor of Northstead* to *David and Jonathan* – over thirty plays and a string of other pieces; years in which Drayton had been the background for the entertainment of an enormous legion of loving friends. The church was completely crowded, and equally crowded was St Martin-in-the-Fields in London where a Memorial Service was held on 5 November and where Brian Johnston, speaking with his usual irrepressible humour and from a friendship which had lasted over sixty years, recalled Will's kindness, wit, courage and simple goodness to an enormous congregation.

William Douglas Home largely devoted his life to the theatre and it is as a pre-eminent dramatist, a man of the British stage in the twentieth century, that he was honoured and will be formally remembered. Yet an old friend, meditating on his life, observed that not too much should be made of Will the playwright; 'he was much more than that.'

He was undoubtedly much more than that. Nevertheless the plays, the work, are inextricably woven into the character of the man – the man who was also aspiring politician, reluctant soldier, indomitable racehorse owner, Border grandee at one remove, paterfamilias. The debit and credit columns in the assessment of Will's character are both extensive, and both should be read to strike the balance.

First, the debit side. He was, as a playwright, criticised for writing too much, for writing in consequence some poor plays and for lacking the judgement to throw them away. He was called obstinate for his reluctance to re-write and improve – stubborn (and stubbornness was anyway a family trait) in his resistance to the well-intentioned suggestions of others. First thoughts, he believed, had usually been best. Listening to criticisms of his plays, however constructive, was never his favourite occupation. Lunching with his brother Alec (who had driven to Pitlochry to see *The Perch* and give Will his views), he left the table as soon as Alec began his critique: he said he had some racing bets to place.

Here and there Will may have missed a trick by this obstinacy; pride of creation, protectiveness towards the work of his own hand prevented him (it may be) from turning an occasional failure into a possible success. He sometimes, it was said, used stereotypes instead of the well-rounded, original characters of which his pen was capable. He sometimes 'wrote down' a little. And his constructions – generally inventive – were now and then thin and predictable; and thus failed.

Will sometimes reckoned that the dramatic critics were obtuse, prejudiced and class-conscious rather than quality-conscious in their appraisals. Sometimes he was right, beyond all question; but sometimes he allowed understandable resentment to colour his own attitude to reasonable criticism. Quite early in his career his agent at the time remarked of one of Will's offerings, 'As a play it's not really much good!' Will's reaction was instantly to change his agent (the agent in question, John Barber, then became a distinguished dramatic critic!). He was sometimes thin-skinned (although always good-tempered and courteous); he had been often wounded, and it showed. He did not perceive, particularly during the bad times when it was indeed hard to perceive, that some of the acid in the attacks on him came from a sense of disappointment. Tynan, for instance, reckoned that a considerable talent was too often, in Will, being put to indifferent use; and deplored it.

He was emotionally vulnerable and tended to shrink from the depiction of raw feelings on stage and from their expression in life. His humour gave him an escape route and he too often took it – flying from a human predicament which demanded too uncomfortable a degree of seriousness; evading an issue; compromising; trivialising. He recognised this in himself and the effort to conquer it is sometimes evident, but seldom successful. A character of Will's, on stage, may be approaching real emotional crisis, but frequently wit beckons, intervenes, saves the situation; or betrays it.

This deep emotional reserve as a playwright derived from Will's extreme sensitivity as a person – in earlier life taking the form of acute shyness. Reserve was anyway another Home family characteristic; in Will, at its best, it could be termed delicacy, at its worst inhibition and something not far from prudery. He could enjoy, and introduce into his plays, a bawdy laugh, but built walls round his feelings; and his wit made the walls near-impregnable.

The most extreme – and most persistent – manifestation of this sensitivity was Will's reluctance to recognise or describe, on stage or off it, anything or anybody genuinely evil. Evil demands condemnation. Will loathed to condemn. Evil calls forth a serious, an unequivocal, even an heroic response. Will had a taste for equivocation, disliked heroics, and reckoned that seriousness – conviction – should more often than not be tempered by tolerance and understanding; and humour. Evil, however – real evil – does not admit of tolerance and Will, therefore, preferred to turn away from it. He preferred to allow evil a good exit line, a word of indulgence. Condemnation had to be leavened with a jest.

This sometimes reduced his range as a dramatist. At the extremes dramatic tension needs confrontation between evil and good. Will detested confrontation. Just as he always looked for the good in people – one of the most significant and endearing points on the credit side of his account – so he was often reluctant to face disagreeable facts if they looked like leading to condemnation or criticism, especially of those he loved. He looked away. He dodged. And he looked away from consequences of his views or his actions if they appeared likely to be upsetting. There was an element of irresponsibility here.

All this, inevitably, led to his own type-casting as a writer of light comedies; and since his light comedies were more often than not set in the drawing rooms of the class he knew best – his own – he was first categorised and later pilloried as a limited and frivolous chronicler of the higher reaches of the social scene; and nothing more. Attempts to transcend this categorisation were, inevitably in the prevailing cultural and political climate, faulted as unconvincing. Sometimes they were. They were also faulted as naive, simplistic and in poor taste. Naive and simplistic some of Will's more serious attempts may have been (but only some); in poor taste they seldom were, except in the particularly humourless eyes of the new puritans.

Easier to criticise are the political attitudes Will from time to time adopted – and some of the criticisms are similar to those levelled at the worst of his plays. He looked at the political issues of his time from an exceedingly over-simplified point of view. This was particularly so in the matter of peace and war, the matter about which he felt most passionately and which, in material terms, was his undoing. He supposed, with too unrigorous a mind, that peace between nations (even nations at war but particularly nations about to contemplate going to war) can be attained by a simple readiness to see things from an opposite angle. He nourished some illusions; he liked a well-turned quotable phrase and, being above all a man of wit, he sometimes supposed that a neat epigram must necessarily indicate sound judgement. He personalised and simplified in his mind issues of international politics which were in reality complex, which involved the interplay of historical and economic compulsions of immense difficulty, and which depended on public opinions seldom resembling the straightforward sum of good-hearted, decent people in which Will longed to believe. This naivety showed a reluctance to use his mind with the penetrative energy of which it was capable, a reluctance some thought culpably evasive. It was similar to – often coincided with – that lack of readiness to face evil, to confront difficult reality, which diluted the force of some of his dramatic work.

Because he saw political issues starkly but with unjustified over-simplification, Will, frequently in life, took a line, wrote, argued – and on the most memorable occasion acted – in a way which is difficult to justify by the calm light of reason. And, in doing so, he sometimes let others down and saddened them. The most vivid example of this – Le Havre, 1944 – was regarded by a few with sympathy even at the time; was recalled with greater understanding as the years went on; but had power to outrage others as long as such things were remembered. To some, both at the time and in retrospect, Will's irresponsibility in taking a commission when he felt as he did remained deplorable, and his refusal to obey an order in battle reprehensible.

He was financially imprudent – he interested himself too little in matters which could affect him crucially unless attended to, left too much to others. He had no understanding, and no desire to acquire understanding, of the principles of financial planning. He made very large sums of money at his best moments and from his best plays, yet suffered financial difficulties in the later years of his life. The fault was largely his. When considering the possibility (often urged upon him) of contributing to a personal pension he simply said 'My royalties will deal with that!' Optimism to excess, perhaps. Laziness perhaps. Generosity beyond any calculation, without question. Aversion from prudent planning certainly.

So much for the debit side.

In professional terms, standing at the head of Will's credit column is his technical expertise. He understood, from the very first, what worked and did not work on stage. He sometimes, like all creative artists, wrote below his own best but it was not for lack of technical and theatrical understanding. He understood actors, actresses and the acting professions. He knew what a good voice could do with a line, what a skilful professional could make of a character, what a sympathetic director could get from a scene. Not for nothing did the best of their profession call him 'an actors' playwright'. He worked and wrote with extraordinary speed and fluency. He 'heard voices' and set them down.

Next was the wit and sparkle of his dialogue itself; what was called his 'loose-wristed' fluency. In spite of his obstinacy over a play's structure, when it reached the cast it was seldom that a line needed changing. His dialogue had rhythm – rhythm and the elisions which carried cast and audience along. His curtain lines seldom failed. He usually gave even minor characters something worthwhile to say and to play. His lines need pace in direction and speaking, and they give an audience an exhilarated sense of being driven by an expert on a highspeed racing track, swerving, accelerating, cornering; or of watching a ball game played by masters of rapidity and grace. His scenes run smoothly, delightfully and above all (in most plays) funnily.

For Will, above all things, made people laugh. He made people laugh in private life, he made people laugh when he made speeches, he made people laugh and laugh again, all over the world, in the theatre. His ideas were original, his constructions entertaining; words adorned situations of inherent humour – or inherent drama. He knew how to produce or maintain tension and his dialogue was always or nearly always credible. He may, to a fault, have created characters who were too generally sympathetic. But they were alive. And they were, when he chose, funny. And, also when he chose, they were moving. When well-produced, Will's plays – seeming so simple and light when read – acquired extra dimensions, and stayed longer in the mind than many of the efforts of more apparently heavyweight dramatists. They will survive and return.

On the credit side of Will's balance must also be set the length of his professional career. *Great Possessions* was produced in 1937; *A Christmas Truce* in 1989. Such a span of creative work can seldom have been bettered, and certainly never bettered by one who was acclaimed as the most gifted writer of light comedies of his age. Will was active, industrious, restless and inventive.[4]

In his theatrical career, with its dramatic ups and downs, its triumphs and disappointments, Will showed enormous resilience and very considerable courage. And this courage had marked the solitary stand he had taken – misguidedly or not is irrelevant – in the Second World War. He had courted punishment and disgrace, and punishment came. He had done so because of what he thought was right, humane, decent. And he had done so in the face of opposition – and in most cases condemnation – by family, friends and the public. He had chosen the path of loneliness, one of the stonier paths which can be trod. He often

---

4. Forty-five plays actually produced, to Shakespeare's thirty-eight – also, it must be admitted, of variable quality!

found himself defending a position virtually alone; and the isolation he found at Le Havre was mirrored in a somewhat milder but still unnerving way by the solitude of his position when the new wave of the theatre broke over him. In neither case did he flinch, and in neither case did he abandon hope or moderate the strength of his convictions.

Yet 'he was much more' than Will the playwright. He was indeed, although the outstanding facets of his character found expression in his plays as well. He was, as has been said, intensely sensitive; and his sensitivity bred a hatred of war, destruction, cruelty, suffering, a hatred which lay at the root of most of his deeper attitudes to life. But above all he hated hatred itself. He could not bear to describe, nor easily contemplate, the savage feelings of one human being for another. His father used to say, 'Think the best of people, expect the best of them, they seldom let you down.' Will remembered that and followed it (an admirable precept extended to most people, it is less reliable applied to horses, but that is another story). He brought out the best in others.

Will's sensitivity, behind his seldom lowered mask of insouciance, may have been excessive. Certainly he was always vulnerable, and certainly he retained to the end what was remarked in him as a young man, a sort of innocence. Above all, however, it led to generosity of spirit. He was completely sincere in his loathing of humbug, of the self-righteousness which he felt lay behind most condemnation – 'Put yourself in the other person's place' was his eternal, simple, straightforward creed. What may be entered in the debit balance as naivety can assuredly be marked up on the other side as charity. There was immense, quiet, undemonstrative love in him. People felt it – often subconsciously, often without fully understanding it. A friend observed that 'If there is a word which conveys the exact opposite of a bully, in all things, that was William.'

This charity, love for his fellows, always unpretentious, always unassuming, generally concealed by humour – this led to considerable material acts of kindness. A friend never applied to Will for help without success, although Will might be as often hard-pressed himself – or soon would be; he seldom knew, and if he guessed he didn't care. And when a friend was unhappy or in trouble, Will's sympathy, perhaps to some extent because he was so markedly undemonstrative, was extraordinarily comforting. Above all, however, charity led to generosity of sentiment, to an instinctive benevolence about others, even when he had little reason. In a profession (like most professions) not always distinguished by kindly views of colleagues, Will was never heard to utter a harsh, or resentful, or embittered word about another. And very few could be remembered saying a disagreeable word about him. The same generosity showed in the handling of his stage characters, possibly to a fault in dramatic terms, but utterly true to their creator's humanity. Few, however unsympathetic, left the stage without being allowed a good line or two, a more agreeable-seeming aspect, a laugh even. Will was saying to them, 'Don't take it to heart! I know there's good in you, after all!'

Will had, to a memorable degree, the gift of friendship, the gift of making others of whatever degree and whatever age feel important, the gift of entering others' lives and drawing others into his own – yet always with that enigmatic, chuckling reserve which contributed so much to his extraordinary attraction. He seemed almost permanently good-humoured, an astonishing gift which might be exasperating yet was, instead, curiously infectious. Some people detected in him a certain inner sadness, firmly concealed always behind the laughter. It may be so. It may be that the stresses of the earlier years never left him alone for long, although he hid it. To the world he showed no melancholy whatsoever. Endlessly entertaining, witty and kind, his wit and kindness were rooted in the sharpness and speed of his mind, and in the goodness of his heart.

An attempt may thus be made to strike a balance in William Douglas Home's character as a playwright and, more importantly, as a man. Nothing of it conveys that most elusive element to trap with words – his personality; and nothing will. Wherever he touched the lives of others he enriched and brought fun to them. Those who had professional dealings with him, men or women of the theatre, agents, lawyers, accountants, whether or not they had found particular encounters difficult, invariably looked on him as the most enchanting and enjoyable of clients. Those who knew him only as a friend knew him to be unique. To the huge mass of his acquaintance who mourned him, who had laughed with him, argued with him, furiously attacked his views or wryly supported them, criticised his attitudes, enjoyed or damned his plays, revelled in his hospitality – to these, perhaps to all of these, he was probably the sweetest-natured, most amusing and most lovable human being they had ever known.

Appendix
Selected playbills

NOW BARABBAS

First produced at the Boltons Theatre, Kensington, on 11th February 1947, with the following cast:

CHARACTERS

Officer King	. .	STANLEY BEARD
4288 Smith .	. .	OWEN HOLDER
3762 Brown .	. .	STANLEY ROSE
1091 O'Brien (Paddy)	.	JULIAN SOMERS
2746 Anderson	. .	HARRY QUASHIE
6145 Spencer	. .	BARRY PHELPS
6146 Roberts	. . .	JOHN MACKWOOD
3804 Medworth	. .	BASIL GORDON
6147 Richards	. .	PETER DOUGHTY
Officer Jackson	. .	DAVID DUNCAN
Tufnell	. .	RICHARD LONGMAN
Officer Jones	. .	PERCY WALSH
Officer Gale	. .	RICHARD FOAT
The Governor	. .	TRISTAN RAWSON
The Chaplain	. .	ANTHONY MARLOWE
Chief Officer Webb	.	JOSS CLEWES
Kitty	. .	JILL BENNETT
Mrs. Brown .	. .	ELSA PALMER
Winnie	. .	BARBARA BIRKENSHAW
8146 Robinson	. .	RAYMOND DUVEEN
'Erb .	. . .	JACQUELINE BOITEAUX

The Play Directed by Colin Chandler

Subsequently presented by Tom Arnold and Linnit and Dunfee Ltd. at the Vaudeville Theatre on 7th March 1947, with the following changes in the cast:

The Chaplain	DENIS WEBB
'Erb	JOHN BARON
Robinson	JOHN LAWSON
Mrs. Brown	VIOLET GOULD
A Warder	RICHARD WIGHTMAN

[*Denis Webb replaced Anthony Marlowe, who was under previous contract to appear elsewhere. The part of 'Winnie' was deleted from the play.*]

THE CHILTERN HUNDREDS

First presented by Linnit & Dunfee Ltd., at the Theatre Royal, Brighton, on 18th August, 1947, and subsequently at the Vaudeville Theatre, London, on 26th August, 1947, with the following cast of characters :

(In the order of their appearance.)

THE EARL OF LISTER (Lord Lieutenant) .	*A. E. Matthews*
THE COUNTESS OF LISTER (His Wife) .	*Marjorie Fielding*
JUNE FARRELL (of the American Embassy) . .	*Leora Dana*
BESSIE	*Diane Hart*
BEECHAM	*Michael Shepley*
LORD PYM (Lord Lister's Son)	*Peter Coke*
LADY CAROLINE SMITH (Lord Lister's Sister) .	*Edith Savile*
MR. CLEGHORN	*Tom Macaulay*

Directed by Colin Chandler

———

SYNOPSIS OF SCENERY

SCENE : The Sitting-room of Lister Castle. Summer, 1945.

ACT I

SCENE 1 . . General Election Result Day. Lunch Time.

SCENE 2 . . . . The next morning. Breakfast Time.

ACT II

SCENE 1 Saturday evening, the following week-end. After Dinner.

SCENE 2 The By-Election. Nomination Day. Breakfast Time.

ACT III

SCENE 1 The By-Election Result Day. A fortnight later. Lunch Time.

SCENE 2 . . . . The same evening. After Dinner.

The Reluctant Debutante

This play was first presented by E. P. Clift in conjunction with Anna Deere Wiman at The Cambridge Theatre, London, on 24th May, 1955, with the following cast of characters:

JIMMY BROADBENT	*Wilfrid Hyde White*
SHEILA BROADBENT (his wife)	*Celia Johnson*
JANE (his daughter)	*Anna Massey*
MABEL CROSSWAITE	*Ambrosine Phillpotts*
CLARISSA (her daughter)	*Anna Steele*
DAVID BULLOCH	*Peter Myers*
DAVID HOYLAKE-JOHNSTON	*John Merivale*
MRS. EDGAR	*Gwynne Whitby*

Directed by JACK MINSTER

Setting by HUTCHINSON SCOTT

The scene is laid throughout in JIMMY BROADBENT's *flat, off Eaton Square, in June.*

ACT ONE

SCENE 1. Breakfast time.
SCENE 2. Cocktail time, the same evening.

ACT TWO

SCENE 1. Early the following morning.
SCENE 2. Breakfast time.

THE SECRETARY BIRD

First produced by Anthony Roye at the Mowlem Theatre, Swanage, on the 9th May 1967, with the following cast of characters:

(in order of their appearance)

HUGH WALFORD	*Anthony Roye*
LIZ WALFORD	*Patrica Leslie*
MRS GRAY	*Betty Woolfe*
MOLLY FORSYTH	*Dona Martyn*
JOHN BROWNLOW	*Robert Dean*

Subsequently produced by John Gale, for Volcano Productions, at the Savoy Theatre, London, on 16th October 1968, with the following cast of characters:

(in order of their appearance)

HUGH WALFORD	*Kenneth More*
LIZ WALFORD	*Jane Downs*
MRS GRAY	*Katherine Parr*
MOLLY FORSYTH	*Judith Arthy*
JOHN BROWNLOW	*Terence Longdon*

The play directed by Philip Dudley

Setting by Hutchinson Scott

The action of the play passes in the living-room of the Walford's country house

ACT I

SCENE 1 Friday night
SCENE 2 Saturday morning

ACT II

SCENE 1 Saturday night
SCENE 2 Sunday morning

Time—the present

THE JOCKEY CLUB STAKES

Produced at the Grand Theatre, Leeds, by Peter
Saunders, on 7th September 1970, and subsequently at the Vaudeville Theatre, London,
WC2, on 30th September 1970, with the following cast of characters:

The Marquis of Candover	Alastair Sim
Lord Coverley De Beaumont	Geoffrey Sumner
Colonel Sir Robert Richardson	Robert Coote
Captain Trevor Jones	Terence Skelton
Miss Hills	Christina Gray
P. Brown	Terence Moran
Lady Ursula Itchin	Julia Lockwood
Lord Green	Wensley Pithey
Tom Glass	Alan White
Charlie Wisden	Brian Hayes
Perch Graham	Barry Walker
Sir Dymock Blackburn, Q.C.	Ernest Clark
Lady Green	Hazel Bainbridge

The play directed by Murray Macdonald.
Decor by Anthony Holland

The action takes place in the Jockey Club
Rooms

ACT I
Scene 1	A Summer Morning
Scene 2	The Following Morning

ACT II
Scene 1	Two Weeks later
	A few days after the Warwick Meeting
Scene 2	It is not yet 2.30 p.m. the same day

Time—the present

LLOYD GEORGE KNEW MY FATHER

First performed under the title **Lady Boothroyd of the By-Pass** by the New Midland Theatre Company, Boston, on 1st February 1972, with the following cast of characters:

Lady Boothroyd (Sheila)	Patricia Leslie
Richardson	Iain Armstrong
General Sir William Boothroyd	Anthony Roye
William Boothroyd, M.P.	Arnold Peters
Maud Boothroyd	Joy Singlehurst
Sally Boothroyd	Penelope Anne Croft
Dickie Horton-Jones	Rayner Bourton
The Rev. Trevor Simmonds	Brian Weston

Designed and directed by Anthony Roye
Lighting by Lawrence Whitfield

Subsequently presented under the title **Lloyd George Knew My Father**, by Ray Cooney and John Gale, by arrangement with Hugh Wontner, on 4th July 1972, at the Savoy Theatre, London, with the following cast of characters:

General Sir William Boothroyd	Ralph Richardson
Lady Sheila Boothroyd	Peggy Ashcroft
Hubert Boothroyd, M.P.	James Grout
Maud Boothroyd	Janet Henfrey
Sally Boothroyd	Suzan Farmer
Simon Green	Simon Cadell
Rev. Trevor Simmonds	David Stoll
Robertson	Alan Barnes

The play directed by Robin Midgley
Setting by Anthony Holland
Lighting by Chris Ellis

The action of the play passes in the sitting-room of Boothroyd Hall, Sir William's home

ACT I
   Scene 1   Saturday morning
   Scene 2   Sunday morning

ACT II
   Scene 1   Sunday evening
   Scene 2   Monday morning

Time – the present

THE DAME OF SARK

An Oxford Theatre Festival Production, first presented at Wyndham's Theatre, London, by Ray Cooney on the 17th October 1974, with the following cast of characters:

Bob Hathaway	Alan Gifford
Sibyl Hathaway	Celia Johnson
Cecile	Jill Raymond
Major Lanz	John Pennington
Dr Braun	Nicholas Loukes
Colonel von Schmettau	Tony Britton
Wilhelm Muller	Peter Settelen
Colonel Graham	Nicholas Courtney
Jim Robinson	Hugh Wooldridge
Mr Bishop	Martin Carroll
Mrs Bishop	Brenda Duncan
The Cowman	Scott Taylor

The play directed by Charles Hickman
Setting by Anthony Holland

The action takes place in the drawing-room of the Seigneurie on Sark

SCENE 1	1940	Summer
SCENE 2	1941	Spring
SCENE 3	1942	Autumn
SCENE 4	1943	Winter
SCENE 5	1944	Summer
SCENE 6	1945	Summer

Period—the Second World War

INDEX

Index